Object Management in Distributed Database Systems for Stationary and Mobile Computing Environments: A Competitive Approach

Network Theory and Applications

Volume 12

OBJECT MANAGEMENT IN DISTRIBUTED DATABASE SYSTEMS FOR STATIONARY AND MOBILE COMPUTING ENVIRONMENTS: A COMPETITIVE APPROACH

WUJUAN LIN
Department of Electrical and Computer Engineering
National University of Singapore
4 Engineering Drive 3, Singapore 117576

BHARADWAJ VEERAVALLI
Department of Electrical and Computer Engineering
National University of Singapore
4 Engineering Drive 3, Singapore 117576

Springer-Science+Business Media, B.V.

ISBN 978-1-4613-4823-8 ISBN 978-1-4419-9176-8 (eBook)
DOI 10.1007/978-1-4419-9176-8

Library of Congress Cataloging-in-Publication

Lin, Wujuan / Veeravalli, Bharadwaj
Object Management in Distributed Database Systems for Stationary and Mobile Computing Environments: A Competitive Approach

---

Printed on acid-free paper.

Dedicated to:

Parent's,
Wife Hu Xiaohong,
Brother Wuqiang Lin,
and all my Teachers

– Wujuan Lin

Parent's(late),
Wife Lavanya,
Daughter Tanya,
Brother Sivakumar and
his family,
all my friends,
and all my Teachers
who got me here

–Bharadwaj Veeravalli

Contents

List of Figures

List of Tables

Preface

Network-based computing domain unifies all best research efforts presented from single computer systems to networked systems to render overwhelming computational power for several modern day applications. Although this power is expected to grow with respect to time due to technological advancements, application requirements impose a continuous thrust on network utilization and on the resources to deliver supreme quality of service. Strictly speaking, network-based computing domain has no confined scope and each element offers considerable challenges. Any modern day networked application strongly thrives on efficient data storage and management system, which is essentially a *Database System*. There have been number of books-to-date in this domain that discuss fundamental principles of designing a database system. Research in this domain is now far matured and many researchers are venturing in this domain continuously due to a wide variety of challenges posed. In this book, our domain of interest is in exposing the underlying key challenges in designing algorithms to handle unpredictable requests that arrive at a *Distributed Database System*(DDBS) and evaluating their performance. These requests are otherwise called as *on-line* requests arriving at a system to process. *Transactions* in an on-line Banking service, Airline Reservation system, Video-on-Demand system, etc, are few examples of on-line requests.

Our venture in this book is somewhat distinct in approach from any standard text books on Database Systems and geared towards providing a strong foundation for researchers in this and allied areas of research, after acquiring required fundamental knowledge in this area. The mathematical rigor and approach required for analysis at times become serious requirements for an advanced level researcher. Also, handling on-line requests posses a key challenge to the algorithm/system designers in this domain, as the applicability of the readily available solutions for handling *off-line* requests become infeasible, if not will be inefficient. Further, the key factor in any distributed system is in the way of which *control* of activities of the system is entertained, i.e., either by *centralized* or *decentralized* fashion. Finally, coupled with the domain context - whether the context is in providing services in *wired/stationary computing environments* or in *wireless/mobile computing environments*, service providers must take into consideration on handling requests in these two domains. Especially, a stringent constraint imposed in a mobile computing environment is in the use of available bandwidth, which in turn reflects in cost incurred to render or avail the service. All these facts provided a strong motivation for this book project after serious observations on several design challenges in the database domain in stationary and mobile computing environments.

Interestingly, several issues that are akin to a wide variety of other application domains also manifest in database domain and form non-trivial component issues to address. For instance, network caching is one of the most popularly spoken problems in the *World-Wide-Web* research and computer systems. However, in the context of database systems, these issues manifest in generating *replicas* (multiple copies) and staging them (caching) at vantage sites for increasing the *availability*. Coupled with these issues, concept of data migration which is a major concern in the web-caching domain, forms an additional issue, should the storage capacities at a node are somewhat limited. Collectively, in this book, we attempt to identify main concerns and factors present in the design of a *data (in general, object) management system* for a DDBS that handles on-line and real-time requests. Typically, we address on *What comprises an object management system, in general?*, *What issues become mainly relevant to this problem domain?*, *How to design algorithms for DDBSs with centralized and decentralized control?*, *What will be the design challenges for a mobile computing environment?*, etc, to quote a few.

One of the modern day mathematical tools that became imperative and very apt to analyze problems in this domain is *Competitive Analysis*. The concept of *competitiveness* was first introduced by Sleator and Tarjan in 1985, in the context of searching a linked list of elements and the most popular paging problem. This tool is particularly elegant in analyzing on-line algorithms and very powerful in quantifying their performance. In this book, we expose the key concepts and several techniques using in competitive analysis, to analyze a wide variety of problems. Each of these techniques is rigorously presented with several examples akin to different application domains so as to make the reader experience the value and applicability of competitive analysis in other domains.

The material in this book is organized into 7 chapters. We give a brief description of the contents of each chapter below.

In Chapter 1, we first explore the reasons that lead to a DDBS. We then broadly classify DDBS suitable for different application domains - centralized/decentralized controls, stationary/mobile computing environments, and real-time/non-real-time service requirements of requests. To some extent, in this chapter we will deal with issues that are inherent in realizing a real-life DDBS such as *object allocation*, *object replication* and *concurrency control*. We discuss and compare these issues in various categories of DDBSs which will be further discussed in later chapters. We also introduce some common definitions and terminology to clarify concepts and constituent fundamental elements of a DDBS such as node, object, communication network, etc. We then present some primary advantages that can be obtained from a DDBS. Finally, we discuss on several performance metrics that are commonly used to evaluate the system performance of DDBSs and introduce the performance metric and mention on one of the most powerful analytical techniques - *competitive analysis*, which will be used throughout this book to analyze the algorithms that handle on-line requests in DDBSs. Readers who are familiar with basic understanding of object management process (OMP), the subject matter of this book, can directly start with Chapter 3 to learn Competitive Analysis techniques.

In Chapter 2, we present a general approach to the entire object management process. We consider four different application domains, wherein the type of objects is different to each domain context. The application domains we focus are *Hierarchical Memory and Remote Memory Paging Systems*, *Video-on-Reservation Systems*, *Caching/Storage on World Wide Web and/or LAN Systems*, and *Distributed Database Systems.* We discuss issues involved in OMP in each of the above domains. We also draw attention to common issues and discuss on how these are handled in each of the domains. We conclude this chapter by providing an example which points to the dependencies among several issues in an OMP and their importance level. This chapter, on the whole, exposes several application domains that share issues commonly found in OMP.

In Chapter 3, we present an invaluable and powerful mathematical tool - Competitive Analysis, used for analyzing on-line algorithms to be designed in later chapters. This chapter introduces the reader to fundamental concepts in competitive analysis quickly through several illustrative examples using a well-known paging algorithm LRU. We will also introduce several techniques present in competitive analysis to analyze the problems. The mathematical techniques acquired here will be of direct use in understanding the design and analysis of algorithms in later chapters.

In Chapter 4, we consider OMP in DDBSs in stationary computing environments (SCEs). The emphasis here will be to design algorithms to handle on-line requests and analyze the performance of the system. We categorize the system into two types - system with centralized control and system with decentralized control and present the analysis separately. We use mathematical models to describe the cost associated with processing the requests and present several deterministic on-line algorithms for these cases. We will also consider the system availability constraints in the problem (model) and quantify the performance of the algorithms.

In Chapter 5, we focus on OMP in DDBSs in mobile computing environments (MCEs). We modify the cost models of algorithms presented in Chapter 4 to suit the conditions of a MCE and carry out similar analysis as in Chapter 4 under mobile computing context. We also modify one of the above algorithms to handle the OMP in a real-time DDBS to show the design challenges in a MCE.

It must be noted that there have been numerous studies in the area of DDBS on a variety of issues and it is beyond the scope of this book to deal with all of them. All the above studies until Chapter 5 do not explicitly assume any knowledge on topology of the underlying network infrastructure. However, to appreciate the usefulness of the techniques developed, one would be inclined to apply the tools and techniques to some of the known topologies. In a way, this becomes a useful exercise for readers. Also, conducting performance studies on known topologies is always a natural interest to implementation specialists and researchers, as small scale networks on everyday use predominantly use known architectures such as ring networks, mesh networks, tree networks, etc. In Chapter 6, we consider the OMP in some regular network topologies. Typically, we present a randomized on-line algorithm for object replication in Star Networks and a randomized on-line algorithm for object migration in Multi-Level Generic Tree Networks. We use competitive analysis to quantify the performance of these two randomized on-line algorithms. A quick glimpse on concepts presented in Chapter 3 would be helpful to understand the contents of this chapter.

In Chapter 7, we conclude the book by highlighting the importance of competitive analysis and its power in analyzing the performance of on-line algorithms. Although the major focus was on DDBSs in this book, the concepts and issues seem to be applicable to a wide variety of application domains as exemplified in Chapter 2.

In conclusion, material for each chapter is carefully considered from very recent literature and organized in a way to improve the readability through several numerical examples. Also, fundamental concepts and techniques presented in Chapter 3 are considered from very important part of the existing classical literature since 1980s. To the best possible extent, wherever applicable, numerical examples are designed and explained in a way to improve the overall clarity in understanding the key concepts.

The organization and presentation of the book are pitched at a research monograph level and the contributions of this book are largely from a theoretical standpoint stressing on underlying concepts and techniques. All the concepts and issues addressed in this book pertaining to a problem context is demonstrated via illustrative examples. This, we believe, will ease the understanding of underlying concepts as well as the readability of the contents. The material covered in this book can be used by graduate students who want to start their research in the area of distributed database systems. A very modest pre-requisite knowledge of discrete mathematics, basic linear algebra and calculus is expected. A systematic treatment on some important common issues present in the DDBS domain and in other domains is exposed to help a beginner to gain a broad outlook on applicability of the concepts. This book is also useful for those who wish to quickly learn competitive analysis and their applicability to several other domains. For an advanced researcher, this book comes very helpful in rendering state-of-the-art adaptive algorithms for different DDBSs in handling on-line and real-time requests. The mathematical rigor will be exposed in a step-by-step manner in the way that can be easily understandable. Finally, for teachers, this book comes as a very direct reference to introduce competitive analysis (Chapter 3) as there is no strong binding to DDBS alone. The material in Chapter 3 can be taught independently in about 6 hours lecture. Also, parts of the Chapters 4, 5 and 6 can be a part of Distributed Databases course, at an advanced level. For algorithm/system designers, the contents of Chapters 4 through 6 render valuable clues in designing algorithms and tuning them to handle on-line requests in an actual DDBS in practice. Further, this book presents several interesting materials to operations research community and management scientists since cost optimization and object management are after all the main emphases of the book.

Acknowledgments

First of all, we would like to thank Professor Cauligi Raghavendra, Department of EECS, USC CA, LA, USA, for giving this unique opportunity to publish this monograph as a part of NETA series. The first meeting of the second author with him in USC during summer 2002 was illuminating and had provided considerable interest in pursuing this paramount project. His quick support in providing pointers to Kluwer Academic Publishers and to kick start this project was truly laudable. Both the authors would like to acknowledge the great support from Mr. John R. Martindale, Senior Publishing Editor and Ms. Angela Quilici, Editorial Assistant of Kluwer Academic Publishers for providing time-to-time support in clarifying several issues in this process. We would like to render our deepest appreciation and thanks to Professor Ouri Wolfson, Department of EECS, University of Illinois, Chicago, IL, USA, for his insightful comments on parts of this work in its early stages.

The first author would like to take this opportunity to thank his wife Hu Xiaohong for her patience, understanding, and encouragement provided throughout the long duration of this project. He is greatly indebted to his mentor, Professor Bharadwaj Veeravalli (the second author), for all the support, valuable suggestions and insightful comments that made this text possible. He would also like to thank all his friends in Open Source Software Laboratory (OSSL), Department of ECE, NUS, Singapore, for rendering technical and moral support during this book writing project.

The second author would like to thank his wonderful wife, Lavanya for her patience, understanding, and encouragement rendered throughout the book writing process. He would like to thank his daughter Tanya for keeping him awake during long night hours, in a way, helping to complete the task on time. He would like to thank his brother Sivakumar and his family for all the encouragement provided during this time. He would like to render special thanks to (his Gurus!) Professor Debasish Ghose and Professor Venkatraman Mani, Department of Aerospace Engineering, Indian Institute of Science, Bangalore, India, who had always a word of encouragement on any research endeavor undertaken by him. The terrific research experience gained over two-and-a-half years of stay with them during PhD days(January 1992-July 1994) had really inculcated certain discipline and systematic research habits to produce high quality research. He would also like to pass a special thanks to his friend and colleague Professor Tom, Department of EE, SUNY, Stony Brook, NY, USA, who always had a great deal of interest in all his work and had provided several insightful comments. Finally, he would like to say a BIG THANK YOU to all his friends in NUS with Department of ECE, NUS, for providing a conducive and joyful ambience. Special thanks to *The Tea Club* members who had discussions, almost everyday, on all topics ranging from Iraq War to everyday life in Singapore! Thanks Guys!

Chapter 1

INTRODUCTION TO DISTRIBUTED DATABASE SYSTEMS

1. Why a Distributed Database?

Databases come in many flavors. We use databases in our daily activities such as airline reservations, banking transactions via an ATM machine, searching information in the Internet by using a search engine, borrowing books from a library, etc. Have you ever thought about *where* and *how* the data are accessed and managed?

Database systems evolved as the need for shared data keep increasing. A very good example to realize the truth behind this statement is a *Video-on-Demand* (VOD) system to which several users subscribe to access movies on a regular basis. In this case, the database is a *movie* database comprising movies stored in a particular style. In particular, the rapid proliferation in computer hardware technology coupled with the underlying communications technology made a grand success for the advent of database systems. The service offering capabilities were further enhanced by the use of modern day computer architectures such as SISD (*single instruction stream over a single data stream*) to MIMD (*multiple instruction streams over multiple data streams*)[KH93], together with the use of sophisticated operating systems exclusively developed for architectures with multiple CPUs[1][PJF97]. As the size of corporate offices, government organizations, educational sectors, etc, grow with time, need for sharing the available computer and communication facilities becomes a clever solution without incurring additional investment overheads. In turn, this demands for devising efficient technologies and methods to disseminate the required data to the users at the required times. Con-

[1]These are also referred to as *Multiprocessor architectures*.

sequently, data organization, management, delivery, storage, etc, form imperative components in rendering services to several application domains mentioned above. In order to simplify the control mechanism in such sophisticated systems, the computer and communication facilities were traditionally biased towards a *centralized* style of operation. In a centralized database system, all the data are collected into a single database, as shown in Figure 1.1, where the *Database Management System* (DBMS) is essentially a software component that provides services for accessing the data stored in the database.

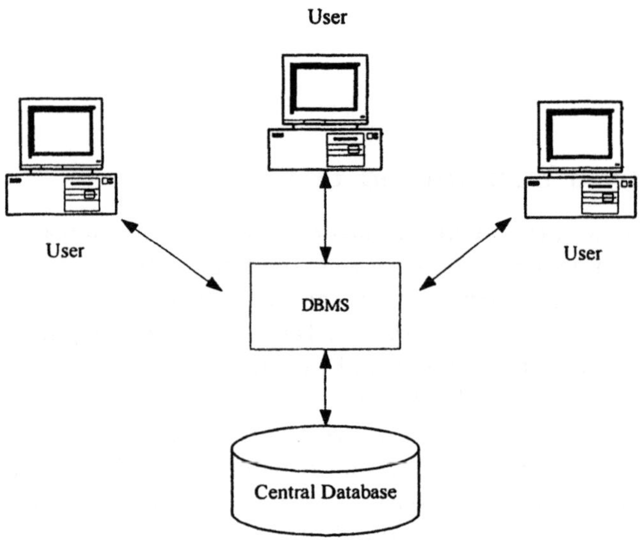

Figure 1.1. A centralized database system architecture

Obviously, the use of centralized database systems makes sense if the user domain is somewhat smaller in size and possibly confined to a smaller geographical area. However, industrial organizations, educational bodies with multi-campuses, transactions between several banks, etc, require a decentralized way of operational style due to geographic separation. Thus, exercising a single point control to coordinate and store all the required data for such systems will be highly inefficient. For instance, users may undergo long waiting times to access the centralized database. Managing and using a single large size database for such diversified applications are prohibitively complex and long communication time between the database and the users, etc, are some of the disadvantages we can immediately comprehend. Essentially, the motivation to take into account the geographic nature of distribution for diversified application domains and reducing the overall cost become dominating factors that lead to a *Distributed Database System* (DDBS), where the data are distributed among server locations of the system.

It may be noted that in the context of database systems, a more generic term to refer to data would be *object*. Especially, with the currently existing different types of media such as audio, video, text files, graphics, animations, etc, the context in which each of these media is used (or in use) depends on the underlying applications. Consequently, we can refer to these individual types of media as audio data, video data, text data, and so on. More generally, with the advent of modern day *object-oriented* engineering approach, special attributes/properties can also be captured in the definition for each of these types of data. Thus, it makes more sense to refer to each of these types simply as *objects*. The definition and use of this terminology *object* are very apt especially in the context of databases systems. Thus, an object, in general, may refer to an indivisible entity ranging from a small text file to a large volume multimedia file, depending on the underlying application.

Further, a DDBS does not simply imply objects distribution alone. Additionally, the service nature of a DDBS should mimic a centralized database system. In other words, as far as the users are concerned, the distributed nature of object distribution/service infrastructure must be made completely transparent[2] and the database system performs as a single and locally accessible database management system to the end users. Thus, although the objects are distributed in the system, unified (centralized) facilities must be enforced for the end users to access the database and for the system administrators to manage the database. Indeed, one of the attractions to manage a DDBS is that it can provide a unified command and control mechanism for a geographically distributed system.

2. What is a DDBS?

A simplified architecture of a DDBS is shown in Figure 1.2. The *Object Management Process* (OMP) in Figure 1.2 is an element in a DDBS that is similar to the DBMS in a centralized database system. We will discuss the OMP in different application domains in Chapter 2.

It should be noted that the database in a DDBS may consist of all the objects in a DDBS or may have a portion of the total set. The decision on how the objects are to be distributed in the system is based on the

[2]Refer to [ODV94, pp.45] for more details.

underlying applications and system performance. From Figure 1.2, we observe that the basic elements of a DDBS comprise objects, nodes, communication sub-systems and OMPs. Sometimes owing to enormous volume of objects to be stored, a DDBS may consist of additional storage units attached to the nodes. As shown in Figure 1.2, a node in a DDBS

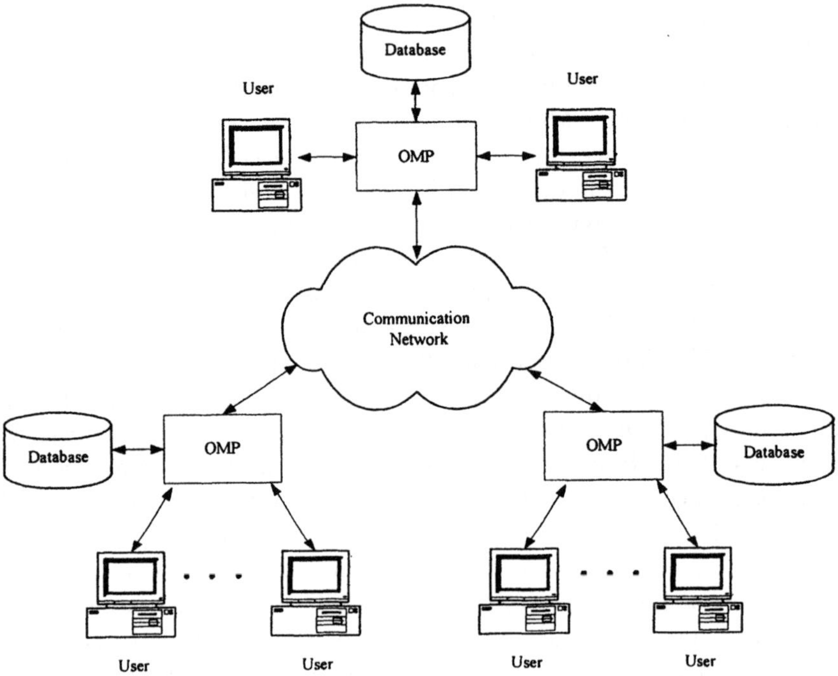

Figure 1.2. A distributed database system architecture

is a complete computer system and a DDBS may consist of several such individual nodes. Each node has independent processing and storage capabilities. Below, we list major components of a node.

- Identity of the node (name)
- Processor architecture (uni-processor or multi-processor)
- Main memory (cache and/or disk)
- Communication devices
- Directory of objects stored in the node

- Route information (the path to a destination node on the network)

The nodes in the system are connected via communication networks, which acts as a conduit through which objects can flow between different nodes. The communication medium may be pairs of twisted wires, coaxial cables, optical fibers or wireless mediums, with data transmission speeds ranging from tens of kilobytes up to a hundred megabytes per second or more. Further, there can be different topologies of the communication networks. We illustrate some commonly used topologies in Figure 1.3.

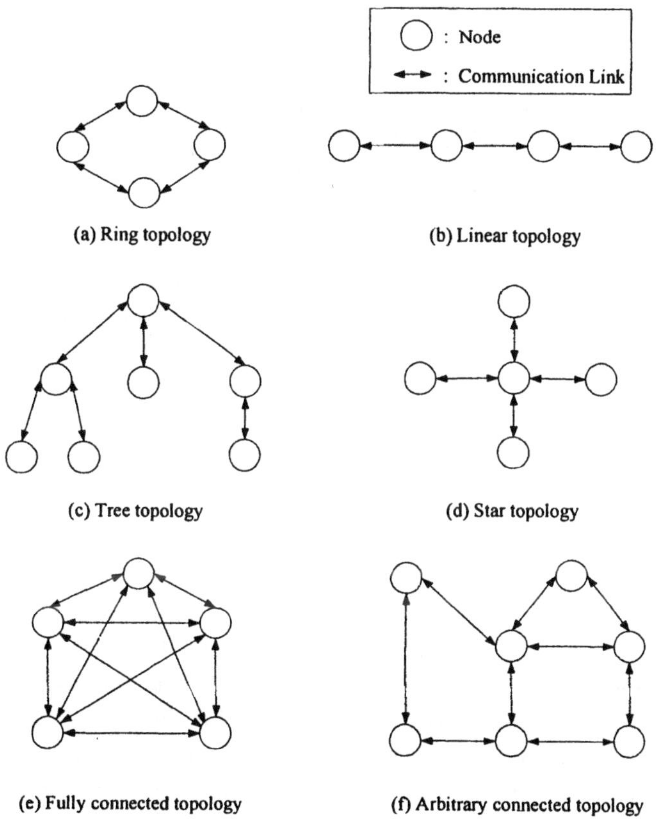

Figure 1.3. Network topologies

It should be noted that the system reliabilities of various network topologies are different. Essentially, the transmission speed and reliability of the communication network will strongly affect the overall performance of a DDBS.

Apart from physical layer issues mentioned above, some additional issues have to be solved when the objects are to be distributed/managed in several locations in the system. These issues include,

- Object Allocation: Determining the locations to hold an object when the object is created (Choosing vantage locations for the respective objects)
- Object Location: Determining the locations of an object whenever an end user wishes to access it (Equivalent to searching locations to find the desired objects)
- Object Replication: Replicating the same object in several locations for performance and reliability considerations (This operation creates multiple copies to exist on the system)
- Object Migration: Migrating an object from one location to another location whenever it is required
- Object Consistency: Maintaining consistency between multiple copies of the same object in different locations due to any modifications of objects elsewhere

The above issues are the most important and widely studied problems in a DDBS. We will formally discuss them in detail in Chapter 2. We now introduce an important process by which servicing is carried out in a DDBS.

Transaction

A service rendering nature of a DDBS typically consists of retrieving objects and/or modifying them as per the requests from clients. Now, to retrieve or modify (update) an object, the node has to issue a *transaction* to the DDBS. Formally, a transaction[3] can be defined as a sequence of database operations carried out by a single node or an application program in a *secured way* as an indivisible unit. Thus, a transaction is an indivisible entity. The basic information in a transaction comprises:

- Transaction identity
- Requested object identity

[3] In this book, we use "transaction" and "request" interchangeably.

- Type of operations to be performed on the object (retrieve/read or update/write)
- Identity of the node that initiated the transaction
- Identity of the destination node which has the requested object or knows the locations of the requested object

Further, several end users may simultaneously issue several transactions for the same object in a DDBS. Hence, the DDBS is expected to support the multiple client accesses. However, in such a situation, transactions may transfer the database from one consistent state to another consistent state and the object consistency may be violated during the processing of transactions, especially when some of the transactions are issued to update the database. Therefore, a *concurrency control* mechanism, such as *time-stamps*[Reed83] and *locking*[BHG87] mechanism, is required to handle these concurrent transactions in such a way that the object consistency will be maintained more-or-less at all times in a DDBS. We will brief on the concurrency control mechanism in Chapter 2. Astute readers are referred to [DJ92, GR93] for further reading, as it is beyond the scope of this book to consider transaction processing in detail.

3. Classification of DDBSs

As indicated in the beginning of this chapter, a DDBS exists in several flavors. In different application domains, different types of DDBS have been realized. For instance, considering the control mechanism, DDBSs can be classified as either with a *Centralized Control* or with a *Decentralized Control.* In Figure 1.4, we show a classification of DDBSs

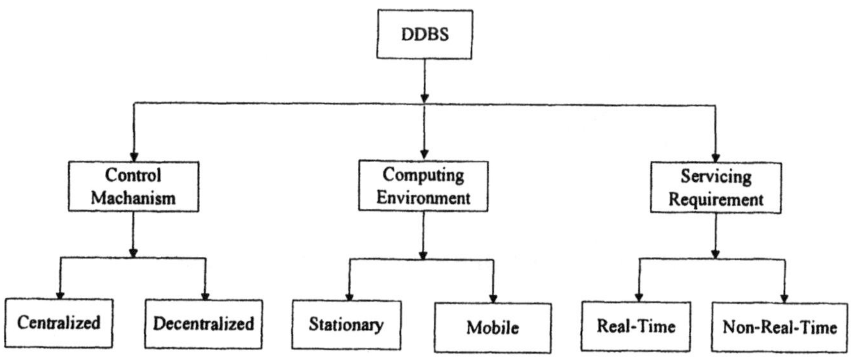

Figure 1.4. Classification of DDBSs

based on independent features that are in place in the design of a DDBS for a specific application. Depending on application requirements, the designers can choose what type of DDBS they are looking for. Thus, for instance, an application may demand designing a DDBS that has a decentralized control mechanism for servicing real-time transactions in a mobile environment, and so on. We shall brief on each of the categories of DDBS below.

3.1 Centralized Control and Decentralized Control

The design of a DDBS can favor two types of control mechanisms namely, either *centralized* control or *decentralized* control, respectively. In a centralized control DDBS there is a *central control unit* (CCU) to which all the transactions arrive for processing. The concurrency control is taken care in the CCU to maintain the object consistency as well as to *serialize* the transactions[4], as shown in Figure 1.5.

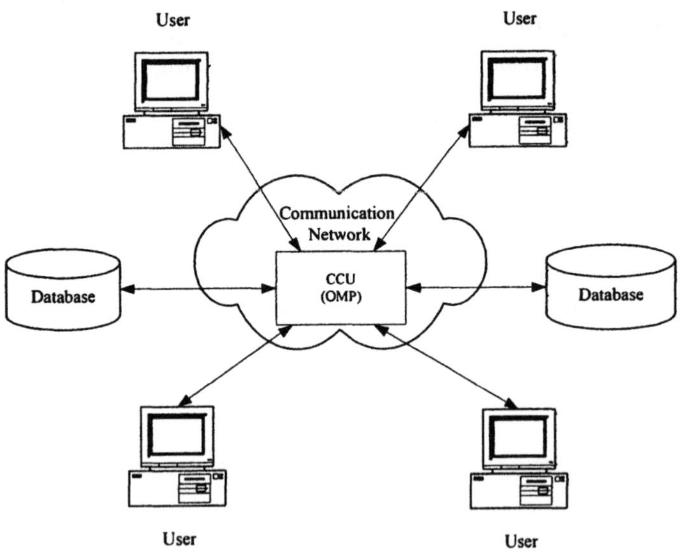

Figure 1.5. A DDBS with a centralized control

[4]Refer to Chapter 2 and [BK91, NRP95, SWH98].

In a decentralized control DDBS, the system does not have a CCU. The concurrency control and security control mechanisms are distributed in the system[5]. Figure 1.2 is an example of a DDBS with a decentralized control. Essentially, with a centralized control, the system reliability of a DDBS is never guaranteed as there is a single point failure. However, the security control and concurrency control, arriving at a consensus, can be relatively taken care easily. On the other hand, for decentralized control, the system reliability is extremely high, but the above mentioned additional issues require somewhat sophisticated treatment. Therefore, the choices of these control mechanisms are usually based on the underlying application requirements and each has its own advantages and disadvantages.

3.2 Stationary Computing Environment and Mobile Computing Environment

Traditionally, a DDBS consists of several stationary nodes (computers) in the system. The location of a node in the system does not change. The internodes communication is implemented via wired links, such as pairs of twisted wires and optical fibers. We usually consider this environment as *Stationary Computing Environment* (SCE). In fact, whatever we have discussed so far applies to SCE domain directly. Recently, due to the technological advancement in realizing sophisticated computing devices and wireless communication technologies promising lower monetary cost rates, the widespread use of mobile computing devices, such as laptops, handhold personal digital assistants (PDAs), have become popular among users. In this domain, a DDBS is expected to support a (computer) network of mobile hosts (MHs). In such a *Mobile Computing Environment* (MCE), thc internodes communication is implemented via wireless medium which has a limited amount of bandwidth to use.

Basically, a MCE aims to provide a continuous network connectivity to MHs regardless of their locations. However, there are several problems when designing a DDBS in a MCE that pose many challenges to the database system/algorithm designers. For example, in a MCE, a MH can move from one location to another (mobility), or the MH may be frequently switched off to save power (disconnection). Under such circumstances, the overall network topology may change dynamically as connectivity is essentially lost. Further, the storage capacities on the MHs as well as the bandwidth availability on the wireless network are all limited, and hence, the issues in designing a DDBS mentioned earlier,

[5]These two control mechanisms can be implemented in the OMPs.

such as the object location and object replication, are more difficult in a MCE when compared to that in a SCE. Above all, monetary costs involved in processing a transaction using a mobile device is more costly when compared to the pricing rates in a SCE.

3.3 Real-Time Servicing Requirement and Non-Real-Time Servicing Requirement

As mentioned earlier, in order to access objects, transactions will be issued to the DDBS by the end users. It should be noted that the transaction requests may not be attended immediately after arriving at the system. Basically, the *response time* of a transaction includes communication time, queuing time (or waiting time due to the concurrency control in the nodes) and processing time. Consequently, the end users may undergo long undesired waiting times to obtain the results of transactions. This waiting time may not be time-critical in a *Non-Real-Time* DDBS. However, in some application domains such as on-line banking transactions, VOD, automated stock trading, telephone call routings, etc [HX00], a quick response for a transaction is expected. DDBSs in such time-critical domains are classified as *Real-Time Distributed Database Systems* (RTDDBSs) and have attracted considerable research interest in recent years. Besides the basic information mentioned in Section 2, a transaction in a RTDDBS consists of a time constraint (imposed by the transaction), which requires the system to service it *on or before* the time constraint. Such time constraint imposed by a transaction is usually defined as *deadline*, which is measured in time units. In different application domains, the consequences for not satisfying the time constraints may be different. Therefore, depending on the different consequences of the time constraints being violated, the nature of deadlines can be classified into three categories: *hard deadlines*, *firm deadlines* and *soft deadlines* [PJF97].

When the system considers a transaction with a hard deadline requirement, it is highly vital for the system to meet its deadline and the system will be penalized if the hard deadline is missed. Further, there will be no benefit if the system processes this transaction after the deadline. On the other hand, the system is not penalized if it misses a firm deadline imposed by a transaction. Similar to the previous case, here too, there is no benefit in completing the transaction after the specified deadline for this category. Finally, in the case of transactions imposing soft deadlines, there will be always a benefit to the system even if it misses the deadline. However, the benefit may decline proportionally depending on the lateness of completion. Further, in all the above cases, it should be noted that the goal of a RTDDBS is to meet as many deadlines as possible before attempting to maximize the system performance, although the consequences of missing the deadlines may be different.

Essentially, a RTDDBS has all of the requirements of traditional database systems, such as concurrency control and security control. It must not only maintain the consistency constraints of objects but also, even more importantly, guarantee the time constraints imposed by each transaction at the same time. In other words, designing a RTDDBS must combine the principles developed in traditional database systems and *real-time* systems. This persuasive dual requirement makes the object management process more complex and difficult in a RTDDBS than that in a conventional (non-real-time) DDBS.

4. Advantages of DDBSs

As mentioned earlier, one of the objectives in designing a DDBS is to provide easy access to the objects. As the objects are distributed in the system, this objective may entertain both the authorized and unauthorized accesses to the objects. Hence, there is always a persistent security problem in a DDBS, which may lead to *data leak*, unless some *security control* mechanisms are proposed. Clearly, the security problem also exists in a centralized database system. However, it is more difficult to implement the security control mechanisms in a DDBS when compared to a centralized database system, because it is difficult to decide about a vantage location for exercising the control mechanism in the system. Unquestionably, the *security control* and the *concurrency control* will complicate the design as well as implementation of a DDBS. However, there are many obvious advantages of a DDBS that can compensate for the additional complexity. The following are some immediate perceivable advantages that a user can obtain from a DDBS.

- Rapid response
  In a DDBS, objects can be stored at the locations where they are frequently accessed. As a result, most of the retrieving transactions can be satisfied locally or satisfied by a closer node. Further, transactions can be serviced concurrently in the system. Therefore, the response time of a transaction is reduced when compared to a centralized database system where all the objects are located at one place.

- High availability and reliability
  An object can be replicated in several nodes in a DDBS, depending on its "importance" or demand. Thus we say that the system has increased the *availability* of the objects so as to facilitate easy and fast access for end users. Further, when objects are replicated elsewhere

on the network, even if one node fails to operate, the transactions associated with the failed node can still be satisfied by redirecting to other relevant nodes holding the requested objects, and the servicing of other transactions are not interrupted. Therefore, object availability and the system *reliability* are *maximized* by using redundant copies. These issues will be discussed in detail in Chapter 2 when we describe an OMP.

- High system scalability
  One of the attractive features of a DDBS is in allowing easy alteration of the physical size of the system under consideration. It is easy for a DDBS to add/remove nodes to satisfy the performance requirement without changing the existing components in the system.

- Improved performance
  Due to object replication, transactions on the same object can be serviced simultaneously in a DDBS. As a result, the communication and the computing processes are distributed in the system, and hence, the system performance is largely improved.

5. Performance Metrics and Related Issues

There are several criteria to evaluate the performance of a DDBS, such as maximizing the *fraction of the transactions* that can be serviced without missing their *deadlines* (or equivalently, minimizing the fraction of transactions that are blocked from service, referred to as *blocking probability*), minimizing the total monetary cost of servicing the transactions, maximizing the *system resources utilization rate*, maximizing the system reliability, designing algorithms with acceptable/minimum *complexity*[6], minimizing the *mean response time* of transactions, etc. The choice of a performance metric usually stems from the underlying application requirements. For instance, considering a RTDDBS, the expected number of transactions to be handled will be very large when we consider applications such as on-line banking. In this situation, the system can choose to have two different important performance criteria - maximizing the system reliability and/or minimizing the mean response time of processing a transaction. On the other hand, in providing a mobile service, a service provider may consider minimizing the blocking probability and maximizing the system resource utilization rate, as available *bandwidth* of mobile services is somewhat limited to use. Thus blocking probability

[6]This can also be equivalently thought of as designing polynomial time bound algorithms.

and system utilization rate become added performance metrics to the above mentioned metrics in our previous on-line banking example.

In this book, we are primarily concerned with exposing the underlying challenges in designing algorithms for efficiently handling *on-line* requests by DDBSs. These algorithms form a part of OMP to be discussed in detail in Chapter 2. Since most of the modern day applications are confronted with an *embarrassingly* large number of requests to be handled, the use of conventional algorithms suitable for small-scale systems and for systems that receive requests infrequently, will be highly detrimental on any performance metric. Our goal is to systematically design and analyze algorithms for DDBSs (centralized and decentralized) in SECs and MCEs to handle on-line requests (both real-time and non-real-time). We will use *Competitive Analysis* to conduct our analysis on the performance of the algorithms. In Chapter 3, we will introduce this technique, which is a valuable tool in analyzing algorithms that can handle on-line requests. Throughout this book, our performance metric of interest is to minimize the total cost of servicing the transactions that arrive at the DDBS. We will more formally define this metric in later chapters.

6. Concluding Remarks

In this chapter we first explored the reasons that lead to a DDBS. We then systematically exposed several components in a DDBS and classified DDBS based on independent features that are in place in its design for a specific application. We have introduced some important issues in realizing a real-life DDBS such as object allocation, object replication, concurrency control, etc, and compared them across different classifications of DDBS introduced above. We also introduced the notion of transaction processing and discussed on several flavors of handling transactions driven by deadline constraints. Astute readers can refer to standard text books and classical literature to extract more details on the issues discussed in this chapter. Further, we have discussed the main advantages that can be achieved in designing a DDBS. The issues and the terminology used in this chapter will be used throughout the book later in our discussions and serves as a valuable quick reference for the readers. Finally, we discussed on several performance metrics, which are commonly used to evaluate the system performance of DDBSs, and mentioned on the performance analysis technique, i.e., competitive analysis which will be used throughout this book to analyze the algorithms that handle on-line requests in DDBSs. Readers who are familiar with basic understanding of OMP can directly start with Chapter 3 to learn Competitive Analysis techniques.

Chapter 2

OBJECT MANAGEMENT PROCESS, ISSUES AND APPLICATION EXAMPLES

In this chapter, we will introduce *Object Management Process* (OMP) in a more generalized sense. As mentioned in Chapter 1, an object, in general, may refer to an indivisible entity ranging from a small text file to a large volume multimedia file, depending on the underlying application. For instance, in database systems these objects can be categorized systematically in the form of text files, audio clips, graphic files, video clips ranging from small to large sizes and can be indexed in a clever manner to aid faster retrieval. Thus, an object is an entity defined by its *type* and *size*. Further, some objects can be altered, i.e., they may be "edited" which means that the size of such objects is a varying quantity. Additionally, in a network system, transferring an object from one node to another may be required by some application which will consume a varying network bandwidth. *Managing* the objects on a network system is an important issue which we call *Object Management Process* (OMP). We will introduce some methodologies of OMP and some performance metrics that are commonly used to quantify the performance of these methodologies. This OMP typically involves:

- *tracking where exactly the original source of an object resides*
- *deciding on the number of copies of an object required at present*
- *allowing copies to relocate to another site on the network as required*
- *guaranteeing consistency among the currently existing copies*
- *broadcasting/multicasting information pertaining to any changes to a copy of an object at any node to other relevant nodes*

- *continuously looking for vantage sites on which objects can be permanently/temporarily stored/located*

Each of the above issues results in the use of enormous amount of resources for processing and may incur overheads, depending on the type of requests submitted to the system. We will look into each of these issues comprising an OMP and specifically quote some application domains wherein each of these issues may be more meaningful. We will now introduce some terminology used in the literature in OMP.

Firstly, the process by which the requested objects are discovered, selected and delivered from neighboring sites is undertaken by an algorithm referred to as *object location algorithm.* Thus, when this algorithm is invoked, it locates the requested object and depending on the flexibility of its design it may be allowed to deliver the requested object to the desired site. Secondly, from common sense perspective, availing network based services seems more economical and faster than any conventional types of services. For instance, it may be cheaper to subscribe to a network-based multimedia movie-on-demand (MOD) service with a service provider than to approach a video rental store for video cassettes/compact discs every time. Further, such network based services offer complete flexibility in allowing the clients to interact with the system. Thus, on a network, it is expected that multiple copies of an object are to be "injected" or "created" such that accessing becomes faster and more requests could be supported. Consequently, *object replication* takes an imperative role in an OMP. However, replicating too many copies may give raise to additional overheads such as maintaining consistency among the copies (when objects can be edited), requiring design of efficient *object consistency* algorithms. The role of object consistency algorithms is to ensure that each available copy of an object on the network is consistent. In simplest sense, this could be based on *time-stamping* technique [AW98] in which the recency of an object is tested using a time-stamp and from where the object was fetched. Finally, in order to ensure consistency, broadcasting or multicasting algorithms can be used, depending on the application under consideration. Predominantly, multicasting algorithms are desired, as copies of the objects exist only in few sites. Further, it may be possible that one may need to redesign conventional multicasting algorithms to suit the current needs of the problem context. For instance, if links are not available in a planned route between a source site and a destination site, an in-between site can route the object via other available best paths at that time instant. Thus, the underlying network topology may dynamically change with respect to resource availability constraints. Hence, conventional multicasting algorithms suited for static case[1] may not be directly applicable in OMP wherein dynamic changes in the network topology take place.

Although replication is desired, when exactly a replication is required is often due to several criteria, depending on the underlying applications. In a MOD system, less popular movies may not be replicated frequently and stored on the network, as the popularity profile may be demanding. Also, when the available storage (or network bandwidth) becomes a bottleneck, replication may be impossible. In some systems, depending on the demand profile, *fixed* number of copies are allowed to exist at some vantage sites. Thus, the problem of replication is closely coupled with issues pertaining to resource availability. In some systems *object migration* may be an alternative solution to object replication. In such cases, if resources are barely available and if the existing copies are few in number, then in lieu of replicating the object in other sites, an existing copy can be "moved" from its current site to any remote (chosen) site. Also, this process of migration can be based on the "importance" of the object at a site. For example, if an object is needed most in a site j and if a copy exists at a site i at which this object is less demanded, then object can be allowed to migrate to site j. These crucial object migration decisions also form a part of OMP. Thus, on the whole, OMP involves the choice of selecting the best possible algorithms for every issue in place for the currently existing network configuration, demand profile of the objects, resource availability constraints. As mentioned before, we will see the following four application domains that directly use the above mentioned OMP with respect to their needs and constraints.

- Hierarchical Memory and Remote Memory Paging Systems
- Video-on-Reservation Systems
- Caching/Storage on World Wide Web and/or LAN Systems
- Distributed Database Systems

We have specifically chosen these application domains because the nature of objects under consideration is different in each domain and imparts different types of constraints.

1. OMP in Hierarchical Memory and Remote Memory Paging Systems

We will first consider a hierarchical memory system that is commonly used in the design of a computer system and extend our discussion to a

[1] Network topology does not change with respect to time or resource availabilities.

remote memory system. Designing strategies for efficient management of the available memory bandwidth and space always posses a challenging problem. From traditional to modern day computer architectures, the performance improvement was shown to be significant when memory management is carried out in a clever manner [KH93]. In the traditional architectures, the memory hierarchy was envisioned to range from tiny registers to tapes and disks as a means of storage media. The definition of an object in this case depends on the level concerned in the memory hierarchy.

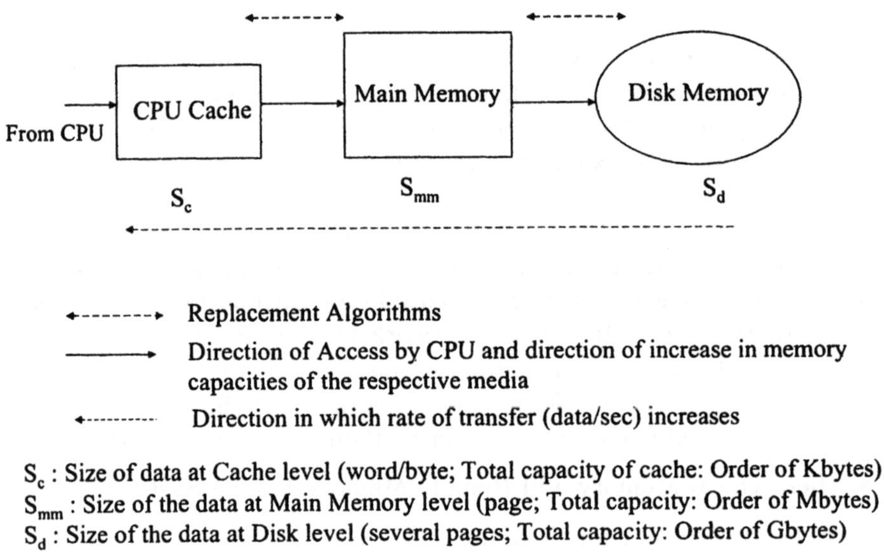

Figure 2.1. Typical memory hierarchy in a single computer system. The figure shows where the replacement algorithms operate, the sizes of the respective media, basic accessible size in each media, direction of access priority, and direction in which data transfer rates increase

At CPU level, an object assumes a size of in bytes, at cache level an object is of size expressed in *cache lines/pages* (typically blocks of bytes), at a main memory level an object is of size *pages* (several blocks of bytes[2]), and finally at disk level it could be large segments comprising several pages, depending on the underlying memory management. At

[2] A page is a fixed size entity as viewed by an operating system.

this single processor level, OMP refers to decisions to be made to allow easier and faster access to the required datum from the memory system. Now, within a memory system, considering a three level hierarchy as an example (refer to Figure 2.1), when a request for a page is generated, it is first searched in the cache (owing to its high access speeds) and if it is found then we say that we have a *hit*. However, if there is a *miss* (datum not found at the desired level), then next higher level is accessed to look for the desired datum and this process continues.

As exemplified in several text books and literature, from performance perspective it may be desirable to retain some most frequently accessed objects in the cache in the hope that there may be some "near" future requests for these objects. However, when there is a miss, a decision has to be taken on which object to be evicted from the cache (or at the level that is currently under consideration) so as to provide room for the requested object. The algorithms which allow these page/object replacements within a memory system hierarchy are referred to as *page replacement algorithms*. Some most popular algorithms in this category include, least recently used (LRU), most frequently used (MFU), least frequently used (LFU), size-based LRU (S-LRU), etc, to quote a few. We will see the working style of some algorithms later in Chapter 3 when we introduce *on-line* problems. Readers may also refer to any standard text books on this topic [KH93, HVZ02]. Thus, as far as an OMP is concerned, at a single node/site level, the issues are on designing replacement algorithms. Object migration and replication are not relevant to be considered at a single processor system level. However, later we will point out that these are the fundamental techniques that are useful even at system levels (between sites) while making migration/replication decisions in web-caching problems. In fact, we will see several variants of these fundamental replacement algorithms are in place for web-caching problems later in Section 3.

Though the techniques used to reduce the latencies during processing in a single CPU system following the above mentioned hierarchy were successful, the power offered by the advent of current day high speed computers, coupled with the networking technology using high speed interconnection media, was seldom exploited fully. From multiprocessors to multicomputers, the memory system hierarchical architecture can be classified as, (a) *shared main-memory architecture*, (b) *distributed shared virtual memory* (DSVM) and (c) *remote caching architecture* (RCA)[LWY91][3]. With the technological advancement in the

[3]This is one of the earliest work introducing the concept of RCA.

computer hardware side as well as in networking, the current trend is geared towards using remote caching architectures as a means of improving the overall system performance. The key feature of RCA is that sites request (and receive) objects from remote sites with a faster *response time* than even accessing their own local disks. This fact is truly surprising and as the system can see an enlarged virtual memory space. The main difference from shared main-memory architectures is that the sites do not necessarily require the capability of direct read/write into remote memory locations. Further, it has been argued in literature that RCA can use DSVM as a platform. This means that, a particular job is assigned a virtual address that can be either referring to a local or on any remote site. Only when the requested objects[4] cannot be found elsewhere in the network, local disk access is initiated. Thus, RCA has an excellent advantage in presenting an expanded virtual memory space and provides a very large virtual space to a single site.

In the so far literature available in RCA [LWY91, LWY92, LWY93, LWY96], the hierarchy is assumed to contain a local main memory, followed by a remote main memory (accessed via the underlying communications network) and then the local disk, as shown in Figure 2.2. The dark arrows in the figure show the order of priority of object access in RCA architecture. In general, the performance of RCA is mainly centered around the performance on the following three fundamental algorithms.

(a) A *location algorithm* that sites predominantly use to efficiently determine whether a page resides in a remote site or not.

(b) A *replacement algorithm* within a site to determine the page that needs to be swapped out of main memory to make sufficient room for an incoming page.

(c) A *consistency algorithm* to ensure that page updates are propagated to buffered copies elsewhere and that page accesses always reflect the most recent changes carried out.

While all the above algorithms are important, the design of a replacement algorithm is the most crucial part. A good replacement algorithm should promise an overall better performance of the entire system. If the application is such that it is permitted to have only read-only access, then consistency is hardly an issue. However, if there are write operations on the memory pages by the application, then item (c) above is indeed an important issue.

---

[4] An object in a RCA system refers to a page, in general.

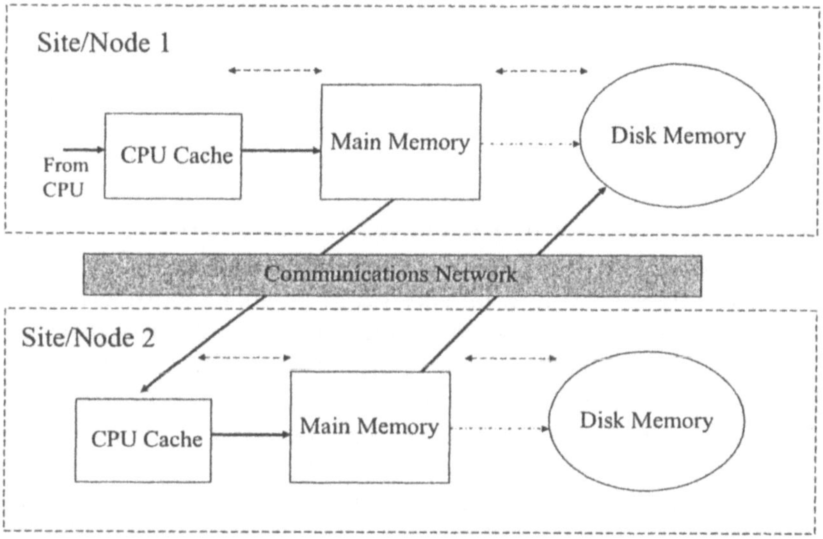

Figure 2.2. Remote Memory Architecture (RCA). The figure shows an access by Site 1 in RCA architecture. The dark arrows show the direction of object access

Before the advent of RCA and after the DSVM model [NL91] for distributed systems, an idea of *remote memory model*[CG90] as a new paradigm that suits distributed systems was in place. This model consists of several client machines, one or more dedicated machines called as remote memory servers, and a communication channel interconnecting them. The client machines share the memory resources located on the remote memory servers. Also, there are other similar models: *remote memory paging system* [FZ91], *adaptive remote paging* [SD91]. Their common feature is to use remote memory as a faster storage medium than the local disk. The basic idea comes from the following fact. The *remote procedure calls* (RPC)[5] over Ethernet consumes approximately only one-tenth of disk access time. But the remote memory model is still different with RCA in the sense that the latter is a symmetric architecture (there are no special remote memory servers and all the machines are both client and server simultaneously), while the former is fundamentally an unsymmetrical architecture (there are special memory servers). Work in [PLKC90, PFSYW91] is convincing in favor of RCA model than a distributed client/server architecture.

[5]Basic work on RPC is reported in [SB89].

With the advent of RCA, the problem is fundamentally treated as a placement problem [LWY92]. The main focus is to obtain an optimal page assignment among sites/nodes on the network so that a minimum average access time[6] is achieved. It is common to formulate these problems as *0-1 nonlinear integer programming* problems [GN72], especially, as a version of the most popular *File Allocation Problem* (FAP) found in the computing literature[7].

Now, for the placement problem of RCA, most algorithms meant for FAP can be used in optimization of page-assignment in RCA system, since there are rigorous studies on algorithms about FAP. An auction algorithm proposed in [BC89] is used to address RCA problem in [LWY91]. But till date, there is no special heuristic strategy for optimization of the RCA problem. For the replacement problem, [LWY93] provides a greedy algorithm and a distributed strategy. Greedy algorithm is a kind of *isolationist* algorithm that considers the value of the page at the local site and this value is used for measuring the importance of the page. On the other hand, the distributed strategy uses "local marginal value" to evaluate the importance of pages. The calculations of "local marginal value" involve the access rates (rate at which requests for pages arrive at the system) at both the local site and remote sites, so that the distributed strategy can obtain better performance than greedy algorithm. Nevertheless, distributed strategy costs a lot of overhead processing for sorting all the pages in the system. Another shortcoming of the distributed strategy is that it *needs* a priori access rates information like an optimal algorithm[8]. However, in real life situation, we cannot obtain the exact magnitudes of the access rates. Thus, distributed strategy is not practical to realize like an optimal algorithm. As a result, there exist a set of heuristic one-copy algorithms, referred to as 1CHg (global) and 1CHl(local) [LWY96]. The algorithms assume that only one copy is enough in the whole system (replication is strictly forbidden) to achieve an acceptable performance. The advantage is that the algorithms are simple in operation and easy to implement. However, deficit is also obvious, in the sense that, even when there is enough space in the main-memory and/or some page is particularly important, replication was seldom used. Thus, 1CHg and 1CHl have a limited scope.

Hence, we see that in a RCA system, whenever our objective is to optimize the local performance predominantly, the choice of the algo-

---

[6]This is also referred to as response time and it is defined as the time instant between a request is submitted to the system and the time at which the request is satisfied.

[7]For FAP - Refer to [C69, C72, E74, DF82, W84].

[8]An optimal algorithm, in general, is assumed to have a complete knowledge of access rate information. We will elaborate this in Chapter 3.

rithms such as LRU, LFU, MFU, etc, affects the performance, as every site uses only local information available to it. However, when global performance is our concern, then the combined influence of the choice of replacement policies mentioned above at every node together with page migration and replication between sites is to be considered. Thus, an OMP in such systems lies in our judicious choice of strategies that are to be used to seek an acceptable performance.

2. OMP in Video-on-Reservation Systems

Multimedia personalized services (MPSs) have become very attractive in recent years because of their elegance in making a simple personal computer at home as a conduit for a wide variety of entertainment at an affordable cost. Coupled with the rapid advancement in networking technology, personalized services can be even more attractive due to many distributed applications such as, tele-education, tele-medicine, video conferencing, tele-shopping, video-on-demand, to quote a few. An underlying strong motivation for all these services stems from a promising trade-off between several factors such as the control of the service quality by the users, monetary cost, control on desired viewing times, control on the playback of the desired documents, and control on the types of media (independent on/off control on media types by users). All these factors not only make MPS attractive, but simply outperforms the services offered by the conventional cable TV and video rental services. Further, in recent years, multimedia services have found strong footholds in areas such as business and medicine, coupled with wireless communications technology. However, one of the overriding reasons for its slow pace to reach every home is the high cost of such services. Surveys in [J94] have shown that only about 6% of respondents would be willing to pay more than their cable television rates for such services.

The existing high cost of multimedia services such as *video-on-demand (VOD) can be reduced by considering an alternative service scheme introduced in the literature, referred to as* video-on-reservation(VOR)[WS99, V00, BY02]. Instead of offering an immediate video delivery service, the consumer/customer is allowed to request for a video *in advance*, i.e., the user can demand when he/she would like to view the actual video. The advantage of having a VOR stems from being able to develop an optimal video[9] delivery schedule for the requests of videos from various consumers. Further, since the video requests are known in advance, the system can thrive to generate the best possible distribution scheme (by

[9]An object in VOR system is a video or a multimedia document.

making use of resources in the best possible manner) which can be cost effective to the user. This provides a cheaper alternative than VOD, making it much more appealing. This economic motivation for the consumer provides the opportunity for the VOR service providers to receive the necessary information for optimal schedule planning. In contrast, VOD services require immediate utilization of resources when requests are made, incurring large amounts of cost at the same time.

Further, in the literature, a Personalized Service Agent (PSA) has been proposed as an alternative for communications over the conventional server-client model [KH98], to support such network based services. A PSA is basically a software code that independently travels from server to server performing tasks specified by clients. It has autonomy over the location and timing of its travel and has the ability to halt and restart itself over the network. As the PSA performs its task, it reports results back to the client asynchronously. Responsibilities of a PSA include information retrieval, network management as well as multimedia presentation. By combining a reservation-based multimedia service scheme and utilizing PSAs to implement this scheme, our aim is to design a PSA that is able to assemble the service requests for a multimedia document within a time frame (window), from clients at different sites, and make best possible decisions for scheduling the delivery of the requested multimedia document to the clients such that the cost per user is minimized.

2.1 Multimedia Network Architecture

A multimedia network that combines the current technologies and aids fast and convenient access for consumers to voice, data and video applications, is needed for the PSA to perform its task. By placing *storage server* at each node in a network, performance can be greatly enhanced. If the consumer has to receive the requested multimedia document directly from the original storage server, it would put enormous burden on that server, especially if several requests were made simultaneously. Furthermore, if the document is to be retransmitted all the way from the original storage server to consumers in the same locality each time it is requested for, this would incur unnecessary communication costs. In fact, it has been argued in the literature that successive retransmissions will not yield an optimal cost of servicing all the requests. These considerations result in a push towards designing new network architecture which is more efficient and economical. We typically consider a distributed multimedia network, shown in Figure 2.3. The highest level of this distributed network are a set of *video warehouses* (VWHs). These VWHs contain huge repositories of document resources. Below these are the *intermediate storage* units which are the servers linking consumers to the video warehouses. These servers are linked by high speed connections such as fiber-optics.

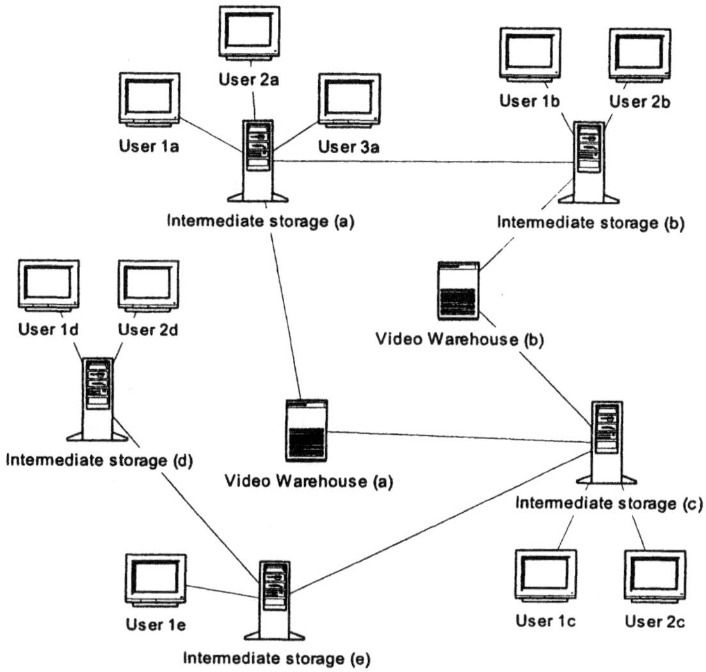

Figure 2.3. A distributed multimedia network for VOR system

The process of requesting a desired document and the way in which scheduling and caching/storing[10] decisions are made can be understood as follows. Typically, the service architecture comprises host of supportive modules, such as service providers, content-base search engines, service agents (these can navigate through catalogues to compose a list of items that closely match the requested media document), network providers, and network directory service facilities, that are involved in the document authentication (assessing the access rights), searching, identification and dissemination processes [PRVS95]. Added to these modules, a PSA interprets and learns about users' profiles and schedules the documents that match their preferences. Thus, the entire service architecture behaves as a centralized control system. In essence, when

[10]We use "caching" and "storing" interchangeably to mean storage of movie at a site.

a user submits his/her request to his/her PSA, the PSA after proper authentication contacts directory services and content-bases to identify a close match between the user request and the available documents. Once authentication is justified, PSA attempts to schedule and deliver the document to the user with the help of network providers at the requested time.

For rendering network-based multimedia services, the problem of movie caching or storage is an important issue to be addressed, as user demands are, in general, random. This problem has been studied extensively, both in the domains of single server systems as well as on network based systems. On a single server system, main concern is to devise strategies that can efficiently store/organize the data in a form that can be easily accessed while servicing a request. Here, the objective would be to optimize the access time[11]. Thus, data organization is one of the important concerns[ORBS94, RV93]. In contrast, on a network-based system the main focus would be to design efficient strategies to optimize the resource utilization thereby minimizing the access times of the requests [DS96, DS97]. This is done by caching the required data that can be used by requests whose requested times are near-by. In a VOR system, users are expected to submit their requests ahead (in advance) of time to avail this service. Since the user requests are known in advance, the system can thrive to optimize the utilization of all the available resources on the network to serve most of the requests successfully (maximizing the number of successful requests). Thus, when a movie is transferred to a client location on or before the desired viewing time, it may traverse intermediate storage sites (or servers) in the system in the planned path. Thus, in view of serving "future" requests, some or all the intermediate servers can store the movie. Thus, these intermediate storage servers act as extra sources to serve the future requests and circumvent the problem of retransmitting the movie every time from a source location.

When a movie is stored at a site for certain amount of duration, then it incurs some storage cost (or otherwise referred to as caching cost) and when the movie is transmitted over a link, it incurs a communication cost. In other words, the cost model has two components - caching cost and communication cost. Thus, the main objective in this domain is to design cost-effective strategies that can decide on - *when* (time to begin caching the movie at a site), *where* (deciding on the location to cache [BP96]) and *how* (number of copies) to cache a movie so that all the user requests can be met. Note that the design of the algorithms

[11]Time to access the desired data on the disk.

must take into account the resource availability, and hence, the decision on "generating" more copies (replications) is crucial. Generating more copies is advantageous from service point of view while cost may be prohibitively higher. In this case, strategic replication is desired which can minimize the total cost. Since resources such as storage capacities at the intermediate sites as well as the network bandwidths are essential commodities in real-life situations, the network topology can undergo changes dynamically depending on resource utilization. This means that, when a decision to remove a movie from a site is to take place in view of infrequent demands, this movie may be "moved" to a most wanted site or can be eliminated (if more than one copy currently exists in the network). Thus, movie migration or minimizing the number of copies in view of releasing the storage space is also an issue to be considered. Only issue that is not of concern in this case is the consistency, as movies are assumed to be non-editable entities. Thus, in the OMP of VOR, consistency is the least concerned issue.

For designing clever strategies for *placing* (caching) the movies, in practice, movie popularity profile is monitored. At every server, the demand for a particular movie is monitored and according to their popularity profile, the movie may be moved to a farther point in the network (if it is less demanded) or further down close to the client (if it is more popular). The popularity of the multimedia documents is usually assumed to follow Zipf's law [N95] which states that the probability of requests for each movie i, i=1,...,M, is inversely proportional to its index, i.e., $p_i = K/i$, where K is a normalization constant given by $\sum_{m=1}^{M}(1/m)$. Thus, depending on the demand, a movie will be stored closer to the service vicinity of the customers, and as demand decreases, the movie will be shifted to remote sites due to capacity constraints in the currently serving server. In the latter case, communication cost (due to downloading) will be more than the caching cost. The objective is to place the movies in a cost-effective manner at various available servers such that the cost of serving the user requests is a minimum. The decision on which movies have to be replicated, and if so, how many times, and in which of the servers, so as to minimize the per user cost is what this problem essentially addresses. An astute reader can further explore other related secondary issues till date from the existing literature [GK00].

3. OMP in Caching/Storage on World Wide Web

With an explosive increase of World Wide Web (WWW) traffic in recent years, the use of web proxies has gained a considerable attention [BO00, W99]. Especially, the interest in the proxy caching problem stems from the challenge posed in designing efficient strategies to avail web based services at a reasonable cost as well to provide complete flexibility in using the services by the users. OMP in this case is much more complicated, as the underlying network, the WWW does not have any fixed/known topology. In general, corporate offices, university campuses and other commercial organizations connect to Internet via a backbone network which is linked to a local proxy server system. Proxy system allows easy access to most frequently used web-pages from its local pool of customers. Sometimes a proxy system may comprise a set of proxies interacting with each other. Here, an object refers to a web-page whose size can range from 1 kilobyte to several kilobytes, depending on the document. For instance, a simple text file may be in order of few kilobytes, however, a graphics or high resolution pictures may be in order of several kilo-bytes. Further, a web-page can also support video streams, in which case interaction by a client may start consuming several kilobytes of static or continuous data[12]. OMP, in this case, uses several variants of replacement algorithms designed originally for memory management in single computer systems as described in Section 1. These algorithms are used when the web-pages need to be replicated as well as when they need to migrate between sites on the web. An additional constraint here is that since not all web-pages are identical in size, one or more pages may need to be replaced in order to allow considerable room for an incoming requested page. Thus, deciding on which of the pages to be evicted from a site is identical to tackling a *subset-sum* problem which is proven to be NP-complete[13]. In addition, careful consideration on access rates[14] for pages that are to be evicted must be given, if not, any inadvertent replacement will lead to a large overhead cost.

We will now focus on several of the variants of page replacement algorithms that are in place for web-caching problems in its OMP. The Figure 2.4 shows a web-proxy architecture, in general. Retrieving the desired object from a proxy cache[15] *before* accessing the main web server has the following advantages[M00]. Firstly, caches are usually "nearer" to the client (user) than the server, and hence, the network traffic and access latencies (time delay to access an object) on original web server is also minimized. Further, to a limited extent, users can obtain the objects even when the original web server cannot permit an access under certain faulty situations (probably because of over-load or breakdown).

---

[12]In general, all these data can be referred to as multimedia data[LG90].

[13]Refer to [CLR94] for subset-sum problem.

[14]Estimation of access rates for a page is yet another issue to be taken care in web-caching problems.

[15]Since these proxies essentially store the web-pages, they are also referred to as *proxy caches* in the literature by some authors.

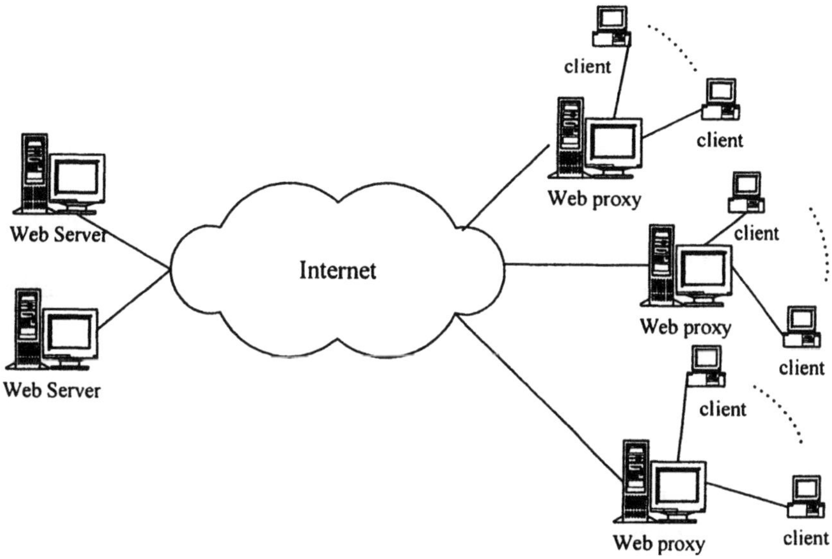

Figure 2.4. A distributed web-proxy system on WWW

A web-caching strategy improves quality of service in two ways. First one is with respect to access time, as accessing the cache is faster than accessing the original server. The other one is the *block ratio*, which is the fraction of the total requests that are unsuccessful (not serviced). Web-caching strategies thrive to minimize this block ratio and a decrease in the block ratio comes mainly from the following reasons.

- When some accesses are shifted from remote original servers to near caches, the congestion in network traffic will be improved. Therefore, more web requests will be accepted.
- Since there exist several copies of an object on the web, the probability of a request failure due to non-existence of an object will be considerably reduced.

In general, a proxy server caches web objects for its clients and shares those cached objects across several users. However, in reality, it has been reported in [DJD99] that there are a very minimum number of identical requests (that demand the same objects) within a set of clients to achieve high hit ratios (fraction of successful requests). This is mainly due to the presence of low-level caches (such as browser cache, a cache present at the client site in his/her browser) that attempt to filter many requests. One of the methods of improving the hit ratio is using a technique referred to as *cooperative proxy caching* in the literature [RCG98]. This is shown to significantly increase the extent to which a cached object can be shared. In the cooperative proxy caching, a client can access several proxies. Hence the possibility of accessing the remote original server is considerably reduced in comparison with the case where a client can access *only one* proxy. In this way, the block ratio decreases and the hit ratio increases.

Further, in the literature, the performance improvement potential for cooperative proxy caching for a large-scale web system has been evaluated quantitatively using a trace-based method as well as an analytical approach [WVSCKL99]. This evaluation shows that cooperative web proxy caching is an effective architecture for small individual caches that together comprise user populations in the tens of thousands of order. Ideally, the proxies must be present in the path connecting the clients and the host servers to provide efficient services by intercepting the client requests [SRT99]. In general, an object accessing process in a cooperative proxy caching environment can be described as follows. If an object is not found in the browser cache of a client, the local (or nearest) proxy cache (hereafter referred to as a *local site*) is usually queried. If the local site does not contain the requested object, the local site attempts to get the object from several neighboring proxies (we refer to these neighboring proxies as *neighboring sites*). However, in the event that none of the neighboring sites have this object, the original web server is queried.

OMP in the case of web caching problem, in general, must also include workload characterization as exemplified in several studies[16] and cache management. OMP in the case of cache management for web system includes the following issues to be addressed.

1. Architecture of caches and the placement of caches (e.g., proxies). There are two kinds of architectures proposed in the literature [RSB99] - mesh (or distributed architecture [PH97]) and hierarchical architecture [CDNSW96]. A performance comparison between these two architectures has been provided and some design guidelines for a large-scale distributed cache environment have been proposed [TDVK98]. In a hierarchical architecture, a client needs to pass *several* hops for accessing an object in a *distant* proxy, while in a distributed architecture, it is inclined to access neighboring and/or directly-connected

[16] Refer to [M95, AW96, ABCD96, B97, DJD99].

proxy. Therefore the latter has less response time. The placement of proxies is the problem of where a proxy (or a set of proxies) should physically reside on the network so as to maximize the global performance, e.g., [LGIDS99]. This is somewhat equivalent to movie placement problem in VOR systems described in Section 2.

2. The object location algorithm that is used to efficiently discover, select and deliver the requested object(s) from neighboring sites, e.g., [AMT99, MNRZFJ98]. In a distributed architecture, the order in which an object is "searched" follows local proxy to a neighboring proxy, and then to the original server. On the other hand, in a hierarchical architecture, the order of looking for an object is from local proxy to a host of parent proxies until an original server.

3. The design of an object placement and replacement algorithms. When the cache space at a local site is sufficient for caching a new object, we *place* the object in the cache. Otherwise, we consider the possibility of replacing other cached object(s) with the new object.

4. An object consistency algorithm which ensures that updates are propagated to the copies elsewhere and no stale objects are present, e.g., [MPKD99]. The design of consistency algorithms is somewhat a crucial requirement when compared to other systems we have discussed before.

5. Cachability of an object - This is to decide on what web objects can be cached to improve the performance of the web system.

Among the above issues, the design of an object replacement and consistency algorithms is challenging and forms an imperative part in deciding the overall performance. The combined influence of these algorithms will promise an overall better performance of the entire system.

In the design of web-object replacement algorithms, one of the useful parameters to quantify is the importance of an object at a site. This quantification is in terms of the gain that can be achieved. This means that using this quantity gain, the replacement algorithm can decide whether or not an object is to be cached at a (local) site. This gain, in general, is defined as the ratio of the *benefit* to the amount of storage cost incurred in caching an object. This benefit could manifest in terms of number of hits [LW00], number of byte-hits, or in terms of amount of response time reduction [SSV97], etc. Thus, for instance, if hit ratio is our concern, then the gain would be simply the ratio of the number of hits (benefit) to the cost, and so on. Although the monetary cost of storage devices (such as RAM, hard-disks, etc) decreases with time as technology advances, research in the direction of designing replacement algorithms continue to spur considerable interest among researchers. Recent studies show that the behavior of web cache hit ratio and byte hit ratio grow in a log-like fashion as a function of cache size while even a slight gain in performance due to replacement algorithms may have an appreciable effect on the network traffic [JBa00]. Further, the growth rate of information content on the web is much higher than the rate at which memory or disk sizes for web caches are likely to grow. In particular, multimedia documents with larger size (more than 3 GBytes) keep increasing on the Internet [GVW96] and the percentage of requests to such large volume multimedia documents may increase more than a linear fashion with respect to time [LW00].

3.1 Who, When and What to Cache on WWW?

In the following, we will systematically discuss on the research efforts that addressed the problem of *who* to cache, *when* to cache and *what* to cache in a web environment.

Firstly, we consider the problem of *who* decides to cache the web objects. In the case of server-initiated strategy, also referred to as *push caching* strategy [B97, MC98], a web server decides on caching the objects. This scheme ensures a strong consistency, however it does not cope up with the rapid changes in request arrival patterns (e.g., a burst request arrival). Also, in this case, the server needs an authority to *command* the proxies to store even unsolicited objects that may not be needed by local users. On the other hand, in the client-initiated strategy, also referred to as *pull caching* strategy, the objects are cached only when a client requests to do so. As opposed to the former strategy, this client-initiated strategy adapts to rapidly changing request arrival pattern. However, in this case, the problem of cache consistency arises.

Secondly, we consider the problem of *when* to cache the web objects. The most common caching strategy is *on-demand caching* [L97]. In this strategy objects are cached upon request by the client, in other words, when there is no request for an object, we will not consider to cache that object in a proxy. In contrast, in the case of *on-command caching* strategy [L97], the proxy is set up to automatically retrieve certain objects or possibly replicate all the objects from a site, at regular time intervals. Prefetching strategy can be treated as a combination of on-demand and on-command caching strategies. In the case of prefetching strategy, an estimate of the future *access probabilities* (i.e., the rate at which requests arrive at the system, also referred to as request rates) is computed and relevant objects are cached for future accesses [FCJ99, JLC00].

Thirdly, when we consider the problem of *what* objects will be cached, two different strategies can be adopted. In the *independent caching* strategy [AWY99, BH98, DA99], every site decides to cache the objects independently, thus only the local site performance is considered, by and large. However, the *cooperative caching* strategy considers the performance of an entire system (i.e., global performance) as well as the performance of local site (i.e., local performance). Hence, independent caching strategy is suitable for single cache environment while the cooperative caching strategy is specifically used in the cooperative caching environment. Before determining which object is cached, the "importance" (or otherwise called as "value") of the objects should be measured. In the independent caching strategy, the importance of the objects is mainly decided by the following four factors.

(F1). *Temporal locality*: This aspect of *locality of reference* suggests that a recently accessed object is likely to be accessed again in the future. According to [JBa00], long-term popularity and short-term temporal correlation among requests (accesses) are two resources of temporal locality[17].

(F2). *Access frequency*: This refers to the rate at which the requests arrive for an object.

(F3). *Object size*: The size of an object is equal to the number of byte hits when that object is found in the cache. Also the size of an object is equal to the space requirement if that object is cached. Therefore an object size has an importance effect on deciding whether or not to cache one object.

(F4). *Miss penalty*: This is equal to the cost of retrieval cost of an object from server upon a miss in a proxy [JBa00].

Table 2.1 gives a taxonomy of existing web cache replacement algorithms ([DV03]) that consider the above four factors. The dark dots indicate the influencing factors for the respective algorithms. In addition to the above factors, *lifetime of an object*, *type of an object*, etc., are also important factors that be considered in the design of replacement algorithms.

The advantages of one replacement algorithm mainly depend on the number of factors involved in this algorithm. A comprehensive performance study of popular replacement algorithms was carried out in the literature [LW00]. This study strongly corroborates the fact considering more factors is apt to generate better replacement algorithms although more factors lead to more complexity. The key aspect of designing a

[17] [SKW99] has a detailed study about temporal locality.

Table 2.1. Taxonomy of existing Web cache replacement algorithms/policies

Algorithms	F1	F2	F3	F4
FIFO				
LRU (including Segmented LRU, EELRU)	•			
LFU (including Perfect LFU, In-Cache LFU)		•		
LFF			•	
Latency				•
LRU-k [NNW93], LRFU [LCCNMC97], LFU-DA [AFJ00]	•	•		
LRUMIN, Var-page-LRU	•		•	
GD (i.e., GreedyDual) [Y91]	•			•
LRV [RV00], GDS [CI97], Size-adjusted LRU [AWY99]	•		•	•
Hybrid [WA97]		•	•	•
GD-LFU [KW99],GDSF [ACDFJ99], GDSP [JB00], LNC-W3 [SSV97], GD* [JBa00]	•	•	•	•

good replacement algorithm is to thoroughly exploit the workload characteristics, which are ever-changing. This comparison is certainly useful to carefully decide on the factors that influence the performance while designing a cooperative caching strategy.

Some Useful Remarks: *Perfect LFU* and *In-Cache LFU* are two variants of LFU. Perfect LFU keeps track of all the past accesses to all the objects (using counters to register these accesses) even when an object is evicted from the cache whereas, In-Cache LFU removes the record of all the past accesses when an object is evicted from the cache. Another version, referred to as *Segmented LRU* [AW97] is a variant of LRU, in which the objects that are referenced only once will be evicted out quickly. *EELRU* [SKW99] performs LRU replacement by default but diverges from LRU an evict page early when it notices that too many pages are being touched in a roughly cyclic pattern that is larger than main memory. *Var-page-LRU* [S88] is a variant of LRU when the page size is variable.

Among the caching algorithms that consider identical set of factors in the design, the difference lies in the amount of overhead incurred and in the manner in which these factors influence the overall performance. In the literature, following methods are available. One way is to combine the above mentioned factors using a heuristic or analytical schemes with some weights assigned to each of these factors, e.g., QoS in [ASF98], utility value in [JB00]. Alternatively, one may prioritize some of the above factors over others (referred to as *key-based policies* [WASAF96]) while combining these factors. Finally, in *regression-based combination* scheme proposed in [FHH99], a past access record is used to do regression calculation to obtain an optimal set of weights for these factors. This approach has two drawbacks. Firstly, the computation involved in the regression calculation is very large and secondly, the regression procedure estimates only the weights of these factors, however fails to determine an exact formula for combination.

Until now, there has been a lot of research for the independent caching algorithm in the single cache environment. In comparison, the research effort, especially for the cooperative caching, is very little in the literature. One typical strategy for cooperative caching is *Gravity/Repulsion-based Replacement Strategy* proposed in the literature [IMMN98].

4. OMP in Distributed Database Systems

OMP in this case is concerned on designing efficient strategies for object replication, placement/allocation, consistency, and replacement algorithms. However, as mentioned in Chapter 1, there are two different environments in which the context of DDBS can be classified. These are, (i) Stationary Computing Environment (SCE) and (ii) Mobile Computing Environment(MCE). In both these domains, the above mentioned issues are common. However, an OMP for DDBS has other issues for these domains that are distinct from the above set of issues. An OMP in this case considers issues pertaining to:

- Access rate and/or request pattern information
- Ordering of requests for processing, also referred to as *Serializability* and Concurrency Control
- Real Time processing requirements of requests
- Characteristics of an object (whether an object is of read type or write type)
- Nature of the requests that arrive[18]
- Controlling strategy for processing the requests (centralized or decentralized)

[18]While concerned about improving the performance of the entire system with respect to some cost measure, OMP may need to consider whether or not the underlying network is *read-intensive* (more read requests than write requests) or *write-intensive* (more write requests than read requests).

- Modeling the cost parameters such as object transferring cost, control-message transferring cost, I/O cost[19]

Further, as the design of distributed systems always favors two types of control mechanisms namely, either *centralized* control or *decentralized* control, respectively, the manner in which the requests are handles also influences the performance of DDBS. The choice of the control strategies usually depends on the application requirements and each has its own advantages and disadvantages. Specifically, as discussed in Chapter 1, with a centralized control system, *fault-tolerance* is seldom guaranteed, as there is a single point failure. However, maintaining consistency of objects, problem of synchronization, arriving at a consensus[20], can be relatively taken care easily. On the other hand, for decentralized control systems, fault-tolerance is extremely high, but the above mentioned additional issues require somewhat sophisticated treatment. In practice, as a rule of thumb the following is in place: when the network span is small in size adopting centralized control with back-up facilities may be more efficient. However, for a large scale system, considering the amount of processing involved for a central controller (and hence, subject to high probability of failure), decentralization may be more efficient. In Chapters 4 through 6, we will rigorously analyze the role of both these control strategies and see how they influence the design of DDBS, especially when real-time processing is sought.

Another important issue in OMP for DDBS is the concept of serializability, i.e., this deals with the ordering of the requests in the way they need to be processed. This issue, under a centralized control, manifests as follows. Since several requests may arrive at a site simultaneously, a serializable controller will serialize the requests in the way they are to be processed. This in turn implies that read and write requests are ordered for processing and that a request is always serviced with the most recent copy of the object in the system. This is allowed provided requests can be processed in any order. However, for some systems wherein FIFO is an enforced service discipline, serializability refers to the arrival time order of requests at a site. The mechanism which accounts serializability is referred to as a *concurrency control mechanism*, which is an imperative module to guarantee serializability.

[19]The first one refers to the cost incurred when an object is transferred from one site to other, the second one is incurred when control messages have to be passed between sites whenever necessary, and the third one is incurred when I/O processing is involved. These will be used in our later Chapters.

[20][AW98] provides a rigorous treatment on these issues in distributed systems.

Now, for a system that has a decentralized control in handling requests, decisions made at a single node to account serializability may not be effective to achieve a global performance. This is because the order in which the requests are to be processed in individual sites may give raise to several unnecessary overheads due to frequent broadcasts of copies in order to maintain consistency among the copies of objects elsewhere. Thus, for two conflicting operations on an object from two different sites, with at least one of them being a write operation (as this will modify the object itself), care must be taken to minimize the overheads and this is done by "ordering" these requests. This can be done by using a *locking* mechanism that is in place in the literature. The basic idea is as follows. Before accessing an object, a transaction acquires a read or a write lock on an object. A *lock* is a mechanism by which a transaction on an object is carried out with a guarantee that no other new transaction that modifies the object can be allowed to transact on that object. Thus, when a site acquires a write lock means that no other sites are allowed to read/write the object till the current transaction is completed. Sometimes this stringent requirement may be relaxed and sites may be allowed to have inconsistent copies. Consequently, this leads to two forms of consistencies namely, *weak consistency* and *strong consistency*. The choice depends on the different levels of consistency requirements of the underlying application.

For a DDBS, serializability can be realized though a *Two-Phase Locking*(TPL) mechanism [BHG87] that is commonly used in practice. Thus, serializability and consistency jointly influence the performance. Further, although we have elaborated on the issue of object replication, in the case of DDBS, the concept of serializability may strongly influence the decision on replication. That is, the performance of replication schemes may also strongly depend on serializability conditions that are enforced. It must be clearly understood that replication, in general, may be due to different decisions. For instance, in VOR system, replication largely depends on resource availabilities and on popularity profile of a movie at a site. However, consistency is a least concerned issue in this case. As addressing all these issues in every problem is a cumbersome task, if not, an impossible task, sometimes it is advantage to simply assume that serializability is taken care or neglected in a problem context. Nevertheless, designing a controller that guarantees serializability is a challenging task.

As far as object replication is concerned, two flavors exist - *static replication scheme* (in which the set of processors in which replicated objects exist is not altered) and *dynamic replication scheme* (in which the set of processors in which replication is carried out is dynamically altered with respect to the demands of the processing requests). Thus, the replication algorithms designed for the latter category is often referred to as *adaptive or dynamic replication algorithms* in the literature. In the existing literature, mathematical models suited for SCEs and MCEs are introduced and *Competitive Analysis*[21] is used to show the superiority of static and dynamic allocation schemes. Much of the literature related to the design of static and dynamic algorithms would be more meaningful after we introduce Competitive Analysis in Chapter 3 and we will elaborate on details of several algorithms later in Chapters 4, 5 and 6.

5. General Discussions on the Design Methodologies in OMP

The above four application domains have highlighted the way in which OMP is to be interpreted and issues within it. Thus, it is clear that depending on an application domain, a top-down approach in deciding the priorities of the underlying issues are to be first considered. If it is possible to generate a priority-chart (diagram identifying priorities among the issues) capturing dependencies between each of the issues, then to some extent, performance goals can be more-or-less set. For instance, in the case of VOR application, a flow-chart capturing the inter-dependency between the issues is shown in Figure 2.5.

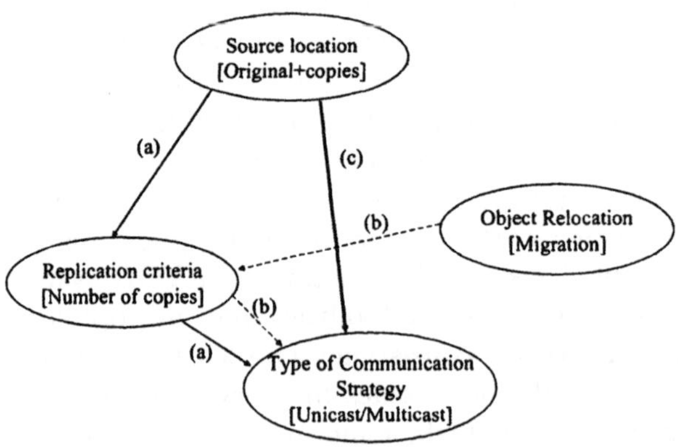

Figure 2.5. Diagram showing influencing issues in the design of OMP for VOR application

[21] Refer to Chapter 3 for detailed treatment on Competitive Analysis.

Assuming the application is to deliver a requested video document to a set of clients, the four major issues in a VOR OMP are: (i) Source location (both original and current copies which can act as temporary sources), (ii) Replication criteria, (iii) Object relocation (or migration), and (iv) Type of communication strategy (unicast/multicast). Thus, in order to deliver the requested movie, a source location is to be chosen first and then a suitable communication strategy is to be decided. It may be noted that in order to decide on which source is to be tapped to serve a request and/or if the number of copies are sufficient as per the current request rate, are highly interdependent factors while creating new copies. Thus, arrows indicating (a) in the figure represents a strong dependency in carrying out source location, replication and the way to carry out these by using a specific choice of communication strategy. Similarly, when an object relocation is to be considered due to current slack in resources then algorithms may prefer checking the currently available number of copies (replication) and may decide whether or not to migrate (or may simply remove the object locally) an object between sites. Since the process also demands decision on the choice of communication strategies, we represent the interaction between factors (iii), (ii) and (iv) by an arrow marked (b) on the figure. Similarly, if algorithms, at any point in time, attempt to locate the currently available sources on the network, the communication strategy directly influences and hence, the dependency is indicated as (c). Thus, in this example, efficient communication strategies are to be given prime importance, then replication criteria has to be decided (may be depending on popularity profile, request rate, resource constraint, cheap storage costs, abundant link bandwidth availability, etc) and then object relocation is to be considered, in that order.

Finally, the request rate is also an important factor that influences the performance of the algorithms designed in an OMP. For off-line processing of requests similar to a VOR application, resource management is the primary focus. However, when the future pattern of requests is completely unknown then designing on-line versions of the algorithms are of paramount challenge. We have seen four major application problems that use OMP in this chapter. In this book, our primary focus is to rigorously analyze the OMP involved in DDBSs, wherein requests that arrive on-line are to be processed. In Chapter 3 we will provide with a basic mathematical tool and present several techniques that are useful to analyze on-line algorithms.

6. Concluding Remarks

This chapter has exposed the fundamental issues involved in an OMP. The notion of an object in a generic sense was discussed. Basic issues involved in an OMP and how they influence the solution was clearly exemplified. All these fundamental issues were identified in four different application domains - Hierarchical memory design, VOR systems, Caching on WWW and DDBS, respectively. In all these domains we have exposed the importance of designing efficient algorithms for tackling variety of issues involved in the respective object management processes. OMP, in general, should be viewed as a collective process comprising all influencing issues that were discussed at the design stage.

After all providing a cost-effective solution being the primary objective, extreme care must be taken to deal with critical issues such as handling on-line requests rates, resource availability constraints, etc. Apart from all the major issues exposed in the design of an OMP, another issue which may affect the performance of the system is *admission-control*, when considering a different objective altogether. To understand this, consider again the VOR application. Under a resource constrained situation while handling on-line requests, suppose the system thrives to maximize the number of requests[22] that can be served successfully, at the top-most level of design, sophisticated *admission control policies*[23] have to be considered. Sometimes, these admission control polices can be an inherent part of the design of OMP. This means that, depending on the modeling style, OMP subsumes the issue of admission control and becomes virtually inseparable. This will be shown later in our design of OMP when serving *real-time* on-line requests. In fact, in Chapter 5, we will distinctly identify the admission-control part of the design of an OMP for a RTDDBS.

[22]This is also referred to as maximizing the throughput of the system.

[23]Policies that determine whether or not a request can be accommodated for successful processing.

Chapter 3

COMPETITIVE ANALYSIS - CONCEPTS AND SOLUTION TECHNIQUES

In this chapter, we address the fundamental concepts of *Competitive Analysis.* Competitive analysis serves as a useful analytical tool in quantifying the performance of *on-line* algorithms. In a way, for an algorithmic designer, this tool aids to fine-tune his/her design to get the solution as closer as possible to an optimal solution. Problems that can be considered for analysis using this analytical tool include K-Server Problem, Paging Problem, Distributed Object Management, Web-Caching[1], Load Balancing in computer networks, Disk Header Scheduling, to quote a few. We first give formal definitions of *competitiveness* for both *deterministic on-line algorithms* and *randomized on-line algorithms.* We then enumerate several techniques in *competitive analysis* such as *Potential Function method, Phase Partition Technique*, and so forth. Several illustrative examples are provided for the ease of understanding to elicit important competitive properties of an *on-line* algorithm.

1. Competitiveness

1.1 On-line Problems

Suppose you are a share-holder of a company. As we know, depending on the response from the consumers, the prices of the stocks may fluctuate (magnitudes are unpredictable). Thus, when the prices rise you may attempt to sell some or all of your shares to profit. Further, you may also wait for further rise in price of the stocks. On the other hand, when the prices fall, you may attempt to buy some more shares in the view of minimizing the average price of each share or simply sell

[1] Refer to Chapter 2 on a brief discussion on some of these topics.

the existing shares to minimize your net loss. Thus, while stocks prices are fluctuating quantities, depending on the current pricing values of the shares, you may need to decide whether or not to buy or sell the shares. In such a case, you are confronted with an *on-line* problem.

Over the past two decades, *on-line* problems are very common in computer science and engineering and have received considerable research interest. To a system designer or a computer scientist, it is imperative to understand on the type of systems that deserve on-line solutions. Predominantly, systems that are expected to service/process a currently submitted request without any knowledge of the future requests to be submitted to the system qualify to look for *on-line* solutions. Thus, on-line problems are completely unaware of behavioral pattern of the incoming requests. The response of on-line algorithms designed to handle such on-line requests would only consider historical data for making any decisions. A completely complementary approach is to design an *off-line* algorithm, which is designed on the basis of a complete knowledge of all the current and the future requests to be processed, such as a VOR system discussed in Chapter 2. However, this attempt is often unrealistic in real-life applications. Many of the algorithms designed to tackle real-life problems are of *on-line* in nature. In these problems, input information is only partially available because some relevant inputs can only arrive in the future and may not be accessible at present. Therefore, an *on-line* algorithm must generate an output without the knowledge of the entire input. Some common *on-line* problems that are applicable in a wide variety of real-life situations are as follows.

- *K-Server Problem*
- *Paging Problem*
- *Distributed Object Management*
- *Disk Header Scheduling*

These problems clearly provide the motivation on why competitive analysis serves as a natural choice in the design and analysis of on-line algorithms.

K-Server Problem:

The *K-Server problem*, introduced by Manasse *et al.* [MMS88], may be defined as follows. We are given a metric space $\mathcal{M}$, which is a set of points with a non-negative symmetric distance function d that satisfies the triangle inequality, i.e., for distinct points x, y, and z we have,

$$\begin{aligned} d(x,x) &= 0 \\ d(x,y) &= d(y,x) > 0 \\ d(x,y) &\leq d(x,z) + d(z,y) \end{aligned} \tag{3.1}$$

Now consider a set $\mathcal{K} \subset \mathcal{M}$ of k points in this metric space $\mathcal{M}$ and imagine that there are k servers that reside on these k points, respectively. Also, let us suppose that each request is submitted to the system to access a specific point $x \in \mathcal{M}$. Suppose that $x \notin \mathcal{K}$, then in order to serve the request, a server has to be made available at that point. This means that one of the $k \in \mathcal{K}$ servers must be "moved" to the requested point. We must serve this request by considering only the current and past requests (requests served so far by the system), which means that the decision on *which* server should be moved to satisfy this request is to be made *on-line.* The cost of satisfying the request is assumed to be proportional to the distance moved by the server. Therefore, we need an *on-line* algorithm to serve a sequence of requests such that the total distance traversed by all the servers is as small as possible. A typical application to this and allied problems arises when we consider minimizing the (monetary) cost of requests by users in a mobile computing environment. In fact we will use mathematical cost models for mobile computing environments and devise strategies to minimize the cost in Chapter 5.

Paging Problem:

We have seen this problem in Chapter 2. Here, we will see this problem from competitive analysis perspective. In other words, we will see how competitive analysis can be used to analyze the paging algorithms. In brief, the *Paging Problem* can be defined as follows. We are given a two-level memory system that consists of a small fast memory (referred to as *cache* memory) and a large slow memory (referred to as *main* memory). Each request specifies a page to be accessed in the fast memory. Without loss of generality, we assume that all pages are of identical size. If the requested page is already in the fast memory, the system need not do anything. Otherwise, a page *fault* (also referred to as a *miss*) is said to have occurred. To handle this situation, a page that is currently residing in the fast memory must be *evicted* and "pushed" to the slow memory so that the requested page can be loaded into the vacated location. This replacement incurs a certain cost, since data must be transferred between the fast memory and the slow memory. Therefore, what is expected to solve the *Paging Prob-*

lem is to design a *page replacement algorithm* which decides on the page to be evicted, whenever a page-fault occurs, from fast memory without knowledge of any future requests. However, it may consider any available historical access pattern information. Typically all the algorithms thrive to make the best use of historical data in the decision making process in different possible ways. The objective of such algorithms is to minimize the total number of page faults incurred on a request sequence.

The *Paging problem* is the most fundamental and practically important on-line problem in computer science. It has been extensively studied since the 1960s. A large variety of page replacement algorithms can be found in the design of memory systems for computers wherein the underlying operating system makes use of these algorithms. In the following, we list four well-known practical *on-line* algorithms used for the *Paging Problem.*

- **LRU**(Least Recently Used): On a fault, evict the page in the fast memory that was requested least recently. This means that out of all pages currently residing in the fast memory choose a page that was never accessed in the recent past.
- **LFU**(Least Frequently Used): On a fault, evict the page in the fast memory that has been requested least frequently. This means that out of all pages currently residing in the fast memory choose a page that was most infrequcntly accessed.
- **FIFO**(First-In First-Out): On a fault, evict the page that has been in the fast memory for the longest time.
- **LIFO**(Last-In First-Out): On a fault, evict the page that was moved to the fast memory most recently.

Further, the *Paging Problem* can also be considered as a special instance of the symmetric *k-Server Problem* in which the distance between any two points in the metric space $\mathcal{M}$ is identical. The slow memory corresponds to the metric space $\mathcal{M}$ and the fast memory corresponds to the k servers occupied points. The cost of swapping the pages between fast and slow memories corresponds to the distance metric in the K-Server Problem.

Finally, implementation of the paging algorithms can found in any standard computer architecture and organization text books[HVZ02, KH93].

Distributed Object Management:

As mentioned in Chapter 1, a DDBS consists of multiple interconnected nodes. Each node consists of a processor and a local memory. Object *replication* and *re-allocation* are essential components of a DDBS to improve the object availability and system performance. Replicas of the objects are distributed in the local memories. A request originating from one processor in the network may request an object either to *read* or to *write*. A read request is satisfied by a replica in the system and a write request, which modifies an object, must be transferred to all the replicas in the remote memories elsewhere. It should be noted that the communication cost of servicing a request associated with a local memory is different from that of servicing a request associated with a remote memory. Consequently, when more replicas are allocated, the average cost of servicing a read request will be smaller, whereas the average cost of servicing a write request will be higher. Therefore, in a *read-intensive network* more replicas are beneficial whereas, in a *write-intensive network* fewer copies are beneficial. In addition, these read/write requests can arrive at the system in an unpredictable (on-line) manner. An *on-line* object allocation and replication algorithm has to determine on *how many replicas of each object are to be created* and to *which processors these replicas are to be allocated* (often referred to as *configurations*) so that a sequence of read/write requests can be processed with minimal total servicing cost. We will see detailed design of algorithms for handling such on-line requests that arrive either at a DDBS or at a RTDDBS later.

Disk Head Scheduling:

Finally, another interesting application of on-line problem is in disk head scheduling. Readers can referred to [SGG00] for details on disk system organization. In brief, a disk is a popular mass-storage device which allows the data stored on it to be accessed in a random fashion. In order to satisfy an I/O request, the disk controller must first move the *head* to the correct track and sector, involving translational and rotational movements. This is like finding someone's home by first finding the street (track) and then the particular house number (sector). Moving the head between cylinders (area that comprises certain amount of tracks) takes a reasonably longer time, referred to as *seek time* in the literature. Since I/O requests arrive randomly and must be satisfied immediately (time-critical!) without knowledge of future requests, design of *on-line* algorithms becomes unavoidable to minimize the total movement of the heads. A number of disk scheduling algorithms are discussed in [SGG00].

Now we are fully set to define an *on-line algorithm* formally as in Table 3.1.

Table 3.1. Definition of an On-line Algorithm

On-line Algorithm: An on-line algorithm ALG is presented with a request sequence consisting of a finite number of requests, $\sigma = \sigma(1), \sigma(2), ..., \sigma(m)$, where $\sigma(i)$ $(1 \leq i \leq m)$ denotes the i-th request in σ. The requests $\sigma(i)$, $i = 1, ...m$, must be served in their order of occurrence, i.e., when serving a request $\sigma(i)$, the algorithm ALG does not know any request $\sigma(i')$ with $i' > i$. Serving these requests incurs cost (defined as per the problem context) and the objective of an *on-line* algorithm is to minimize the total cost of serving the entire request sequence.

In the following, we shall highlight two different categories of *on-line* algorithms found in practice, i.e., *deterministic* on-line algorithms and *randomized* on-line algorithms.

1.2 Deterministic On-line Algorithms

An *on-line* algorithm is said to be *deterministic* if its behavior can be completely predicted from a given input. That is, consider *on-line* requests as inputs. Under identical initial conditions, each time when a certain set of inputs is presented, a deterministic *on-line* algorithm gives out the identical set of outputs and it does not make any random choice. For example, the *Paging Algorithms* LRU, LFU, FIFO, LIFO are all deterministic on-line algorithms, which can predict the page to be evicted from the fast memory whenever a page fault occurs. This is because their behavior strictly follows a "rule" defined in the way they work. This means, for instance, LRU will always attempt to evict a page from the fast memory that was requested least in the recent past. Since this rule is strictly followed, this algorithm (and similarly other paging algorithms mentioned above) is referred to as a deterministic on-line algorithm. Thus, "deterministic" part refers to a fixed working style of the underlying algorithm and "on-line" part refers to the capability to handle on-line requests.

1.3 Randomized On-line Algorithms

Compared to a *deterministic on-line* algorithm, we call an on-line algorithm as a *randomized on-line algorithm* if its behavior is determined not only by the inputs but also driven by any *internal random choice.* For instance, the internal random choices can be solely dictated by a random-number generator. In other words, a randomized algorithm uses random numbers to influence the choices it makes in the course of its computation. Thus, its behavior varies from one execution to another even with an identical and fixed input. As an example, for the *Paging Problem* discussed above, on a page fault, if an *on-line* algorithm *ALG* randomly chooses a page in the fast memory to evict, then *ALG* is considered as a *randomized on-line* algorithm. For more information of *randomize on-line* algorithms, interested readers can refer to [ACN00, BBKTW94, BRICS96, MR95], etc. A randomized strategy is specifically useful when there are many ways in which an algorithm can proceed and when it is difficult to determine which way is guaranteed to be good. If many of the alternatives are good, simply choosing one randomly can yield a good strategy. Usually, a *randomized on-line* algorithm is much simpler to implement with lower overhead when compared to a *deterministic on-line* algorithm. Finally, in the context of distributed systems, randomization has been conclusively proven to be a very powerful analytical tool for designing distributed algorithms. Examples from distributed systems using randomization include, the design of *leader election algorithms*, *mutual exclusion* problem and *consensus* problem[2], to quote a few.

1.4 Definition of Competitiveness

Usually, when addressing an *on-line* problem, we are specifically interested to answer the following questions.

1. Can we design an *on-line* algorithm for the on-line problem?
2. How well does the *on-line* algorithm perform for the problem?
3. What is the best possible performance that an *on-line* algorithm can deliver for the problem?

In general, no *on-line* algorithm can yield an optimum performance (minimum cost) on any request sequence. For example, an *on-line* algorithm ALG^1 may be better than an *on-line* algorithm ALG^2 for one particular sequence of requests and algorithm ALG^2 may be better than ALG^1 for another request sequence. Therefore, in order to evaluate various *on-line* algorithms, we need to choose a performance measure that takes into consideration the *on-line* nature of the problem. In recent years, it has been shown that *competitive analysis* is a powerful tool to analyze the performance of *on-line* algorithms. The concept of

[2]Readers can refer to [AW98] to see the details of these problems.

competitiveness was first introduced by Sleator and Tarjan [ST85] in the context of searching a linked list of elements and the paging problem. As per our above argument, since it makes no sense to compare two on-line algorithms directly, the performance of any on-line algorithm is always quantified upon a comparison against an off-line algorithm that knows the entire request sequence in advance and can obtain an optimal performance. Thus, the better an *on-line* algorithm approximates to an optimal solution, the more competitive it is considered to be.

We now define the competitiveness of a deterministic on-line algorithm as well as the competitiveness of a randomized on-line algorithm as follows. In both the cases, we compare on-line versions with algorithms, often referred to as *adversaries*, and define the competitiveness of on-line algorithms. The concept of adversaries will be easy if we think of an *on-line* problem as a *game* between two players wherein one player is an adversary and the other is an *on-line* algorithm. The adversary is supposed to know the description of the *on-line* algorithm and generates a request sequence σ, which is served one at a time by the *on-line* algorithm. The adversary also has to serve σ, however, it may be charged (priced) the optimum cost to satisfy σ. An optimal off-line algorithm OPT in the definition of competitiveness for a deterministic on-line algorithm ALG can be considered as an adversary that has complete knowledge of ALG. Since ALG is deterministic, OPT can predict the response of ALG over the entire sequence. This kind of adversary is called a *deterministic off-line* adversary [MJA98]. However, for a randomized on-line algorithm ALG', even when the adversary has complete knowledge of ALG', it cannot predict the exact response of ALG' to a given request. This is because of the *randomized* working style of ALG', which is in turn due to a random sequence generator that is purely internal to ALG'.

Now, for deterministic on-line algorithms we define the competitiveness as follows. Let σ be a sequence of requests that arrive at the system. The servicing cost on σ using an algorithm ALG is denoted by $COST_{ALG}(\sigma)$. Formally, a deterministic *on-line* algorithm ALG is said to be c-competitive, if there exist constants c $(c \geq 1)$ and d $(d \geq 0)$ such that for any request sequence σ,

$$COST_{ALG}(\sigma) \leq c \cdot COST_{OPT}(\sigma) + d \tag{3.2}$$

where $COST_{OPT}(\sigma)$ is the cost on σ for an optimal off-line algorithm (deterministic off-line adversary), denoted by OPT, which knows the entire request sequence in advance and can serve the requests with a minimum cost. Further, the factor c is called the *competitive ratio* of the algorithm ALG and d is an additive constant. Thus, constants c and

d define the radius and the *quality*, respectively, of the (near-optimal) solution generated by a deterministic on-line algorithm when compared to an optimal off-line algorithm. Further, when $d = 0$, the algorithm ALG is said to be *strictly* competitive.

When discussing randomized *on-line* algorithms, it is important to define carefully the exact power given to the *adversaries*. Ben-David *et al.* [BBKTW94] introduced three kinds of adversaries for analyzing randomized on-line algorithms.

Oblivious adversary:
An oblivious adversary, as the name indicates, will generate a request in advance without any knowledge of the (randomized) answers of a randomized on-line algorithm (oblivious property) to all the previous requests. In other words, it generates a complete request sequence before any requests are served by the randomized on-line algorithm. The oblivious adversary is charged a cost of the optimum off-line algorithm for that request sequence.

Adaptive on-line adversary:
This adversary may observe the on-line algorithm and generate the next request based on the algorithm's randomized answers to all previous requests. The adversary must serve each request on-line without knowing the random choices made by the randomized on-line algorithm on the present or any future request.

Adaptive off-line adversary:
This adversary also generates a request sequence adaptively as done by an adaptive on-line adversary; however, it is charged an optimum off-line cost for servicing that request sequence.

The essential differences between these categories lie in the way that the adversary decides to generate future requests and the way that the cost is to be incurred for servicing the request sequence generated. Both an oblivious adversary and an adaptive off-line adversary are actually optimal off-line algorithms for the request sequence σ generated, as the cost incurred by these two adversaries to serve σ is exactly the optimal off-line cost. However, there is a fundamental difference between an oblivious adversary and an adaptive off-line adversary. An oblivious adversary generates the request sequence σ independently of the random choices made by the randomized on-line algorithm, and hence the cost incurred by the oblivious adversary for servicing σ is a fixed quantity. On the other hand, an adaptive off-line algorithm generates the request sequence σ depending upon the random choices made by the randomized on-line algorithm. That is, σ is a random variable and therefore the cost incurred by the adaptive off-line adversary for servicing σ is a random variable as well. Finally, in the case of an adaptive on-line adversary, the request sequence generated and the cost incurred for the adaptive on-line adversary are random variables as above description for an adaptive off-line adversary. However, it should be noted that the cost incurred by the adaptive on-line adversary may not be coincided with the optimal off-line cost as the adaptive on-line adversary has to serve the request sequence on-line.

We are now set to define the competitiveness of a randomized on-line algorithm. Formally, a randomized on-line algorithm ALG is called c-competitive against an oblivious adversary ADV if there exist constants c ($c \geq 1$) and d ($d \geq 0$), such that for any request sequence σ generated by the oblivious adversary,

$$\mathbf{E}[COST_{ALG}(\sigma)] \leq c \cdot COST_{ADV}(\sigma) + d \tag{3.3}$$

where $\mathbf{E}[\cdot]$ is the mathematical expectation operator taken over all the random choices made by ALG. As usual, c is the competitive ratio of algorithm ALG and d is an additive constant.

Similarly, a randomized on-line algorithm is said to be c-competitive against an adaptive on-line/off-line adversary ADV if there exist constants c ($c \geq 1$) and d ($d \geq 0$), such that for any request sequence σ generated by the adaptive on-line/off-line adversary,

$$\mathbf{E}[COST_{ALG}(\sigma) - c \cdot COST_{ADV}(\sigma)] \leq d \tag{3.4}$$

By linearity property of expectation operator, we can equivalently express Equation (3.4) as,

$$E[COST_{ALG}(\sigma)] \leq c \cdot E[COST_{ADV}(\sigma)] + d \tag{3.5}$$

Furthermore, Ben-David *et al.* [BBKTW94] investigated the relative strength of the adversaries with respect to an arbitrary on-line problem and propounded the following significant results.

Theorem 3.1: If there is a randomized on-line algorithm that is c-competitive against any ***adaptive off-line adversary***, then there also exists a c-competitive deterministic on-line algorithm.

Theorem 3.2: If ALG is a c-competitive randomized algorithm against any ***adaptive on-line adversary*** and if there is a d-competitive algorithm against any ***oblivious adversary***, then ALG is $(c \cdot d)$-competitive against any ***adaptive off-line adversary***.

An immediate consequence of the above two theorems is the following corollary.

Corollary 3.1: If there exists a c-competitive randomized algorithm against any ***adaptive on-line adversary***, then there is a c^2-competitive deterministic algorithm.

2. Techniques of Competitive Analysis

Performing competitive analysis for on-line algorithms is a paramount challenge to an algorithmic designer. Once we propose an on-line algorithm, as mentioned earlier, we are interested to answer the question that "How well does our *on-line* algorithm perform for the targeted problem?" Therefore, we need to compare the performance of our on-line algorithm with that of other relevant on-line algorithms for the same problem. In this book, we focus on the competitive analysis mentioned above to compare the performance of different on-line algorithms on the same on-line problem. Generally, in order to analyze the competitiveness of an on-line algorithm, we need to use mathematical methods to show that the inequalities in Equation (3.2) (deterministic) or in Equations (3.3)/(3.5) (randomized) hold for the on-line algorithm. In the following, we introduce some common competitive analysis techniques, such as *Potential Function, Phase Partition,* etc.

2.1 Potential Function

We now present an important proof technique, called *Potential Function method* that can be used to analyze the competitiveness for deterministic and randomized on-line algorithms. Firstly, let us consider an example to understand what this potential function means and its relevance in our context. In the theory of gravitation, as a result of the gravitational attraction of the Earth, an object can "store energy" depending on its position. This stored energy is referred to as *gravitational potential energy.* The gravitational potential energy of an object is directly proportional to its height above the zero position (a reference position), and hence, to determine the gravitational potential energy of an object, a zero height position must first be arbitrarily assigned. Typically, the ground (surface of the earth) is considered to be a position of zero height. For example, in Figure 3.1, when we lift the ball up, the *work* we have done will be transferred and stored as potential energy. The higher we lift the ball the more potential energy is stored. Therefore, the amount of potential energy being stored is a function of where we locate the ball, a function of how high we lift it up. We call this function as a potential function.

This concept of potential function is used in competitive analysis to analyze the performance of an on-line algorithm. This mathematical method basically quantifies the energy stored by the system as a function of the positions of the system components. Typically, a potential function will measure the "distance" from the *on-line* algorithm's configuration to the configuration of its adversary. We will now see how a

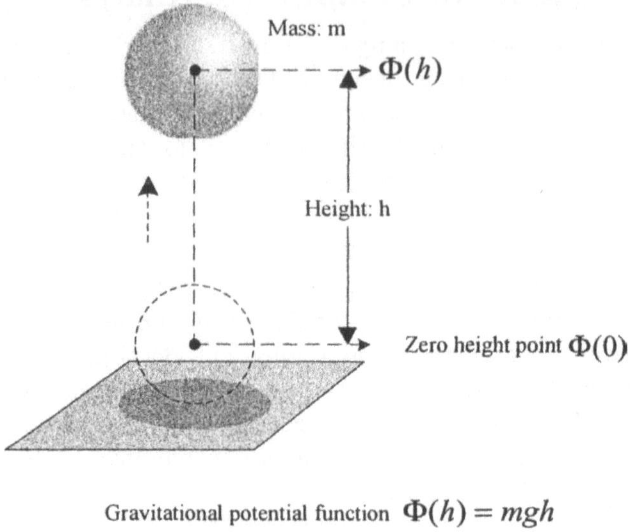

Figure 3.1. Illustation of gravitational potential function

potential function method can be used to analyze an on-line algorithm and see what "energy" and "potential" actually mean in our context.

For instance, let us consider a request sequence $\sigma = \sigma(1), \sigma(2), ..., \sigma(m)$ that arrives at a DDBS. For each request $\sigma(t)$, $1 \leq t \leq m$, we denote $COST_{ALG}(\sigma(t))$ and $COST_{ADV}(\sigma(t))$ as the cost of an on-line algorithm ALG and the cost of the adversary ADV on $\sigma(t)$, respectively[3]. Suppose further that ALG and ADV service σ simultaneously. A potential function maps the system configurations of ADV and ALG to a real number Φ. Let $\Phi(t)$ denote the value of the potential function after ADV and ALG serve $\sigma(t)$. Then we verify the following.

$$COST_{ALG}(\sigma(t)) + \Phi(t) - \Phi(t-1) \leq c \cdot COST_{ADV}(\sigma(t)) \tag{3.6}$$

Summing up Equation (3.6) for all $t = 1, ..., m$, we obtain,

$$\sum_{t=1}^{m} COST_{ALG}(\sigma(t)) + \Phi(m) - \Phi(0) \leq c \cdot \sum_{t=1}^{m} COST_{ADV}(\sigma(t)) \tag{3.7}$$

i.e.,

$$COST_{ALG}(\sigma) \leq c \cdot COST_{ADV}(\sigma) + [\Phi(0) - \Phi(m)] \tag{3.8}$$

[3]For a randomized on-line algorithm, we will consider the expected cost on $\sigma(t)$.

Thus, if we can show that for any request $\sigma(t)$, the above inequality in Equation (3.7) holds, then we can prove that the on-line algorithm ALG is c-competitive. Here, $\Phi(0)$ is the initial potential value[4] of the system (corresponds to the zero height point in our Figure 3.1), and $(\Phi(t)-\Phi(t-1))$ is the *change in potential* that occurs during the processing of $\sigma(t)$. Typically, a potential function is *chosen* such that $\Phi(t)$ is always non-negative. However, it should be noted that using a potential function to derive the competitive ratio of an on-line algorithm is a difficult task, as the challenge lies in constructing an apt function $\Phi(t)$ and showing that Equation (3.7) holds for each request in σ. In general, potential functions will be found by trial and error and depend on problem context.

2.2 Phase Partition Technique

This is another proof technique that is commonly used in the competitive analysis of on-line algorithms. *Phase Partition Technique* may prove to be an alternative whenever it is difficult to construct a potential function to prove the competitiveness of an on-line algorithm. We now introduce this technique in detail. As usual, let us suppose that we are given a request sequence $\sigma = \sigma(1), \sigma(2), ..., \sigma(m)$ that arrives at a DDBS. We partition σ into *phases* $P(0), P(1), P(2), ..., P(r)$ based on an on-line algorithm ALG that we need to analyze. Each phase comprises a set of requests and may not contain $m/(r+1)$ requests exactly. It should be noted that for different on-line algorithms, the partition methods might be different.

For each request phase $P(i)$, $0 \leq i \leq r$, we denote $COST_{ALG}(P(i))$ and $COST_{ADV}(P(i))$ as the cost of an on-line algorithm ALG and the cost of the adversary on $P(i)$, respectively[5]. Now, if we can obtain that for any request phase $P(i)$,

$$COST_{ALG}(P(i)) \leq c \cdot COST_{ADV}(P(i)) + d_i \tag{3.9}$$

where d_i is an additive constant, then summing up Equation (3.9) for all $i = 0, ..., r$, we obtain,

$$\sum_{i=0}^{r} COST_{ALG}(P(i)) \leq c \cdot \sum_{i=0}^{r} COST_{ADV}(P(i)) + \sum_{i=0}^{r} d_i \tag{3.10}$$

i.e.,

$$COST_{ALG}(\sigma) \leq c \cdot COST_{ADV}(\sigma) + d \tag{3.11}$$

[4] A potential function $\Phi(t)$ is called *strict* iff $\Phi(0) = 0$ [BFR92].

[5] Again, for a randomized on-line algorithm, we will consider the expected cost on $P(i)$.

where $d = \sum_{i=0}^{r} d_i$ is an additive constant. Thus, we can prove that the on-line algorithm ALG is c-competitive. Similar to potential function method, here too, the challenge lies in constructing a partition of the given request sequence into phases such that Equation (3.9) holds for each phase $P(i)$. In the next section, we shall present some examples to see the workings of these two methods in detail.

3. Examples: Competitive Analysis for LRU Algorithm

As an example, we now discuss on how to analyze the competitiveness of LRU paging algorithm using the *Potential Function* method and *Phase Partition* technique, to ease our understanding of these methods.

3.1 Using Potential Function

Let us assume that the size of the fast memory in our paging problem is k pages. This means that at any time instant the fast memory can hold at most k pages. In [BRICS96], S.Albers has shown that the LRU paging algorithm is k-competitive using the potential function method.

Proof: Let us consider an arbitrary request sequence $\sigma = \sigma(1), \sigma(2), \ldots, \sigma(m)$, where $\sigma(t)(1 \leq t \leq m)$ denotes the t-th request in σ. At any instant, we denote S_{LRU} as the set of pages that reside in the fast memory using LRU algorithm. Similarly, we denote S_{OPT} as the set of pages that reside in the fast memory using an optimal algorithm OPT. Here, the *optimal algorithm* OPT is an *adversary* of LRU algorithm. Assume that we have an integer function $w(x)$ for LRU, which assigns integer weights from the range $[0, k]$ to the pages in the system. In addition, if page p is in S_{LRU}, then $0 < w(p) \leq k$; otherwise, page p is not in S_{LRU}, and $w(p) = 0$. In other words, for each page that resides in fast memory, a positive weight is assigned, and for each page not in fast memory, a zero weight is assigned. We assume that initially, the fast memory is empty. Thus, we start with $w(p) = 0$ for every page p in the system. Now, let us consider that LRU serves a request $\sigma(t) = p$ (requested page is, say, p) in σ. If a page fault occurs, LRU must load page p to the fast memory, then $w(q)$ *for each page* $q \in S_{LRU}$ will be decreased by 1, and the page, say z, whose $w(z) = 0$[6] will be evicted from the fast memory. Further, for the requested page p, $w(p) = k$. On the other hand, if $p \in S_{LRU}$, then for each page $q \in S_{LRU}$ that $w(q) > w(p)$, $w(q)$ is decreased by 1, and $w(p)$ is set to k. Hence, $w(q) < w(p)$, for all $q \in S_{LRU}$ after the

[6]We look for that page whose weight has become zero after we decrease its weight from its current value.

request $\sigma(t) = p$ is serviced. Therefore, it should be noted that the value $w(p)$ for a page p is dynamically adjusted when servicing the requests in σ. With this working philosophy, we now construct a potential function as follows. Let

$$\Phi(t) = \sum_{p \in \{S_{LRU} - S_{OPT}\}} w(p) \tag{3.12}$$

where $S_{LRU} - S_{OPT}$ denotes the set of pages that are in S_{LRU} but not in S_{OPT} and $\Phi(t)$ is the value of the potential function after OPT and LRU served the request $\sigma(t)$. Without loss of generality, we assume that LRU and OPT initially start with the same fast memory, and hence, $\Phi(0) = 0$. As mentioned above, if we can show that for any request $\sigma(t)$ $(1 \leq t \leq m)$,

$$COST_{LRU}(\sigma(t)) + [\Phi(t) - \Phi(t-1)] \leq k \cdot COST_{OPT}(\sigma(t)) \tag{3.13}$$

then we are convinced that LRU algorithm is k-competitive.

To this end, let us consider an arbitrary request $\sigma(t)$ which requests for page p. Without loss of generality, we assume that OPT serves this request first and then LRU serves it secondly. For OPT algorithm, we need to consider following two distinct cases. When OPT serves $\sigma(t)$, if there is no page fault, then the servicing cost is 0 and the potential remains unchanged. On the other hand, if there is a page fault, then the servicing cost for OPT is 1. Furthermore, OPT might evict a page, say q, that is currently a member of the set S_{LRU}, in which case the potential increases by $w(q)$. It should be noted that $w(q) \leq k$ in our potential function. Therefore, the potential can increase by at most k.

Now we consider the case when LRU serves the request $\sigma(t)$. Similar to the OPT algorithm, here too we should consider the following two cases. When servicing $\sigma(t)$, if LRU does not have a page fault, then the servicing cost is 0 and the potential value decreases or remains unchanged. On the other hand, if there is a page fault occurred, then the servicing cost for LRU on this request is 1. In this case, we need to determine the change in potential. We know that when LRU serves $\sigma(t)$, page p was a member of the set S_{OPT}. This implies that there must be a page q that is only in S_{LRU}, i.e., there must exist at least one page $q \in \{S_{LRU} - S_{OPT}\}$. When the page fault occurred, if q is evicted from the fast memory by LRU, then the potential value decreases by $w(q) \geq 1$. Otherwise, LRU will evict a page in both S_{LRU} and S_{OPT}, which does not influence the potential, and then page p is loaded into the fast memory. As a result, $w(q)$ must be decreased by 1. Hence, the potential value must decrease by at least 1 in this case.

Thus, we observe the following from the above arguments. We have shown that when OPT has a fault on $\sigma(t)$, the potential increases by at most k, and when LRU has a fault on $\sigma(t)$, the potential decreases by at least 1. Thus, we can conclude that Equation (3.13) must hold, and hence, we realize that LRU paging algorithm is k-competitive. ■

Alternatively, in order to prove that LRU paging algorithm is k-competitive, instead of Equation (3.12) one can also define a potential function as follows.

$$\Phi(t) = \sum_{p \in S_{OPT}} (k - w(p)) \tag{3.14}$$

The proof is similar to that we present above and we leave it to interested readers to verify. ■

3.2 Using Phase Partition Techniques

We now introduce two *Phase Partition* techniques, called **Heuristic 1** and **Heuristic 2** to show that LRU paging algorithm is k-competitive.

Heuristic 1

Proof[7]*:* Consider an arbitrary request sequence $\sigma = \sigma(1), \sigma(2), ..., \sigma(m)$ that arrives at a DDBS, where $\sigma(t)$ $(1 \leq t \leq m)$ denotes the t-th request in σ. Without loss of generality, we assume that LRU and an optimal off-line algorithm OPT initially start with the same fast memory, where the OPT algorithm serves as an adversary of LRU.

We now use the Heuristic 1 to partition σ into *phases* $P(0), P(1), P(2)$, ..., $P(r)$, such that LRU has at most k faults on $P(0)$ and exactly k faults on $P(i)$, for every $1 \leq i \leq r$. Such a partitioning can be obtained as follows. We start at the end of sequence σ and scan the request sequence backwards. As shown in Figure 3.2, whenever we have seen k faults

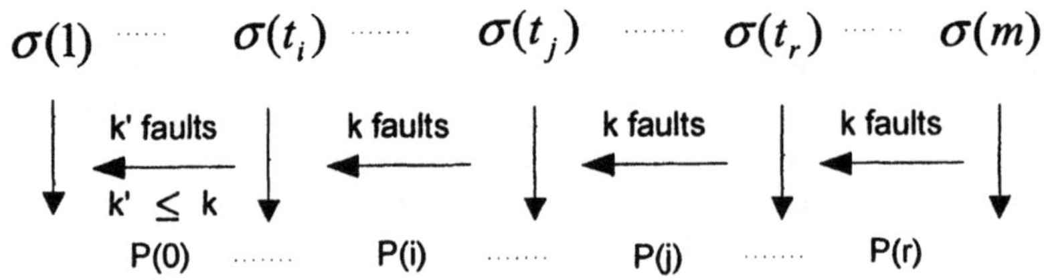

Figure 3.2. Illustration of phase partition technique – Heuristic 1

[7]This method was first presented by Sleator and Tarjan [ST85], and S.Albers presented a simplified version in [BRICS96].

made by LRU, we cut off a new phase. In the remainder of this proof we will show that OPT has at least one page fault during each phase. In fact, this should be sufficient to complete our proof. Note that in this technique, we do an analysis on the responses after the entire sequence is served by LRU.

For phase $P(0)$, since LRU and OPT start with identical initial set of pages in the fast memory, OPT must have a page fault on the first request on which LRU has a fault. Thus it should be no surprise to realize,

$$COST_{LRU}(P(0)) \leq k \cdot COST_{OPT}(P(0)) \tag{3.15}$$

Now let us consider an arbitrary phase $P(i)$, $1 \leq i \leq r$. Let $\sigma(t_i)$ be the first request in $P(i)$ and let $\sigma(t_{i+1} - 1)$ be the last request in $P(i)$. Furthermore, Let p be the page that is last requested in $P(i-1)$, i.e., $\sigma(t_i - 1) = p$. We now state an important lemma as follows.

Lemma 3.1: $P(i)$ $(1 \leq i \leq r)$ contains requests to k distinct pages that are different from page p.

Since OPT has page p in its fast memory at the beginning of $P(i)$, if Lemma 3.1 holds, then OPT cannot have all the k pages different from p in its fast memory simultaneously. Thus, OPT must have at least one page fault when it serves the requests in $P(i)$, which implies that,

$$COST_{LRU}(P(i)) \leq k \cdot COST_{OPT}(P(i)) \tag{3.16}$$

and hence, from Equation (3.15) and Equation (3.16), we can prove that LRU paging algorithm is k-competitive. Therefore, it remains to prove Lemma 3.1.

In order to prove Lemma 3.1, we need to consider following three cases.

Case 1: LRU faults twice on a page q in $P(i)$, i.e., LRU has a fault on both $\sigma(s_1) = q$ and $\sigma(s_2) = q$, where $t_i \leq s_1 < s_2 \leq t_{i+1} - 1$.

Case 2: The k requests on which LRU has a fault in $P(i)$ are to k distinct pages and these pages are also different from p.

Case 3: The k requests on which LRU has a fault in $P(i)$ are to k distinct pages but on one of the faults, page p is requested.

For Case 1, it should be noted that page q is in the fast memory immediately after LRU serves $\sigma(s_1)$. Since LRU has a fault on $\sigma(s_2)$, page q must be evicted from the fast memory at some request $\sigma(t)$ with $s_1 < t < s_2$. We know that according to the working strategy of LRU, when q is evicted, it is the least recently requested page in the fast memory. Thus the subsequence $\sigma(s_1), ..., \sigma(t)$ must contain requests to $k+1$ distinct pages, at least k of which must be different from p, and hence, Lemma 3.1 holds.

Lemma 3.1 is clearly held in Case 2.

Finally, in Case 3, it should be noted that page p is in the fast memory at the beginning of $p(i)$. Since on one of the faults in $P(i)$, page p is requested. Thus, at some request $\sigma(t)$ with $t_i < t \leq t_{i+1} - 1$, page p must be evicted from the fast memory. Similarly to Case 1, we obtain that the subsequence $\sigma(t_i - 1), \sigma(t_i), ..., \sigma(t)$ must contain $k+1$ distinct pages, k of which must be different from p, and hence, Lemma 3.1 holds.

From the above three cases, we prove Lemma 3.1. Therefore, Equation (3.16) is held for all the request phase $P(i)(1 \leq i \leq r)$. From Equation (3.15) and Equation (3.16), we obtain that,

$$\sum_{i=0}^{r} COST_{LRU}(P(i)) \leq k \cdot \sum_{i=0}^{r} COST_{OPT}(P(i)) \tag{3.17}$$

i.e.,

$$COST_{LRU}(\sigma) \leq k \cdot COST_{OPT}(\sigma) \tag{3.18}$$

and hence the proof. ■

Heuristic 2

We now use another phase partition technique - Heuristic 2 to prove that LRU paging algorithm is k-competitive.

Proof: Consider an arbitrary request sequence $\sigma = \sigma(1), \sigma(2), ..., \sigma(m)$ arrives at the system, where $\sigma(t)$ $(1 \leq t \leq m)$ denotes the t-th request in σ. As done in Heuristic 1, we assume that LRU and OPT initially start with the same fast memory, where the optimal algorithm OPT is the adversary of LRU. As shown in Figure 3.3, we divide σ into *phases* $P(0), P(1), P(2), ..., P(r)$, such that $P(i)$ $(0 \leq i \leq r-1)$ has a maximal request sequence that contains exactly k distinct page requests. In other words, $P(i+1)$, if it exists, will begin on the request which is the $(k+1)$-th distinct page request since the start of $P(i)$. Further, for the last phase $P(r)$, it may be incomplete and have $k' \leq k$ distinct page requests. Since there are at most[8] k distinct page requests in any request phase $P(i)$ $(0 \leq i \leq r)$, using LRU paging algorithm, once a page is requested, it will not be evicted until the phase $P(i)$ has been completed. Consequently, LRU will not fault twice on the same page in one phase. Therefore, it is clear that LRU incurs at most k page faults when it serves the requests in $P(i)$.

[8] $P(r)$ has $k' \leq k$ distinct page requests.

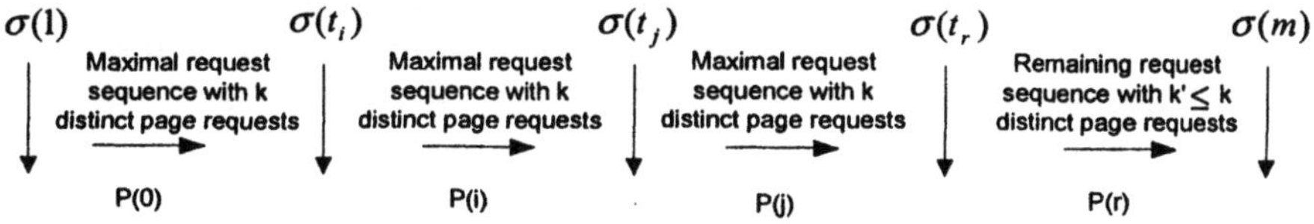

Figure 3.3. Illustration of phase partition technique – Heuristic 2

For any $0 \leq i \leq r-1$, let $\sigma(t_i)$ be the first request of $P(i)$ and consider the request sequence starting from the second request of $P(i)$ to the first request of $P(i+1)$. After OPT serves the request $\sigma(t_i)$, page $\sigma(t_i)$ is in the fast memory, and since there are k distinct page requests in this sequence different from $\sigma(t_i)$, OPT must incur at least one fault to service this request sequence. We charge OPT this cost in servicing $P(i)$ $(0 \leq i \leq r-1)$. For the last phase $P(r)$, since there are not a phase $P(r+1)$ and there are only $k' \leq k$ distinct page requests in $P(r)$, it may possibly incur none page fault for OPT to serve the rest requests[9] in $P(r)$. Therefore, we will ignore the cost for OPT to serve the request sequence $\sigma(t_r+1), ..., \sigma(m)$.

In all, LRU has at most k faults in each phase and we can charge OPT with at least one fault for each phase except the last phase. Hence, we obtain that,

$$\sum_{i=0}^{r} COST_{LRU}(P(i)) \leq k \cdot \sum_{i=0}^{r} COST_{OPT}(P(i)) + k \tag{3.19}$$

i.e.,

$$COST_{LRU}(\sigma) \leq k \cdot COST_{OPT}(\sigma) + k \tag{3.20}$$

and hence the proof. ■

The choice of the above heuristics purely depends on the problem context. With our LRU example, both the techniques are somewhat easy to use, as the difference essentially lies on how to "partition" the sequence into distinct phases.

4. Concluding Remarks

In this chapter we have introduced a mathematical tool - *competitive analysis*, that is useful to analyze the performance of *on-line* algorithms.

[9]It should be noted that the first request $\sigma(t_r)$ in $P(r)$ is already taken into account by OPT.

We presented several well-known on-line problems and introduced two competitive proof techniques, *Potential Function method* and *Phase Partition technique.* For an ease of understanding, we have considered LRU Paging Problem and analyzed its performance using the above two proof techniques. As described earlier in this chapter, a paging algorithm can be considered as a special instance of the symmetric *k-Server Problem* in which many interesting problems remains open. Manasse *et al.* [MMS88] conjectured that there exists a deterministic k-competitive on-line algorithm for the *k-Server Problem* and there is no deterministic on-line algorithm for the *k-Server Problem* that can be better than a competitive ratio k. This is indeed the famous *k-server conjecture* quoted often in the literature. This conjecture holds when the network topology is uniform [ST85], a line [CKV90], or a tree [CL96]. On general metric spaces, only for certain special cases ($k = 2$ and $k = n - 1$, where n is the number of points in the metric space [MMS88]) the k-server problem was solved. Recently, randomized on-line algorithms were proposed to reduce this k-competitive bound of paging algorithms. The *Marking algorithm* presented in [FKLMSY91] is proved to be $2H_k$-competitive, where H_k is the kth harmonic number (H_k is asymptotic to $ln(k)$). An interesting problem when considering randomized algorithms is in deriving a best competitive ratio for a randomized k-server algorithm. The *HARMONIC* algorithm, originally proposed by Raghavan and Snir in [RS89], is a simple and natural randomized on-line algorithm. A lot of research effort was made to analyze the competitiveness of *HARMONIC* algorithm. However, finding an exact competitive ratio of *HARMONIC* algorithm continues to remain as an open problem.

In this chapter, we used LRU paging algorithm as an example to demonstrate the power offered by competitive analysis. Compilation of several results on different application domains can be found in [MR95, BE98]. Our main emphasis in this book is to focus on on-line algorithms used for DDBS and/or RTDDBS. In the following chapters, we will present several deterministic and randomized on-line algorithms in DDBS/RTDDBS and analyze their performance using competitive analysis. Predominantly, we will use *Phase Partition* technique introduced in this chapter.

Chapter 4

OBJECT MANAGEMENT IN STATIONARY COMPUTING ENVIRONMENTS

In this chapter, we address the issues (object allocation and replication) of OMP in the application domain of DDBSs in SCEs. In general, a DDBS consists of n nodes (as shown in Figure 1.2), denoted as $p_1, p_2, ..., p_n$, interconnected via a communication network. Each node consists of a processor and a local memory (database). Replicas of objects are stored in the local memories. All the local memories are private and accessible only by the processors who own them. Internodes communication is carried out by passing messages through the interconnection network. As mentioned in Chapter 3, transactions on objects arriving at a DDBS can be in the form of either read or write operations, referred to as *read requests* or *write requests*, respectively. Requests originating from processors for objects are assumed to arrive at the system concurrently and there exists a concurrency control mechanism to serialize[1] them. Specifically, a read request is serviced with a replica (latest version) of the requested object, while a write request actually modifies (creates a new version) an object. Especially, in order to guarantee the *object consistency* among multiple replicas of an object, every change to an object must be transferred to all the other available replicas in the remote memories elsewhere. In other words, a write request for an object must be propagated to all the processors that have replicas of the object in their respective local memories. Without loss of generality, these read/write requests can arrive at the system in a random manner and they need not exhibit a regular pattern.

[1]Refer to [SWH98, BK91, ORP95] and Section 4 of Chapter 2 for more details.

In a SCE, as mentioned in Chapter 2, there are three types of costs associated with the operations in servicing the requests. The first one is the I/O cost, i.e., the cost of *fetching* an object from the local memory to the processor or *saving* an object from a processor to its local memory. We denote this cost as C_{io}. The other two types of costs are due to communication in the underlying interconnection network, namely, control-message transferring cost and data-message (object) transferring cost. We denote these costs as C_c and C_d, respectively. For instance, a control-message transfer is needed when a processor needs to read an object which is not in its local memory, whereas a data-message is just the object transferred between the processors via the communication network. We know that the I/O operation is only a local operation. It does not utilize any network resources, such as link bandwidth. Furthermore, the size of a control-message is normally much shorter than a data-message. Therefore, it is reasonable to assume $C_d > C_c > C_{io}$ in a SCE. To normalize the cost, we assume that $C_{io} = 1$. This means that C_c is the ratio of a control-message transferring cost to an I/O cost and C_d is the ratio of a data-message transferring cost to an I/O cost.

In a DDBS, objects are usually replicated in the system for improving certain system performance metrics such as *response time*, *monetary cost*, *bandwidth utilization*, etc. Replication also increases the object availability by allowing many nodes to service several requests for the same object concurrently [AW98, VR01, TS02]. Thus, in some cases, the cost of maintaining redundant copies can offset the cost of communication overheads and boost the performance in terms of reliability. However, it should be noted that the performance of the system is very sensitive to the distribution of the replicas among the nodes. This is due to the fact that the cost of servicing a request associated with a local memory is different from the cost of servicing a request associated with a remote memory. Especially, in order to guarantee the consistency of the replicas, every change of an object must be transferred to all the other available replicas in the remote memories elsewhere. Thus, when more replicas are allocated, the average cost of servicing a read request will be smaller, whereas the average cost of servicing a write request will be higher. Therefore, a crucial decision while designing an object allocation and replication algorithm in a DDBS lies in determining *how many replicas of each object* are to be present at any instant in the network, and *in which nodes* these copies of the objects should be allocated. Thus, an object allocation and replication algorithm recommends a set of processors, often referred to as an *object allocation scheme*[2], that need

[2]This is referred to as "Configuration" in Chapter 3.

to have copies of an object. In other words, an object allocation scheme identifies the nodes at which the copies of an object are stored. Obviously, more replicas are beneficial in a read-intensive network, whereas fewer copies are beneficial in a write-intensive network. It is worth noting that any OMP for a DDBS attempts to modify or use this allocation scheme information to seek the most recent (fresh) copy of an object. This object allocation scheme can be a dynamic quantity depending on the strategy used in the design of OMP. Thus, by and large, most of the strategies are geared towards efficient ways of managing this object allocation scheme. Finally, it should be clear that one needs to define an allocation scheme for every object in the system and it is defined as follows.

Formally, we define an *allocation scheme* of an object o, denoted by A_o, on a request *Req* as a set of processors having copies of the latest version of object o in their respective local memories right before request *Req* is serviced, however after the immediately preceding request for object o is serviced. All the processors in the current A_o are called *data-processors* of object o. Other processors that do not belong to the current A_o are considered as *non-data-processors.* Further, we define an *initial request sequence* as follows. An *initial request sequence*, denoted as σ, comprises read/write requests issued for several objects. For example, $\sigma = R_2^{p_4} W_3^{p_1} W_2^{p_3} R_2^{p_7} R_2^{p_8} W_4^{p_2}\ R_1^{p_1} R_3^{p_2}$ is an initial request sequence in which the first request $R_2^{p_4}$ is a read request from processor p_4 requesting for object 2, the second request $W_3^{p_1}$ is a write request from processor p_1 requesting for object 3, and so on. Similarly, we denote σ_o as a *request sequence* in which all the read/write requests are requesting for the same object o. In addition, the allocation scheme on the first request in σ_o is referred to as an *initial allocation scheme* of σ_o, denoted as IA_o.

Designing an intelligent and efficient object allocation and replication on-line algorithm, as mentioned above, always offers considerable challenges to the system designers. There are several criteria to evaluate the performance of a DDBS, such as the *percentage of the transactions* that can be serviced without missing their *deadlines*, the total cost of servicing the transactions, the *system resources utilization rate*, etc. The performance metric in our study here is minimizing the cumulative cost[3] of all the operations involved in servicing read and write requests. Further, in this chapter, in order to improve an object availability and the system reliability, we assume that at any time instant, there exists at least t copies $(1 \leq t \leq n)$[4] for every object in the system. This constraint is often re-

[3]Data-message transferring cost, control-message transferring cost and I/O cost.

[4]n is the number of nodes in the network system.

ferred to as t-availability constraint in the literature [WH98, WJH97] and it will be considered in all the algorithms presented in this chapter and Chapter 5, where we consider the issues of object management in MCEs. In this chapter, we first propose mathematical (cost) models that consider all the above mentioned costs. In the available literature, using these cost models, both the *static* and *dynamic* algorithms are proposed for SCEs. We consider both these versions and present some *deterministic* on-line algorithms in this chapter. While there are several algorithms available in the literature, our choice on these algorithms is based on their simple working styles, simple-to-implement natures, and easy-to-analyze behaviors. Also, for a reader who merely wants to practice competitive analysis, these algorithms serve as excellent examples to realize the power of competitive analysis. Lastly, all these algorithms bear a strong relationship in their design and working styles, and share more-or-less common cost models. Thus, we first introduce a traditional static object allocation scheme, referred to as *Static Allocation* (SA) algorithm and then present three adaptive dynamic object allocation and replication algorithms, referred to as *Dynamic Allocation* (DA) algorithm, *Dynamic Window Mechanism* (DWM) algorithm and *Adaptive Distributed Request Window* (ADRW) algorithm, respectively. Finally, we will use competitive analysis to quantify the performance of all these four algorithms. It may be emphasized that in order to quantify the performance of the algorithms, it is sufficient to consider a single object and analyze the behavior of the algorithms under several influencing factors. For ease of understanding, several numerical examples will be provided when we present the above algorithms.

1. SA Algorithm

In this section, we introduce an OMP with a static object allocation algorithm, SA algorithm. The idea behind the design of SA algorithm is that it keeps a *fixed allocation scheme* of each object in the DDBS at all time. Further, in order to satisfy the t-availability constraint mentioned earlier, we assume that the allocation scheme of an object o is given by a *fixed* processor set $S(o)$ and $|S(o)| = t$. The processors in $S(o)$ are called as *servers*[5] and all the processors in the system know the server set of every object. It should be noted that for different objects, the allocation schemes may be differ.

SA algorithm follows a *read-one-write-all* working style. Essentially, if the system receives a read request issued from a non-data-processor

[5]Hence, $S(o)$ is also referred to as a server set of object o.

p_i for object o, SA algorithm requests a replica of object o from some server $p_j \in S(o)$. As a response, p_j fetches the replica of the object o from its local memory and sends it to p_i. On the other hand, in response to a write request issued from a processor p_i for object o, SA algorithm will send the new version of object o to all the members of $S(o)$. We now present the cost model of SA algorithm to compute the cost of servicing a read request or a write request. We define the cost of servicing a request *Req* by an algorithm A as $COST_A(Req)$.

1.1 Cost Model

Case A (Read request): Consider servicing a read request $R_o^{p_i}$. Then, the cost of servicing this request is given by,

$$COST_{SA}(R_o^{p_i}) = \begin{cases} 1 & \text{if } p_i \in S(o) \\ 1 + C_c + C_d & \text{otherwise} \end{cases} \tag{4.1}$$

In Equation (4.1), if $p_i \in S(o)$, then object o is directly retrieved from its local memory. This process incurs C_{io} units of cost for I/O operation, where $C_{io} = 1$. On the other hand, as mentioned above, if $p_i \notin S(o)$, then p_i sends a read request to a server p_j. After receiving the read request, p_j retrieves object o from its local memory and sends it to processor p_i. This process incurs $(1 + C_c + C_d)$ units of cost.

Case B (Write request): Consider servicing a write request $W_o^{p_i}$. Then, the cost of servicing this request is given by,

$$COST_{SA}(W_o^{p_i}) = \begin{cases} (|S(o)| - 1)C_d + |S(o)| & \text{if } p_i \in S(o) \\ |S(o)|C_d + |S(o)| & \text{otherwise} \end{cases} \tag{4.2}$$

Note that a write request creates a new version of an object. In order to maintain object consistency, the new version must be transferred to all the servers in the system. Therefore, in Equation (4.2), if $p_i \in S(o)$, then object o will be transferred to all the processors in $S(o)$ other than p_i[6], incurring $(|S(o)| - 1)C_d$ units of cost. Whereas, if $p_i \notin S(o)$, then object o will be transferred to all the processors in $S(o)$, incurring $(|S(o)|)C_d$ units of cost. Finally, in both the cases, servers in $S(o)$ will save the object o into their respective local memories, incurring a total of $|S(o)|$ units of cost for I/O operations.

Example 4.1: Consider a request sequence $\sigma_o = W_o^{p_5} R_o^{p_4} R_o^{p_3} W_o^{p_2} R_o^{p_3} R_o^{p_3} R_o^{p_3} R_o^{p_3} R_o^{p_3} W_o^{p_4}$ comprising requests for object o, where $W_o^{p_5}$ is a

[6]Since the new version of object o is already available in processor p_i in this case.

write request from processor p_5 for object o, $R_o^{p_4}$ is a read request from processor p_4 for object o, and so on. We assume that $S(o) = \{p_1, p_2, p_5\}$. According to the above cost model, each read request issued by a processor $p_i \notin S(o)$ will incur $(1 + C_c + C_d)$ units of cost, otherwise $(p_i \in S(o))$ it will incur only one unit cost for I/O operation. On the other hand, a write request issued from a processor $p_i \in S(o)$ or $p_i \notin S(o)$ will incur $(2C_d + 3)$ or $(3C_d + 3)$ units of cost, respectively. We define the cost of servicing a request sequence σ_o with an initial allocation scheme IA_o by an algorithm A as $COST_A(\sigma_o, IA_o)$. Thus, the total cost of servicing the above request sequence σ_o using SA algorithm is given by,

$$COST_{SA}(\sigma_o, S(o)) = 14C_d + 7C_c + 16 \tag{4.3}$$

1.2 Analysis of SA Algorithm

We will now evaluate the performance of SA algorithm using a competitive analysis, specifically using the *Phase Partition* technique introduced in Chapter 3.

Theorem 4.1: For any integer $t^7 \geq 1$, SA algorithm is $(1 + C_c + C_d)$-competitive in a SCE.

Proof: Let us consider an arbitrary request sequence for an object o $\sigma_o = \sigma_o(1), \sigma_o(2), ..., \sigma_o(m)$ arrives at the system, where $\sigma_o(j)$ $(1 \leq j \leq m)$ denotes the j-th request in σ_o. Without loss of generality, we assume that SA algorithm and an optimal algorithm OPT (which also satisfies the t-availability constraint) initially start with the same allocation scheme $S(o)$.

Heuristic 3

We now introduce a new Phase Partition technique, Heuristic 3, which is different from Heuristics 1 and 2 presented in Chapter 3. As shown in Figure 4.1, using Heuristic 3, we partition σ_o into several *phases* $P(0), P(1), P(2), ..., P(r)$, such that $P(0)$ consists of only the read requests before the first write request in σ_o. Further, $P(i)$ $(1 \leq i \leq r)$ consists of a write request followed by all the read requests presented between this write request and the next write request in σ_o. For example, in Figure 4.1, $P(1)$ consists of the first write request $\sigma_o(t_i)$ and all the read request $(\sigma_o(t_i + 1), ..., \sigma_o(t_j - 1))$ presented between $\sigma_o(t_i)$ and the second write request $\sigma_o(t_j)$. It should be noted that given a σ_o, using

[7] Here, t represents the t-availability constraint and $1 \leq t \leq n$, where n is the number of nodes in the network system. We will not mention these hereafter.

Heuristic 3, $P(0)$ may not exist if there are no read requests arriving before the first write request in σ_o. Similarly, $P(i)$ $(1 \le i \le r)$ may not exist if all the requests in σ_o are read requests.

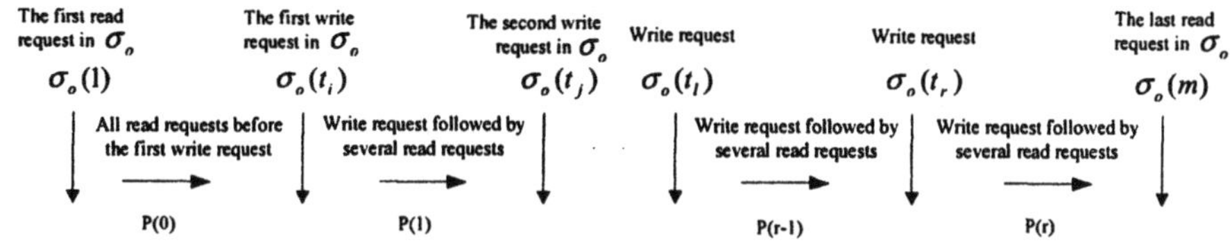

Figure 4.1. Illustration of Phase Partition technique – Heuristic 3

Let us first consider phase $P(0)$, if it exists. From Equation (4.1), we know that each read request in $P(0)$ will incur no more than $(1+C_c+C_d)$ units of cost. On the other hand, for OPT algorithm, each read request will incur at least one unit cost for the I/O operation. Therefore,

$$\begin{aligned} COST_{SA}(P(0), S(o)) &\le (1 + C_c + C_d)|P(0)| \\ &\le (1 + C_c + C_d)COST_{OPT}(P(0), S(o)) \end{aligned} \tag{4.4}$$

where $|P(0)|$ denotes the number of the requests in $P(0)$.

Now, let us consider the analysis for a phase $P(i)$ $(1 \le i \le r)$. We suppose that the initial allocation scheme on the write request in $P(i)$ using the OPT algorithm is $A_o^*(i)$. $A_o^*(i)$ may be different from the server set $S(o)$. However, in order to satisfy the t-availability constraint in the system, the size of the allocation scheme $A_o^*(i)$ must be such that $|A_o^*(i)| \ge t$. Thus, using the OPT algorithm, the write request must incur at least $(t-1)C_d$ units of cost for data-message transferring[8] and t units of cost for I/O operations. Similarly, the rest of the read requests in $P(i)$ must each incur at least one unit cost for I/O operation. Therefore, we can obtain,

$$COST_{OPT}(P(i), A_o^*(i)) \ge (t-1)C_d + t + (|P(i)| - 1) \tag{4.5}$$

On the other hand, from Equation (4.2), we know that the write request in $P(i)$ will incur at most[9] (tC_d+t) units of cost for SA algorithm,

[8]In this case, the allocation scheme includes the processor that issues the write request in $P(i)$.

[9]If the processor issued the write request is not in $S(o)$.

since the allocation scheme of object o is always $S(o)$ and $|S(o)| = t$. Further, each read request in $P(i)$ will incur at most $(1+C_c+C_d)$ units of cost as mentioned before. Thus, we can obtain that,

$$\begin{aligned} COST_{SA}(P(i), S(o)) &\leq tC_d + t + (1 + C_c + C_d)(|P(i)| - 1) \\ &\leq (1 + C_c + C_d)[t + (|P(i)| - 1)] \\ &\leq (1 + C_c + C_d)COST_{OPT}(P(i), A_o^*(i)) \end{aligned} \tag{4.6}$$

From Equation (4.4) and Equation (4.6), we can therefore obtain that,

$$\begin{aligned} &COST_{SA}(\sigma_o, S(o)) = \sum_{i=0}^{r} COST_{SA}(P(i), S(o)) \\ &\leq (1 + C_c + C_d) \left[COST_{OPT}(P(0), S(o)) + \sum_{i=1}^{r} COST_{OPT}(P(i), A_o^*(i)) \right] \\ &= (1 + C_c + C_d)COST_{OPT}(\sigma_o, S(o)) \end{aligned} \tag{4.7}$$

Thus, we clearly observe that SA algorithm is $(1+C_c+C_d)$-competitive in a SCE, and hence the proof. ■

2. DA Algorithm

In this section, we introduce a dynamic object allocation and replication algorithm, referred to as DA algorithm. Object allocation and replication algorithms can be either static or dynamic. As discussed earlier, in a *read-intensive network*, we can obtain a smaller average cost of servicing a read request when more replicas are replicated in the system. On the other hand, in a *write-intensive network* fewer replicas would be beneficial. Since read/write requests may arrive at the system in an unpredictable manner, a fixed object allocation scheme is obviously inefficient for the system. Thus, designing a dynamic object allocation and replication algorithm that can adapt to the random patterns of read/write requests is therefore crucial, so that the request sequence can be processed with a minimal total servicing cost. We now describe the DA algorithm in detail in the next subsection.

2.1 Algorithm Description

Similar to the SA algorithm, in the DA algorithm, we assume that the initial allocation scheme of an object o is given by a fixed server set $S(o)$ and $|S(o)| = t$, which is indeed the consideration of t-availability constraint in the system. Further, we assume that the allocation scheme of an object o A_o always consists of $S(o)$ and several other processors which are not in $S(o)$ and can be changed depending on the read-write request patterns. For example, for processors p_i and p_j ($p_i, p_j \notin S(o)$), the processor set $S(o) \cup \{p_i\} \cup \{p_j\}$ or simply $S(o) \cup \{p_j\}$ can be a possible A_o at some point in time. Furthermore, all the processors in the system are assumed to know the server set of every object in DA algorithm.

We have discussed earlier that there are three types of cost associated with I/O operation, control-message and data-message transferring operations. In DA algorithm, there is another operation, referred to as an object *invalidate* operation which upon execution is to invalidate the replicas of an object o. Since the purpose of this invalidate operation issued by a server (to be discussed in next subsection) is to inform the respective data-processors to invalidate the corresponding replicas, only control-messages need to be sent. Thus, the cost of an "invalidate" operation is equal to the cost of transferring a control-message and we continue to use C_c to denote this "invalidate" cost.

In Section 3 of Chapter 2, we have mentioned that *Temporal Locality*[10] is one of the primary factors for an independent caching strategy to decide the importance of an object. The DA algorithm also considers the *Temporal Locality* property when a processor accesses an object. In other words, when a processor issues a request to access an object it is more likely for this processor to access the same object again in the *near future* (temporal aspect). Therefore, in the DA algorithm, if the system receives a read request issued from a non-data-processor p_i for object o, the DA algorithm requests a replica of object o from some server $p_j \in S(o)$. As done in SA algorithm, p_j will send object o to p_i as a response. The most important process in DA algorithm is that after receiving object o, p_i saves object o into its local memory to save the communication cost for the future expected read requests for object o. We denote this read request as a *saving-read* request. Finally, server p_j will add processor p_i into an invalidate-list[11] for object o, denoted as $inv\_list(p_j, o)$. The key idea behind this operation is that when servicing a following write request for object o from a processor q, the servers of object o can simply send control-messages to the processors in their invalidate-lists for object o, except q (if q is in an invalidate-list), to invalidate the redundant copies of object o in their respective local memories. We summarize the entire workings of DA algorithm in Table 4.1 (in a pseudo-code form) for servicing a read/write request *Req* from processor p_i requesting an object o.

[10]Refer to [KH93, pp.193] for the definition.

[11]An invalidate-list can be considered as a processor set, whose initial value is $\emptyset$.

Table 4.1. DA algorithm

```
Initial conditions: Server set S(o), allocation scheme A_o
If (Req is a read request)
  { If (p_i ∈ A_o)     {Fetch object o from the local memory of p_i;}
      Else     /* Req is a saving-read request */
        {Select a server p_j ∈ S(o) and sends a control-message to p_j;
          p_j fetches object o from its local memory and sends it to p_i;
                /* p_j adds p_i into inv_list(p_j, o) */
          inv_list(p_j, o) = inv_list(p_j, o) ∪ {p_i};
          p_i saves object o into its local memory;
          A_o = A_o ∪ {p_i};
        }
  }
Else     /* Req is a write request */
  { If (p_i ∈ S(o)) /* p_i is a server */
        {p_i sends object o to all the servers in S(o) except p_i;
          All the server in S(o) save object o into their respective local
          memories, send control-messages to the processors in their respective
          invalidate-lists for object o to invalidate the redundant copies, and
          then empty their respective invalidate-lists for object o;
          A_o = S(o);
        }
      Else /* p_i is not a server */
        {p_i sends object o to all the processors in S(o);
          All the servers send control-messages to the processors (except p_i) in
          their respective invalidate-lists for object o to invalidate the redundant
          copies;
          A_o = S(o) ∪ {p_i};
          All the processors in A_o save object o into their respective local
          memories;
          All the servers remove the processors (except p_i) from their respective
          invalidate-lists for object o;
          If (p_i is not in any invalidate-list for object o)
              {p_i indicates some server to add it into the corresponding
                invalidate-list;
              }
        }
  }
```

According to Table 4.1, we can now present the cost model of DA algorithm to service a read and a write request, respectively, as carried out below.

2.2 Cost Model

Case A (Read request): Consider servicing a read request $R_o^{p_i}$ and let A_o be the allocation scheme of object o on this request. Then,

$$COST_{DA}(R_o^{p_i}) = \begin{cases} 1 & \text{if } p_i \in A_o \\ 2 + C_c + C_d & \text{otherwise} \end{cases} \quad (4.8)$$

In Equation (4.8), if $p_i \in A_o$, then object o is simply retrieved from its local memory. This will incur only one unit cost for I/O operation. On the other hand, as mentioned above, if $p_i \notin A_o$ (p_i is a non-data-processor), then p_i will send a control-message to a server p_j to inform about the read request. As a response, p_j retrieves object o from its local memory and sends it to p_i. This process will incur $(1 + C_c + C_d)$ units of cost. Further, p_i saves object o into its local memory (saving-read), incurring one unit cost for an I/O operation, and thus, the total servicing cost will be $(2 + C_c + C_d)$ units. Finally, server p_j will add processor p_i into its invalidate-list $inv\_list(p_j, o)$.

Case B (Write request): Consider servicing a write request $W_o^{p_i}$ and let $S(o)$ be the server set of object o. Then,

$$COST_{DA}(W_o^{p_i}) = \begin{cases} (|S(o)| - 1)C_d + |S(o)| \\ \qquad + \sum_{p \in S(o)} (|inv\_list(p,o)|C_c) & \text{if } p_i \in S(o) \\ \\ |S(o)|C_d + (|S(o)| + 1) \\ \qquad + \sum_{p \in S(o)} (|inv\_list(p,o) - \{p_i\}|C_c) \\ & \text{otherwise} \end{cases} \quad (4.9)$$

where $inv\_list(p, o) - \{p_i\}$ denotes the set of processors in $inv\_list(p, o)$ except processor p_i. We know that each data-message transferring will incur C_d units of cost. Therefore, the number of processors to which the new version of object o created by $W_o^{p_i}$ must be transferred should be as small as possible. On the other hand, we must satisfy the t-availability constraint of object o in the system. Thus, when servicing a write request $W_o^{p_i}$, if $p_i \in S(o)$, then object o will be transferred to all the servers in $S(o)$ other than p_i, incurring $(|S(o)| - 1)C_d$ units of cost. Whereas, if $p_i \notin S(o)$, then object o will be transferred to all the servers in $S(o)$, incurring $|S(o)|C_d$ units of cost. In both the cases, processors in $S(o) \cup \{p_i\}$ will save the object o into their respective local memories, incurring a total cost of $(|S(o) \cup \{p_i\}|)$ units.

From the above description, we know that when DA algorithm services $W_o^{p_i}$, some data-processors may not obtain the new version of object o.

Therefore, after receiving the new version of object o from processor p_i, all the servers in $S(o)$ will send control-messages to the processors in their corresponding invalidate-lists except processor p_i (if p_i is in an invalidate-list) to invalidate the outdated replicas of object o and remove these processors from their corresponding invalidate-lists. Finally, if processor $p_i \notin S(o)$ and p_i is not in any invalidate-list for object o, then p_i will indicate some server in $S(o)$ to add itself into the corresponding invalidate-list. The purpose of this process is to invalidate the copy of object o in processor p_i when the DA algorithm services a following write request from another processor for object o.

Example 4.2: Let us consider the same example presented in Example 4.1, where $\sigma_o = W_o^{p_5} R_o^{p_4} R_o^{p_3} W_o^{p_2} R_o^{p_3} R_o^{p_3} R_o^{p_3} R_o^{p_3} R_o^{p_3} W_o^{p_4}$ and $IA_o = S(o) = \{p_1, p_2, p_5\}$. Note that, in this example, the t-availability constraint in the system is 3. We can compute the cost of servicing σ_o using DA algorithm as follows. The first request $W_o^{p_5}$ will incur $[1+2(1+C_d)]$ units of cost, where the first one unit cost is the cost for processor p_5 to save object o into its local memory, and the cost $2(1+C_d)$ is the cost for p_5 to transfer object o to the servers p_1 and p_2, and then these two servers save object o into their respective local memories. As a saving-read request, the second request $R_o^{p_4}$ will incur $(2 + C_c + C_d)$ units of cost according to Equation (4.8) and now the allocation scheme is $A_o = \{p_1, p_2, p_4, p_5\}$. Similarly, for the last request $W_o^{p_4}$, $A_o = \{p_1, p_2, p_3, p_5\}$ and the servicing cost is $C_c + [1 + 3(1 + C_d)]$, where the first part C_c is the cost to invalidate the outdated replica in processor p_3, the rest of the cost components are similar to that explained for the first request $W_o^{p_5}$. Finally, after servicing the last request, $A_o = \{p_1, p_2, p_4, p_5\}$. Table 4.2 shows the adjustment of A_o when DA algorithm services each of the requests in σ_o.

As a result, the total cost of servicing σ_o using DA algorithm is given by,

$$COST_{DA}(\sigma_o, S(o)) = 10C_d + 6C_c + 20 \tag{4.10}$$

From Equation (4.3) and Equation (4.10), we obtain

$$COST_{SA}(\sigma_o, S(o)) - COST_{DA}(\sigma_o, S(o)) = (4C_d + C_c - 4) > 0$$
$$\text{(since } C_d > C_c > 1)$$

Hence, in the above example, $COST_{SA}(\sigma_o, S(o)) > COST_{DA}(\sigma_o, S(o))$ for the same request sequence and the same initial allocation scheme, and therefore the total servicing cost is improved by using DA algorithm.

Table 4.2. The adjustment of A_o when DA algorithm services σ_o

	Request	A_o (after serving the request)
1	$W_o^{p_5}$	$\{p_1, p_2, p_5\}$
2	$R_o^{p_4}$	$\{p_1, p_2, p_4, p_5\}$
3	$R_o^{p_3}$	$\{p_1, p_2, p_3, p_4, p_5\}$
4	$W_o^{p_2}$	$\{p_1, p_2, p_5\}$
5	$R_o^{p_3}$	$\{p_1, p_2, p_3, p_5\}$
6	$R_o^{p_3}$	$\{p_1, p_2, p_3, p_5\}$
7	$R_o^{p_3}$	$\{p_1, p_2, p_3, p_5\}$
8	$R_o^{p_3}$	$\{p_1, p_2, p_3, p_5\}$
9	$R_o^{p_3}$	$\{p_1, p_2, p_3, p_5\}$
10	$W_o^{p_4}$	$\{p_1, p_2, p_4, p_5\}$

2.3 Analysis of DA Algorithm

The above described example exemplifies the fact that DA algorithm clearly adapts to the changing request patterns and shows its use in minimizing the overall servicing cost. In this subsection, we use competitive analysis technique presented in the proof of SA algorithm, Phase Partition Heuristic 3, to study the performance of DA algorithm. We consider an arbitrary request sequence for object o, $\sigma_o = \sigma_o(1), \sigma_o(2), ..., \sigma_o(m)$, arrives at the system, where $\sigma_o(j)$ $(1 \leq j \leq m)$ denotes the j-th request in σ_o. We know that using Heuristic 3, σ_o will be partitioned into *phases* $P(0), P(1), P(2), ..., P(r)$ (refer to Section 1.2). Further, we assume that the initial allocation scheme of each phase $P(i)$ $(0 \leq i \leq r)$ is $IA_o(i)$ when DA algorithm services σ_o. As usual, without loss of generality, we assume that DA algorithm and an optimal algorithm OPT (which also satisfies the t-availability constraint) initially start with the same initial allocation scheme $IA_o = IA_o(0) = S(o)$. We first state two important lemmas associated with the servicing of each phase and then use the results of these lemmas to show that DA algorithm is $(2+C_c)$-competitive in a SCE.

Lemma 4.1: Given a σ_o with an IA_o, $COST_{DA}(P(0), IA_o) \leq (2 + C_c)COST_{OPT}(P(0), IA_o)$ in a SCE.

Proof: Let $N(0)$ be the set of processors which are not in IA_o and have issued read requests in $P(0)$. From Equation (4.8), the first read requests issued by the processors in $N(0)$ will each incur $(2 + C_c + C_d)$ units of cost for DA algorithm. The rest of the read requests are all issued from data-processors when DA algorithm services them, and hence will each incur one unit cost for I/O operation. Further, we should consider servicing the anticipated write request in $P(1)$. If $P(1)$ exists, according to the cost model in Equation (4.9), control-messages must be transferred to invalidate the redundant replicas in $N(0)$ to maintain the object consistency. Therefore, the total cost for DA algorithm to service the read requests in $P(0)$ is given by,

$$COST_{DA}(P(0), IA_o) \leq |N(0)|(2+C_c+C_d)+(|P(0)|-|N(0)|)+|N(0)|C_c \tag{4.11}$$

For OPT algorithm, since the processors in $N(0)$ have no replicas of object o in their local memories, data-massages must be transferred to these processors and incur a total of $|N(0)|C_d$ units of cost. Further, each read request must incur at least one unit cost for I/O operation. Hence, the total cost computed by OPT algorithm for servicing $P(0)$ is,

$$COST_{OPT}(P(0), IA_o) \geq |N(0)|C_d + |P(0)| \tag{4.12}$$

Thus, the difference between Equation (4.11) and Equation (4.12) is,

$$\begin{aligned}
& COST_{DA}(P(0), IA_o) - COST_{OPT}(P(0), IA_o) \\
\leq\ & 2|N(0)|C_c + |N(0)| \\
\leq\ & (|N(0)|C_d + |P(0)|) + |P(0)|C_c \quad (\text{since } C_c < C_d, |N(0)| \leq |P(0)|) \\
\leq\ & (1 + C_c)COST_{OPT}(P(0), IA_o)
\end{aligned}$$

Alternatively,

$$COST_{DA}(P(0), IA_o) \leq (2 + C_c)COST_{OPT}(P(0), IA_o) \tag{4.13}$$

Hence the proof. ■

The above lemma derives the competitive ratio for phase $P(0)$. For phases $P(i)(1 \leq i \leq r)$, following lemma derives the competitive ratio.

Lemma 4.2: Given a σ_o with an IA_o, $COST_{DA}(P(i), IA_o(i)) \leq (2 + C_c)COST_{OPT}(P(i), IA^*_o(i)) + K$, where $1 \leq i \leq r$, $IA^*_o(i)$ is the initial allocation scheme of object o on $P(i)$ using the OPT algorithm, and $K \geq 0$ is an additive constant.

Proof: Without loss of generality, let us suppose that the first request in $P(i)$ $(1 \leq i \leq r)$, which is indeed a write request issued from any processor in the system for object o, denoted by W_o^*. We define $N(i)$ as the set of processors which have issued read requests in $P(i)$ and do not belong to the A_o after servicing the first write request W_o^*. According to Equation (4.9), using DA algorithm, a write request will incur at most[12] $|S(o)|C_d$ units of cost due to data-messages transferring and $(|S(o)|+1)$ units of cost for I/O operations. Additionally, control-messages must be sent to invalidate the redundant replicas elsewhere in the system. Since the cost of sending "invalidate" messages to all the processors in $N(i-1)$ is already accounted while analyzing $P(i-1)$[13], referring to Equation (4.9), we note that the cost to invalidate the redundant copies of object o is at most[14] C_c. Therefore, using DA algorithm, the cost for servicing the first write request W_o^* in $P(i)$ is given by,

$$COST_{DA}(W_o^*) \leq |S(o)|C_d + (|S(o)|+1) + C_c \tag{4.14}$$

The rest of the requests in $P(i)$ are all read requests. The cost of servicing these read requests is similar to Equation (4.11) in the analysis of $P(0)$. We present it as follows,

$$\sum_{j=1}^{|P(i)|-1} COST_{DA}(\text{the } j^{th} \text{ read request in } P(i))$$

$$\leq |N(i)|(2 + C_c + C_d) + (|P(i)| - |N(i)| - 1) + |N(i)|C_c \tag{4.15}$$

It should be noted that as done in Lemma 4.1, the cost to invalidate the replicas in $N(i)$ when servicing the expected write request in $P(i+1)$ is calculated in Equation (4.15). Thus, from Equation (4.14) and Equation (4.15), the total cost for servicing the requests in $P(i)$ using DA algorithm is given by,

$$\begin{aligned} COST_{DA}(P(i), A_o(i)) &= COST_{DA}(W_o^*) \\ &\quad + \sum_{j=1}^{|P(i)|-1} COST_{DA}(\text{the } j^{th} \text{ read request in } P(i)) \\ &\leq (|S(o)| + |N(i)|)C_d + (2|N(i)| + 1)C_c + (|P(i)| + |N(i)| + |S(o)|) \end{aligned} \tag{4.16}$$

[12] When the processor issued the write request does not belong to $S(o)$.

[13] Refer to the analysis in $P(0)$ and the analysis of the read requests in $P(i)$ $(1 \leq i \leq r)$ that will be presented later.

[14] To invalidate the redundant copy in the processor which issued the write request in $P(i-1)$ $(2 \leq i \leq r)$, if this processor does not belong to $S(o)$.

For the OPT algorithm, every read request incurs at least one unit cost for I/O operation. We define $N'(i)$ as the set of processors that issued read requests in $P(i)$. There are two cases we need to consider as follows.

Case A: If $|N'(i)| > t$, then the first write request W_o^* in $P(i)$ will incur at least t units of cost for I/O operations and $(t-1)C_d$ units of cost for data-message transferring due to the consideration of the t-availability constraint in the system. Further, there are at least number of $(|N'(i)| - t)$ processors which issued read requests in $P(i)$ and are not in the allocation scheme after the OPT algorithm services the write request W_o^*. Thus, to these processors, data-messages must be transferred. Finally, each read request incurs at least one unit cost for I/O operation. Hence, the total cost[15] of servicing the requests in $P(i)$ for the OPT algorithm is given by,

$$\begin{aligned} COST_{OPT}(P(i), IA_o^*(i)) &\geq (t-1)C_d + t + (|N'(i)| - t)C_d \\ &\qquad + (|P(i)| - 1) \\ &= (|N'(i)| - 1)C_d + t + (|P(i)| - 1) \quad (4.17) \end{aligned}$$

Thus, the difference between Equation (4.16) and Equation (4.17) is,

$$\begin{aligned} &COST_{DA}(P(i), IA_o(i)) - COST_{OPT}(P(i), IA_o^*(i)) \\ &\leq \ (t + |N(i)| - |N'(i)| + 1)C_d + (2|N(i)| + 1)C_c + (|N(i)| + 1) \\ &\qquad\qquad (\text{since } |S(o)| = t) \\ &\leq \ (|N'(i)| - 1)C_d + (2|N(i)| + 1)C_c + 2C_d + (|N(i)| + 1) \\ &\qquad\qquad (\text{since } |N'(i)| > t, |N'(i)| \geq |N(i)|, |P(i)| \geq |N'(i)| + 1) \\ &\leq \ (|N'(i)| - 1)C_d + t + (|P(i)| - 1) + 2|N(i)|C_c + 2C_d + C_c \\ &\leq \ COST_{OPT}(P(i), IA_o^*(i)) + C_c COST_{OPT}(P(i), IA_o^*(i)) + K_1 \end{aligned}$$

where $K_1 = (2C_d + C_c)$ is an additive constant. Therefore, we obtain,

$$COST_{DA}(P(i), IA_o(i)) \leq (2 + C_c) COST_{OPT}(P(i), IA_o^*(i)) + K_1 \quad (4.18)$$

Case B: If $|N'(i)| \leq t$, then the first write request W_o^* will incur at least t units of cost for I/O operations and $(t-1)C_d$ units of cost for

[15] An optimal algorithm may not serve the requests in $P(i)$ as explained in this case. However, the total servicng cost of $P(i)$ must satisfy the inequality in Equation (4.17), when the t-availability constraint is considered.

data-message transferring, since OPT algorithm can send the object o to all the processors in $N'(i)$ when servicing the first write request W_o^*. Hence, the total cost of servicing the requests in $P(i)$ for the OPT algorithm is given by,

$$COST_{OPT}(P(i), IA_o^*(i)) \geq (t-1)C_d + t + (|P(i)| - 1) \quad (4.19)$$

In this case, the difference between Equation (4.16) and Equation (4.19) is,

$$\begin{aligned}
& COST_{DA}(P(i), IA_o(i)) - COST_{OPT}(P(i), IA_o^*(i)) \\
\leq\ & (|N(i)|+1)C_d + (2|N(i)|+1)C_c + |N(i)| + 1 \\
\leq\ & (t-1)C_d + t + (|P(i)|-1) + 2|N(i)|C_c + 2C_d + C_c \\
& \qquad\qquad (\text{since } |N(i)| \leq |N'(i)| \leq t, |P(i)| \geq |N'(i)| + 1) \\
\leq\ & COST_{OPT}(P(i), IA_o^*(i)) + C_c COST_{OPT}(P(i), IA_o^*(i)) + K_2
\end{aligned}$$

where $K_2 = (2C_d + C_c)$ is an additive constant. Therefore, we can obtain that,

$$COST_{DA}(P(i), IA_o(i)) \leq (2 + C_c)COST_{OPT}(P(i), IA_o^*(i)) + K_2 \quad (4.20)$$

Thus, from Equation (4.18) and Equation (4.20) the result of Lemma 4.2 is immediate. Hence the proof. ■

The significance of the above two lemmas is as follows. For request patterns in $P(0)$ and phase $P(i)$ $(1 \leq i \leq r)$, Lemmas 4.1 and 4.2 assure that the total cost of the DA algorithm on $P(i)$ $(0 \leq i \leq r)$ is at most $(2 + C_c)$ times worse than that of an optimal algorithm which also satisfies the t-availability constraint. This interesting property will play a crucial role in proving our main theorem for a SCE below.

Theorem 4.2: For any integer $t \geq 1$, DA algorithm is $(2 + C_c)$-competitive in a SCE.

Proof: From the results of Lemma 4.1 and Lemma 4.2, we know that for an arbitrary σ_o with an IA_o,

$$\begin{aligned}
COST_{DA}(\sigma_o, IA_o) &= \sum_{i=0}^{r} COST_{DA}(P(i), IA_o(i)) \\
&\leq (2 + C_c)\sum_{i=0}^{r}(COST_{OPT}(P(i), IA_o^*(i))) + K \\
&= (2 + C_c)COST_{OPT}(\sigma_o, IA_o) + K \qquad (4.21)
\end{aligned}$$

where $IA_o^*(i)$ is the initial allocation scheme of object o on $P(i)$ after servicing the last request in $P(i-1)$ using the OPT algorithm, $IA_o^*(0) =$

IA_o, and $K = \sum_{i=1}^{r} x_i$ $(x_i \in \{K_1, K_2\})$ is an additive constant. It may be noted that $K = \alpha_1 K_1 + \alpha_2 K_2$ $(\alpha_1, \alpha_2 \geq 0)$ is a linear combination of K_1 and K_2 obtained in our analysis of $P(i)$ $(1 \leq i \leq r)$. The values of α_1 and α_2 depend upon the requests in σ_o. Hence the proof. ■

3. DWM Algorithm

The DA algorithm discussed in the previous section is a dynamic object allocation and replication algorithm. It always considers a read request from a non-data-processor as a *saving-read* request. Let us reconsider σ_o in Examples 4.1 and 4.2 where $\sigma_o = W_o^{p_5} R_o^{p_4} R_o^{p_3} W_o^{p_2} R_o^{p_3} R_o^{p_3} R_o^{p_3} R_o^{p_3} R_o^{p_3} W_o^{p_4}$ and $IA_o = S(o) = \{p_1, p_2, p_5\}$. Now, if we do not consider the second and third read requests ($R_o^{p_4}$,$R_o^{p_3}$) as saving-read requests, the total cost of servicing the above σ_o will be,

$$COST(\sigma_o, S(o)) = 10C_d + 4C_c + 18 \tag{4.22}$$

We clearly observe that the cost is smaller than that obtained by DA algorithm in Equation (4.10). Therefore, even if we use a dynamic object allocation and replication algorithm, the most important aspect is to decide whether or not to consider a read request from a non-data-processor as a saving-read request. If we can decide on this issue effectively, then we can further improve the performance (minimize the cost) to a large extent. In fact, DWM algorithm precisely attempts to implement this idea.

DWM algorithm is designed for distributed systems that need centralized controllers. In a centralized control system we have a central control unit (CCU) at which all the requests arrive for processing. Requests for objects can arrive in a concurrent fashion, but we assume that there is a concurrency control mechanism (CCM) to serialize[16] them in such a way that CCU outputs at most one request in a δ time units, with δ chosen to be infinitesimally small. Without loss of generality, we assume that $\delta = 1$. All the requests from CCU form an initial request sequence σ in which the read/write requests can be issued for different objects. Whenever a request is released from CCU as an output, the DWM algorithm will be invoked for servicing, as shown in Figure 4.2. Additionally, our design of DWM algorithm involves a window mechanism, which will be

[16]Refer to Section 3 of Chapter 1 and Section 4 of Chapter 2 for more details of centralized control system and concurrency control mechanism.

explained in Section 3.2. The window mechanism allows a systematic partition of requests to be served and to minimize the total cost.

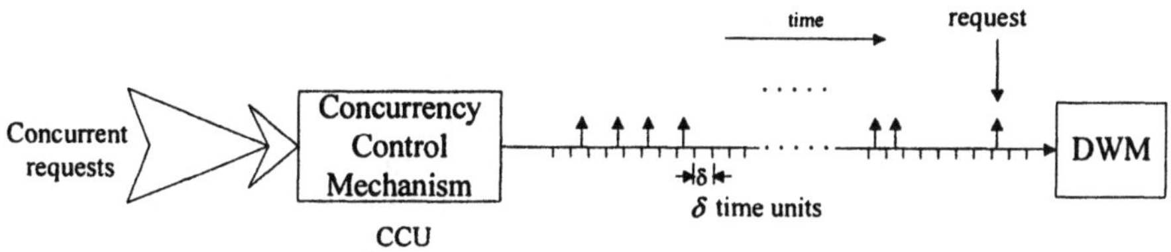

Figure 4.2. **Illustration of the concurrent control mechanism**

Further, similar to DA algorithm, we assume that the initial allocation scheme of an object o in DWM algorithm is given by a fixed server set $S(o)$ and $|S(o)| = t$, which is the consideration of t-availability constraint in the system. Also, we assume that $S(o) \subseteq A_o$ holds for each object o at any time instant and CCU knows the allocation scheme of every object in the system. Additionally, besides the I/O operation, control-message and data-message transferring operations, we also consider the invalidate operation discussed in DA algorithm.

We now present the cost model for DWM algorithm to service a read request and a write request, respectively.

3.1 Cost Model

Given a σ_o, the cost of servicing a request in σ_o is defined as follows.

Case A (Read request): Consider a read request $R_o^{p_i}$ and let A_o be the allocation scheme of object o on this request. Then,

$$COST_{DWM}(R_o^{p_i}) = \begin{cases} 1 & \text{if } p_i \in A_o \\ 1 + C_c + C_d & \text{if } p_i \notin A_o \text{ and } R_o^{p_i} \text{ is not a saving-read request} \\ 2 + C_c + C_d & \text{if } p_i \notin A_o \text{ and } R_o^{p_i} \text{ is a saving-read request} \end{cases} \tag{4.23}$$

If $p_i \in A_o$, then object o is simply retrieved from its local memory. This will only incur one unit cost for I/O operation. On the other hand, if $p_i \notin A_o$, then CCU will send a control-message to a server $p_j \in S(o)$ to inform about the read request. Similarly, p_j retrieves object o from its local memory and sends it to processor p_i as a response. This process will incur $(1+C_c+C_d)$ units of cost. A significant aspect of this model is that after receiving the object o, if p_i saves object o into its local memory (saving-read), then the servicing cost will be one unit higher than that if p_i does not save object o into its local memory (non-saving-read) to account for the extra I/O cost. Further, whether $R_o^{p_i}$ is a saving-read request or not is decided by the CCU. We will further discuss this issue along with the presentation of DWM algorithm.

Case B (Write request): Consider a write request $W_o^{p_i}$ and let A_o be the allocation scheme of object o on this request. Also, let A'_o be the allocation scheme of object o after servicing this request. Then,

$$COST_{DWM}(W_o^{p_i}) = \begin{cases} (|S(o)|-1)C_d + |S(o)| + |A_o - A'_o|C_c & \text{if } p_i \in S(o) \\ |S(o)|C_d + (|S(o)|+1) + |A_o - A'_o|C_c & \text{otherwise} \end{cases} \quad (4.24)$$

where $A_o - A'_o$ denotes the set of processors in A_o but not in A'_o. Similar to that in Equation (4.9), when DWM services $W_o^{p_i}$, if $p_i \in S(o)$, then object o will be transferred to all the servers in $S(o)$ other than p_i, incurring $(|S(o)|-1)C_d$ units of cost. Whereas, if $p_i \notin S(o)$, then object o will be transferred to all the servers in $S(o)$ incurring $|S(o)|C_d$ units of cost. In both the cases, processors in $S(o) \cup \{p_i\}$ will save the object o into their respective local memories, incurring a total cost of $(|S(o) \cup \{p_i\}|)$ units (as $C_{io} = 1$). From the above description, it should be noted that $A'_o = S(o) \cup \{p_i\}$. Further, control-messages must be transferred to the processors in $A_o - A'_o$ to invalidate the redundant copies for the object consistency, incurring total of $|A_o - A'_o|C_c$ units of cost. It should be noted that compared to DA algorithm, there are no invalidate-lists maintained in a server in DWM algorithm, since CCU knows the allocation scheme of every object. Thus the additional operations for tracking redundant copies and invalidating them now become the responsibility of CCU in DWM algorithm.

3.2 Window Mechanism of DWM

As mentioned earlier, our design of DWM algorithm involves a window mechanism. We generate multiple dynamic request windows in the system, one for each requested object. We denote a request window for an object o as $win(o)$. Each request window is of a FIFO type window with size τ to store at most τ number of requests (in τ time units) for the same object. Additionally, for each $win(o)$, we associate a counter TC_o with an initial value set to τ and the value of TC_o is decremented

Table 4.3. Window mechanism of DWM algorithm

```
For (Each time unit)
{ If (There is a request Req for an object o)
      { If (win(o) does not exist)     /* Req is the first request for object o */
            { Generate win(o) and insert Req into win(o);
              TC_o = τ;
            }
        Else      /* Req is not the first request for object o */
            { If (Req is a read request)     { Insert Req into win(o); }
              Else      /* Req is a write request */
                  {Service the requests in win(o);
                                        /*win(o) is empty after servicing*/
                    Insert Req into win(o);
                    TC_o = τ;
                  }
            }
      }
  For (Each currently existed request window win(o') in the system)
        /* No matter whether there is a request in this time unit or not */
      { TC_o'=TC_o' - 1;
        If (TC_o' == 0)
            { Service the requests in win(o');
              Delete win(o');
              Invalidate the copies of o' in processors that
              belong to {A_o' - S(o')};
              A_o' = S(o');
            }
      }
}
```

by one per time unit until it reaches 0. We now describe the window mechanism of the DWM algorithm in Table 4.3.

From Table 4.3, it may be observed that a request window $win(o)$ will be dynamically generated or deleted by the DWM algorithm. We denote the request sequence that is inserted into $win(o)$ during its individual lifetime as σ_o. Suppose a request sequence $\sigma_o = \sigma_o(1), \sigma_o(2), ..., \sigma_o(m)$, where $\sigma_o(i)$ $(1 \leq i \leq m)$ denotes the i-th request in σ_o. From Table 4.3, using the window mechanism of DWM algorithm, σ_o will be essentially partitioned into several phases $P(0), P(1), ..., P(r)$ which are identical to those obtained by using Phase Partition Heuristic 3 (presented in Section 1) to partition σ_o. Now, whenever a phase comes into an existence, DWM algorithm will service the request sequence in that phase without any knowledge of the future phases. However, it may be noted that DWM algorithm need not wait for the entire window $win(o)$ to be filled up for processing.

Example 4.3: Following example will clarify the workings of the window mechanism in DMW algorithm. In Figure 4.3(a), when $TC_o = \tau_1$, a write request $W_o^{p_3}$ arrives at $win(o)$. Thus, the previous three read requests in $win(o)$ form the phase $P(0) =< R_o^{p_1} R_o^{p_2} R_o^{p_1} >$. At this stage, DWM algorithm is then invoked to service $P(0)$. After servicing, $P(0)$ will be *deleted* from $win(o)$ and $W_o^{p_3}$ is *inserted* into $win(o)$. Similarly, in Figure 4.3(b), when $TC_o = \tau_2$, a write request $W_o^{p_1}$ arrives at $win(o)$, and hence phase $P(1) =< W_o^{p_3} R_o^{p_2} >$ is formed. In Figure 4.3(c), since $TC_o = 0$, the last phase $P(2) =< W_o^{p_1} R_o^{p_3} R_o^{p_4} >$ is formed. After servicing $P(2)$, $win(o)$ will be deleted from the system. Thus, in this example, we consider the request sequence as a concatenation of sequences in P(0), P(1), and P(2), i.e., $\sigma_o = R_o^{p_1} R_o^{p_2} R_o^{p_1} W_o^{p_3} R_o^{p_2} W_o^{p_1} R_o^{p_3} R_o^{p_4}$.

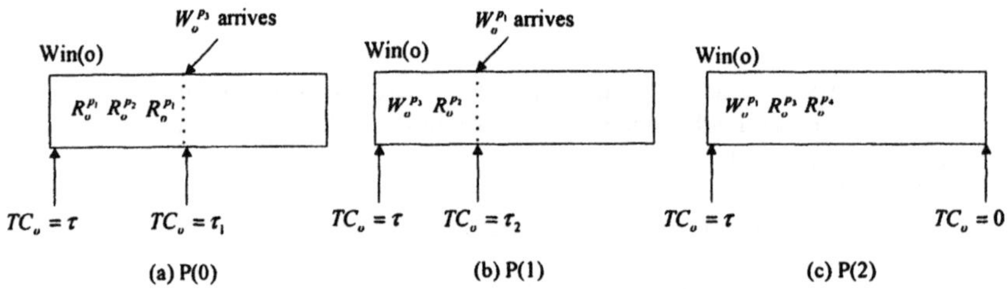

Figure 4.3. An example of the working policy of window mechanism in DWM

Finally, it should be noted that the window mechanism can guarantee that the queuing delay of a request in the system is at most τ time units. In DWM algorithm, if the value of counter TC_o reaches 0 then a request sequence σ_o is formed. After servicing the last phase of σ_o, $win(o)$ is deleted and DWM algorithm will reset the allocation scheme of object o to $S(o)$, which is indeed the server set of object o. The next request for object o will be considered as the first request for object o and $win(o)$ will be again generated by the window mechanism. Similarly, the request sequence that is inserted into the new $win(o)$ during its lifetime is considered as a new request sequence σ_o.

The reason for DWM algorithm to reset the allocation scheme of an object o to $S(o)$ after servicing the last phase of σ_o is due to the consideration of following two extreme cases.

Case 1: In Figure 4.4(a), during the time period starting from $TC_o = \tau'$ to $TC_o = 0$, which is a relatively long time period for the system there are no requests arriving at $win(o)$. In this case, it is wiser to consider object o as an object which is rarely accessed in the system. Hence, after servicing σ_o, we should reduce the cardinality of A_o. On the other hand, we should satisfy the t-availability constraint in the system. Therefore, we reset A_o to $S(o)$, where $|S(o)| = t$.

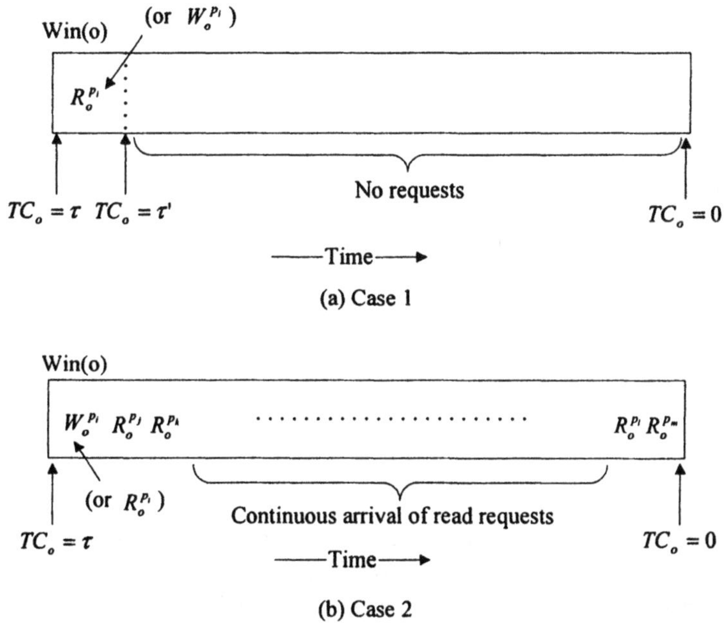

Figure 4.4. Illustration of two extrme cases in DWM algorithm

Case 2: In Figure 4.4(b), read requests for object o keep arriving at $win(o)$ till $TC_o = 0$. In this case, we consider that the requests for object o are read-intensive, and hence, we may need to rearrange the server set $S(o)$ to $S'(o)$ for improving the system performance. However, since future request patterns are unpredictable, there is no sufficient information for us to decide which processor should be included in $S'(o)$. Thus, after servicing σ_o we simply assume that $S'(o) = S(o)$ and reset A_o to $S(o)$ for servicing a new σ_o in the future.

From the above description, it may be noted that the parameter τ is a key parameter in the DWM algorithm. Different values of τ may influence the performance of the system. Obviously, the value of τ should not be too small. For example, let us consider an extreme case where $\tau = 1$. If $\tau = 1$, then each request will form a request sequence and the request windows will be generated and deleted in one time unit. This will undesirably consume most of the computing capacity of CCU. On the other hand, if the value of τ is too large then a request may suffer a large queuing delay in the system, which may not be tolerable in some application domains, especially in a *Real-Time* DDBS. Therefore, to seek a reasonable performance by the DWM algorithm, we should choose a value of τ depending on the underlying application requirements.

Below, we shall see how DWM algorithm services the requests in each phase of σ_o to minimize the cumulative servicing costs.

3.3 Servicing of Phases

1. Servicing of $P(0)$

As mentioned earlier, $P(0)$ in σ_o consists of all the read requests before the first write request in σ_o. We suppose that the initial allocation scheme of object o on $P(0)$ is $IA_o(0)$. Let $N(0)$ be the set of processors which are not in $IA_o(0)$ and have issued read requests in $P(0)$. Further, let $n_r(p,0)$ be the total number of read requests issued by processor p in phase $P(0)$. We define

$$\Delta(0) = (\sum_{p \in N(0)} (n_r(p,0)) - |N(0)|)(C_c + C_d) \tag{4.25}$$

According to Equation (4.23) discussed in the cost model, if we do not consider any of the read request from the processors in $N(0)$ as a saving-read request, then the total cost of servicing read requests issued from processors in $N(0)$ will be

$$\sum_{p \in N(0)} (n_r(p,0))(1 + C_c + C_d) \tag{4.26}$$

On the other hand, if we consider the first read request from each of the processors in $N(0)$ as a saving-read request, then the rest of the read requests from these processors will each incur only I/O cost. Hence, the cost of servicing these read requests will be

$$\begin{aligned} & |N(0)|(2 + C_c + C_d) + (\sum_{p \in N(0)} (n_r(p,0)) - |N(0)|) \\ = \; & |N(0)|(1 + C_c + C_d) + \sum_{p \in N(0)} (n_r(p,0)) \end{aligned} \tag{4.27}$$

Furthermore, we should consider servicing the expected write request in $P(1)$. If $P(1)$ exists, then referring to the description of Equation (4.24), when we consider the first read request from each of the processors in $N(0)$ as a saving-read request, CCU must send at most $|N(0)|$

number of control-messages to invalidate the redundant replicas of object o in these processors (belonging to $N(0)$) when servicing the write request in $P(1)$. On the other hand, if $P(1)$ does not exist, then $P(0)$ is the last phase of σ_o. As mentioned before, in this case, the DWM algorithm will reset A_o to $S(o)$. Thus, when we consider the first read request from each of the processors in $N(0)$ as a saving-read request, CCU will similarly send control-messages to all the processors in $N(0)$ to invalidate the redundant replicas of object o after servicing $P(0)$. Therefore, in both these two cases, the total servicing cost for the read requests issued from processors in $N(0)$ would be

$$|N(0)|(1 + C_c + C_d) + \sum_{p \in N(0)} (n_r(p,0)) + |N(0)|C_c \tag{4.28}$$

The difference between Equation (4.26) and Equation (4.28) is then given by,

$$\left(\sum_{p \in N(0)} (n_r(p,0)) - |N(0)|\right)(1 + C_c + C_d) - \sum_{p \in N(0)} (n_r(p,0)) - |N(0)|C_c$$

$$= \left(\sum_{p \in N(0)} (n_r(p,0)) - |N(0)|\right)(C_c + C_d) - |N(0)| - |N(0)|C_c$$

$$= \Delta(0) - |N(0)| - |N(0)|C_c \tag{4.29}$$

Thus, there exists a cost trade-off between whether or not we consider the first read request from each of the processors in $N(0)$ as a saving-read request. In DWM algorithm, if $\Delta(0) > (|N(0)| + |N(0)|C_c)$, then DWM indeed considers these requests mentioned above as saving-read requests. Otherwise, if $\Delta(0) \leq (|N(0)| + |N(0)|C_c)$, DWM algorithm will not consider any of the read requests from processors in $N(0)$ as a saving-read request.

Example 4.4: As an example, we suppose that in σ_o, $P(0) =< R_o^{p_1} R_o^{p_2} R_o^{p_3} R_o^{p_4} R_o^{p_3} R_o^{p_3} R_o^{p_2} >$, and $IA_o(0)$ is $\{p_1, p_2, p_5\}$. We assume that $C_c = 2$, $C_d = 3$, then $\Delta(0) = 2(C_c + C_d) = 10$, and $(|N(0)| + |N(0)|C_c) = 2 + 2 * 2 = 6$. We note that $\Delta(0) > (|N(0)| + |N(0)|C_c)$. Therefore, DWM considers the third and the fourth requests as saving-read requests. However, if $P(0) =< R_o^{p_2} R_o^{p_3} R_o^{p_1} R_o^{p_4} R_o^{p_2} R_o^{p_5} R_o^{p_3} >$, then with the same values of $IA_o(0)$, C_c and C_d as above, we note that $\Delta(0) = 5 < (|N(0)| + |N(0)|C_c) = 6$, and hence, we should not consider the second, fourth, and seventh requests as saving-read requests.

2. Servicing of $P(i)$ $(1 \leq i \leq r)$

Now let us consider the servicing of DWM for $P(i)$ $(1 \leq i \leq r)$ in σ_o. $P(i)$ consists of a write request followed by all the read requests presented between this write request and the next write request in σ_o. DWM algorithm first services the write request according to Equation (4.24). The servicing of the rest of the read requests in $P(i)$ is almost similar to that in $P(0)$. We define

$$\Delta(i) = \left(\sum_{p \in N(i)} (n_r(p,i)) - |N(i)| \right)(C_c + C_d) \tag{4.30}$$

where $n_r(p,i)$ is the total number of read requests issued by processor p in phase $P(i)$, and $N(i)$ is the set of processors which are not in the allocation scheme of object o after servicing the first write request and have issued read requests in $P(i)$. This is the key difference between (4.25) and (4.30). Thus, as done in $P(0)$, when servicing $P(i)$, if $\Delta(i) > (|N(i)| + |N(i)|C_c)$, then DWM considers all the first read requests from processors in $N(i)$ as saving-read requests. Otherwise, DWM will not consider any of the read requests from processors in $N(i)$ as a saving-read request.

3.4 Analysis of DWM Algorithm

In this subsection, we shall verify the performance of DWM algorithm using a competitive analysis. We consider an arbitrary request sequence $\sigma_o = \sigma_o(1), \sigma_o(2), ..., \sigma_o(m)$, where $\sigma_o(j)$ $(1 \leq j \leq m)$ denotes the j-th request in σ_o. Based on the window mechanism of DWM algorithm, we know that σ_o will be essentially partitioned into several phases $P(0), P(1), P(2), ..., P(r)$. As mentioned earlier, $P(0)$ consists of all the read requests before the first write request in σ_o and $P(i)$ $(1 \leq i \leq r)$ consists of a write request followed by several read requests. The competitive analysis for DWM algorithm to be presented below is similar to that in DA algorithm. We first state two important lemmas associated with the servicing of each phase and then show that DWM algorithm indeed delivers a competitive ratio of $(2+2\frac{C_c}{C_d})$ in a SCE. Furthermore, we assume that the initial allocation scheme of each phase $P(i)$ $(0 \leq i \leq r)$ is $IA_o(i)$ when DWM algorithm services σ_o. Without loss of generality, we assume that DWM algorithm and an optimal algorithm OPT (which also satisfies the t-availability constraint) initially start with the same initial allocation scheme $IA_o = IA_o(0) = S(o)$ and both satisfy the t-availability constraint.

Lemma 4.3: Given a σ_o with an IA_o, $COST_{DWM}(P(0), IA_o) \leq (2 + 2\frac{C_c}{C_d})COST_{OPT}(P(0),$
$IA_o)$ in a SCE.

Proof: Let $N(0)$ be the set of processors which are not in IA_o and have issued read requests in $P(0)$. To analysis the servicing of the read requests in $P(0)$, we need to consider the following two conditions to be analyzed.

Condition 1: Referring to Equation (4.25) (Servicing of $P(0)$), if $\Delta(0) > |N(0)|+|N(0)|C_c$, then we should consider the first read requests issued by the processors in $N(0)$ as saving-read requests.

In this case, the servicing of $P(0)$ using DWM algorithm is the same as that using DA algorithm. From Equation (4.23), the first read requests issued by the processors in $N(0)$ will each incur $(2 + C_c + C_d)$ units of cost for DWM algorithm. The rest of the read requests are all issued from data processors when DWM algorithm services them, and hence, each will incur one unit cost for I/O operation. Further, as mentioned in Section 3.3, we should consider servicing the expected write request in $P(1)$. If $P(1)$ exists, according to the cost model in Equation (4.24), control-messages must be transferred to invalidate the redundant replicas in the processors belonging to $N(0)$ when servicing the write request in $P(1)$. On the other hand, if $P(1)$ does not exist, which means that $P(0)$ is the last phase of σ_o, then after servicing $P(0)$, the DWM algorithm will reset A_o to $S(o)$. Thus, CCU must also send control-messages to all the processors in $N(0)$ to invalidate the redundant replicas of object o after servicing $P(0)$. Therefore, in this case, the total cost for DWM algorithm to service the read requests in $P(0)$ is given by,

$$
\begin{aligned}
&COST_{DWM}(P(0), IA_o) \\
&= |N(0)|(2 + C_c + C_d) + (|P(0)| - |N(0)|) + |N(0)|C_c \quad (4.31)
\end{aligned}
$$

Similarly, for an OPT algorithm, the total cost for servicing $P(0)$ is the same as Equation (4.12). We rewrite it as follows.

$$
COST_{OPT}(P(0), IA_o) \geq |N(0)|C_d + |P(0)| \qquad (4.32)
$$

Thus, the difference between Equation (4.31) and Equation (4.32) is,

$$
\begin{aligned}
& COST_{DWM}(P(0), IA_o) - COST_{OPT}(P(0), IA_o) \\
\leq\ & 2|N(0)|C_c + |N(0)| \\
\leq\ & |N(0)|C_d + |P(0)| + 2|N(0)|C_c \quad (\text{since } C_c < C_d, |N(0)| \leq |P(0)|) \\
\leq\ & COST_{OPT}(P(0), IA_o) + 2\frac{C_c}{C_d} COST_{OPT}(P(0), IA_o)
\end{aligned}
$$

Therefore, we obtain,

$$
COST_{DWM}(P(0), IA_o) \leq (2 + 2\frac{C_c}{C_d}) COST_{OPT}(P(0), IA_o) \qquad (4.33)
$$

Condition 2: Referring to Equation (4.25), if $\Delta(0) \leq |N(0)|+|N(0)|C_c$, then we will not consider any of the read requests issued by the processors in $N(0)$ as a saving-read request.

In this case, the servicing of $P(0)$ using DWM algorithm is the same as that using SA algorithm. All the read requests issued by the processors in $N(0)$ will each incur $(1+C_c+C_d)$ units of cost. The other read requests will each incur one unit cost for I/O operation. Further, no matter whether $P(0)$ is the last phase of σ_o or not, there is no "invalidate" control-message sent by CCU in this case. Hence, the total cost for DWM algorithm to service the read requests in $P(0)$ is given by,

$$
\begin{aligned}
&COST_{DWM}(P(0), IA_o) \\
&= \sum_{p \in N(0)} (n_r(p,0))(1 + C_c + C_d) + (|P(0)| - \sum_{p \in N(0)} (n_r(p,0))) \quad (4.34)
\end{aligned}
$$

For the OPT algorithm, the cost for servicing $P(0)$ is still given by Equation (4.32).

Thus, the difference between Equation (4.34) and Equation (4.32) is,

$$
\begin{aligned}
&COST_{DWM}(P(0), IA_o) - COST_{OPT}(P(0), IA_o) \\
&\quad \leq (\sum_{p \in N(0)} (n_r(p,0)) - |N(0)|)(C_c + C_d) + |N(0)|C_c \\
&\quad = \Delta(0) + |N(0)|C_c
\end{aligned}
$$

From Condition 2, we obtain,

$$
\begin{aligned}
&COST_{DWM}(P(0), IA_o) - COST_{OPT}(P(0), IA_o) \\
&\leq |N(0)| + |N(0)|C_c + |N(0)|C_c \\
&\leq |N(0)|C_d + |P(0)| + 2|N(0)|C_c \quad (\text{since } C_c < C_d, |N(0)| \leq |P(0)|) \\
&\leq COST_{OPT}(P(0), IA_o) + 2\frac{C_c}{C_d} COST_{OPT}(P(0), IA_o)
\end{aligned}
$$

Therefore, we have,

$$
COST_{DWM}(P(0), IA_o) \leq (2 + 2\frac{C_c}{C_d}) COST_{OPT}(P(0), IA_o) \quad (4.35)
$$

From Equation (4.33) and Equation (4.35), for both the conditions 1 and 2, it is shown that,

$$
COST_{DWM}(P(0), IA_o) \leq (2 + 2\frac{C_c}{C_d}) COST_{OPT}(P(0), IA_o)
$$

Hence the proof of Lemma 4.3. ■

Lemma 4.4: Given a σ_o with an IA_o, $COST_{DWM}(P(i), IA_o(i)) \leq (2 + 2\frac{C_c}{C_d})COST_{OPT}(P(i), IA_o^*(i)) + K$, where $1 \leq i \leq r$, $IA_o^*(i)$ is the initial allocation scheme of object o on $P(i)$ using the OPT algorithm and K is an additive constant.

Proof: As done in the competitive analysis of $P(i)$ in DA algorithm, let us suppose that the first request in $P(i)$ $(1 \leq i \leq r)$ is W_o^*, where W_o^* denotes a write request issued from any processor in the system for object o. According to Equation (4.24), using DWM algorithm, a write request will incur at most $|S(o)|C_d$ units of cost due to data-messages transferring and $(|S(o)| + 1)$ units of cost for I/O operations. Additionally, CCU must send control-messages to invalidate the redundant replicas elsewhere in the system. Since the cost of sending "invalidate" messages to all the processors in $N(i-1)$ is already accounted while analyzing $P(i-1)$[17], referring to Equation (4.24), we note that the cost to invalidate the redundant copies of object o is at most[18] C_c. Therefore, using DWM algorithm, the cost for servicing the first write request W_o^* in $P(i)$ is given by,

$$COST_{DWM}(W_o^*) \leq |S(o)|C_d + (|S(o)| + 1) + C_c \qquad (4.36)$$

The rest of the requests in $P(i)$ are all read requests. We define $N(i)$ as the set of processors which have issued read requests in $P(i)$ and do not belong to A_o after servicing the first write request W_o^*. To analysis the servicing of the rest read requests in $P(i)$, we must consider two conditions as follows.

Condition 1: Referring to Equation (4.30) (Servicing of $P(i)$), if $\Delta(i) > |N(i)| + |N(i)|C_c$, then we should consider the first read requests issued by the processors in $N(i)$ as saving-read requests.

In this case, the servicing of the read requests in $P(i)$ using DWM algorithm is similar to that using DA algorithm. That is the first read requests issued by the processors in $N(i)$ will each incur $(2 + C_c + C_d)$ units of cost, and the rest of the read requests will each incur one unit cost for I/O operation. Further, as discussed in the proof of Lemma 4.3, we should consider servicing the expected write request in $P(i+1)$. If $P(i+1)$ exists, according to the cost model in Equation (4.24), control-messages must be transferred to invalidate the redundant replicas in the processors belonging to $N(i)$ when servicing the write request in

[17]Refer to the competitive analysis of $P(i)$ $(1 \leq i \leq r)$ in DA algorithm.

[18]To invalidate the redundant copy in the processor which issued the write request in $P(i-1)$ $(2 \leq i \leq r)$, if this processor does not belong to $S(o)$.

$P(i+1)$. As mentioned above, it should be noted that the cost for sending "invalidate" control-message to the processor issued the write request in $P(i)$, if the processor does not belong to $S(o)$, is calculated in the analyzing of $P(i+1)$. On the other hand, if $P(i+1)$ does not exist, which means that $P(i)$ is the last phase of σ_o, then after servicing $P(i)$, the DWM algorithm will reset A_o to $S(o)$. In this case, CCU must similarly send control-messages to the processors in $N(i)$ to invalidate the redundant replicas of object o. Additionally, CCU may also send such an "invalidate" control-message to the processor which issued the write request in $P(i)$ if this processor does not belong to $S(o)$. Thus, when $P(i)$ is the last phase of σ_o, the number of "invalidate" control-messages sent by CCU is at most $(|N(i)|+1)$. Therefore, in this case, the total cost for DWM algorithm to service the requests in $P(i)$ is given by,

$$\sum_{j=1}^{|P(i)|-1} COST_{DWM}(\text{the } j^{th} \text{ read request in } P(i))$$

$$\leq |N(i)|(2+C_c+C_d) + (|P(i)| - |N(i)| - 1) + (|N(i)|+1)C_c \quad (4.37)$$

As done in the competitive analysis of DA algorithm, the cost to invalidate the replicas in $N(i)$ when servicing the expected write request in $P(i+1)$ is calculated in Equation (4.37). Thus, from Equation (4.36) and Equation (4.37), the total cost for servicing the requests in $P(i)$ using DWM algorithm is given by,

$$COST_{DWM}(P(i), A_o(i)) = COST_{DWM}(W_o^*)$$
$$+ \sum_{j=1}^{|P(i)|-1} COST_{DWM}(\text{the } j^{th} \text{ read request in } P(i))$$
$$\leq (|S(o)| + |N(i)|)C_d + (2|N(i)|+2)C_c + (|P(i)| + |N(i)| + |S(o)|) \quad (4.38)$$

For the OPT algorithm, every read request incur at least one unit for I/O cost. Let $N'(i)$ be the set of processors that issue read requests in $P(i)$. There are two cases we need to consider as follows.

Case A: If $|N'(i)| > t$, then the total cost of servicing the requests in $P(i)$ for the OPT algorithm is the same as Equation (4.17).

Thus, the difference between Equation (4.38) and Equation (4.17) is,

$$COST_{DWM}(P(i), IA_o(i)) - COST_{OPT}(P(i), IA_o^*(i))$$

$$\leq (t + |N(i)| - |N'(i)| + 1)C_d + (2|N(i)| + 2)C_c + (|N(i)| + 1) \quad \text{(since } |S(o)| = t\text{)}$$
$$\leq (|N'(i)| - 1)C_d + 2(|N'(i)| - 1)C_c + 2C_d + 4C_c + (|N(i)| + 1) \quad \text{(for } |N'(i)| > t, |N'(i)| \geq |N(i)|, |P(i)| \geq |N'(i)| + 1\text{)}$$
$$\leq (|N'(i)| - 1)C_d + t + (|P(i)| - 1) + 2(|N'(i)| - 1)C_c + 2C_d + 4C_c$$
$$\leq COST_{OPT}(P(i), IA_o^*(i)) + 2\frac{C_c}{C_d}COST_{OPT}(P(i), IA_o^*(i)) + K_3$$

where $K_3 = (2C_d + 4C_c)$ is a constant. Therefore, we obtain,

$$COST_{DWM}(P(i), IA_o(i)) \leq (2 + 2\frac{C_c}{C_d})COST_{OPT}(P(i), IA_o^*(i)) + K_3 \quad (4.39)$$

Case B: If $|N'(i)| \leq t$, then the total cost of servicing the requests in $P(i)$ for the OPT algorithm is the same as Equation (4.19).

In this case, the difference between Equation (4.38) and Equation (4.19) is,

$$\begin{aligned}
& COST_{DWM}(P(i), IA_o(i)) - COST_{OPT}(P(i), IA_o^*(i)) \\
\leq\ & (|N(i)| + 1)C_d + (2|N(i)| + 2)C_c + |N(i)| + 1 \\
\leq\ & (t - 1)C_d + t + (|P(i)| - 1) + 2(t - 1)C_c + 2C_d + 4C_c \\
& \quad \text{(since } |N(i)| \leq |N'(i)| \leq t, |P(i)| \geq |N'(i)| + 1\text{)} \\
\leq\ & COST_{OPT}(P(i), IA_o^*(i)) + 2\frac{C_c}{C_d}COST_{OPT}(P(i), IA_o^*(i)) + K_4
\end{aligned}$$

where $K_4 = (2C_d + 4C_c)$ is a constant. Therefore, we can obtain that,

$$COST_{DWM}(P(i), IA_o(i)) \leq (2 + 2\frac{C_c}{C_d})COST_{OPT}(P(i), IA_o^*(i)) + K_4 \quad (4.40)$$

Condition 2: Referring to Equation (4.30)(Servicing of $P(i)$), if $\Delta(i) \leq |N(i)| + |N(i)|C_c$, then we will not consider any of the read requests issued by the processors in $N(i)$ as a saving-read request.

In this case, the servicing of the rest read requests in $P(i)$ using DWM algorithm is similar to that using SA algorithm. All the read requests issued by the processors in $N(i)$ will each incur $(1+C_c+C_d)$ units of cost. The other read requests will each incur one unit cost for I/O operation. Further, if $P(i)$ is the last phase of σ_o, then due to the requirement of resetting A_o to $S(o)$, an additional "invalidate" control-message must be sent to the processor which issued the write request in $P(i)$ if this processor does not belong to $S(o)$. On the other hand, if $P(i+1)$ exists, since we do not consider any of the read requests issued by the processors in $N(i)$ as a saving-read request, no control-messages are required to sent to processors in $N(i)$ when servicing the write request in $P(i+1)$. Hence, the total cost for servicing $P(i)$ using DWM algorithm is given by,

$$\begin{aligned} COST_{DWM}(P(i), IA_o(i)) &= COST_{DWM}(W_o^*) \\ &+ \sum_{j=1}^{|P(i)|-1} COST_{DWM}(\text{the } j^{th} \text{ read request in } P(i)) \\ &\leq |S(o)|C_d + (|S(o)|+1) + C_c + \sum_{p \in N(i)} (n_r(p,i))(1 + C_c + C_d) \\ &+(|P(i)| - \sum_{p \in N(i)} (n_r(p,i))) + C_c \end{aligned} \tag{4.41}$$

For the optimal algorithm, we still consider two cases as before.

Case A: If $|N'(i)| > t$, then the total cost for servicing $P(i)$ using the OPT algorithm is the same as Equation (4.17).

Thus, the difference between Equation (4.41) and Equation (4.17) is,

$$\begin{aligned} & COST_{DWM}(P(i), IA_o(i)) - COST_{OPT}(P(i), IA_o^*(i)) \\ & \leq (\sum_{p \in N(i)} (n_r(p,i)) - |N'(i)| + |S(o)| + 1)C_d \\ & \qquad +(\sum_{p \in N(i)} (n_r(p,i)) + 2)C_c + 2 \\ & \leq |S(o)|C_d + (\sum_{p \in N(i)} (n_r(p,i)) - |N(i)|)(C_c + C_d) \\ & \qquad +(|N(i)| + 2)C_c + C_d + 2 \\ & \leq |S(o)|C_d + \Delta(i) + (|N(i)| + 2)C_c + C_d + 2 \end{aligned}$$

Using Condition 2, we obtain,

$$\begin{aligned} & COST_{DWM}(P(i), IA_o(i)) - COST_{OPT}(P(i), IA_o^*(i)) \\ & \leq |S(o)|C_d + 2|N(i)|C_c + |N(i)| + C_d + 2C_c + 2 \\ & \leq (|N'(i)| - 1)C_d + t + (|P(i)| - 1) + 2(|N'(i)| - 1)C_c \\ & \qquad +2C_d + 4C_c + 1 \\ & \qquad (\text{since } |N'(i)| > t, |N'(i)| \geq |N(i)|, |P(i)| \geq |N'(i)| + 1) \\ & \leq COST_{OPT}(P(i), IA_o^*(i)) + 2\frac{C_c}{C_d} COST_{OPT}(P(i), IA_o^*(i)) + K_5 \end{aligned}$$

where $K_5 = (2C_d + 4C_c + 1)$ is a constant. Therefore, we have,

$$COST_{DWM}(P(i), IA_o(i)) \leq (2 + 2\frac{C_c}{C_d})COST_{OPT}(P(i), IA_o^*(i)) + K_5 \quad (4.42)$$

Case B: If $|N'(i)| \leq t$, then the total cost of servicing $P(i)$ for the OPT algorithm is the same as Equation (4.19).

Thus, the difference between Equation (4.41) and Equation (4.19) is,

$$\begin{aligned} & COST_{DWM}(P(i), IA_o(i)) - COST_{OPT}(P(i), IA_o^*(i)) \\ \leq & \sum_{p \in N(i)} (n_r(p,i))(C_c + C_d) + C_d + 2C_c + 2 \\ = & \Delta(i) + |N(i)|(C_c + C_d) + C_d + 2C_c + 2 \end{aligned}$$

Using Condition 2, we can obtain,

$$\begin{aligned} & COST_{DWM}(P(i), IA_o(i)) - COST_{OPT}(P(i), IA_o^*(i)) \\ \leq & |N(i)|C_d + 2|N(i)|C_c + |N(i)| + C_d + 2C_c + 2 \\ \leq & (t-1)C_d + t + (|P(i) - 1) + 2(t-1)C_c + 2C_d + 4C_c + 1 \\ & (\text{ since } |N(i)| \leq |N'(i)| \leq t, |P(i)| \geq |N'(i)| + 1) \\ \leq & COST_{OPT}(P(i), IA_o^*(i)) + 2\frac{C_c}{C_d}COST_{OPT}(P(i), IA_o^*(i)) + K_6 \end{aligned}$$

where $K_6 = (2C_d + 4C_c + 1)$ is a constant. Therefore, we have,

$$COST_{DWM}(P(i), IA_o(i)) \leq (2 + 2\frac{C_c}{C_d})COST_{OPT}(P(i), IA_o^*(i)) + K_6 \quad (4.43)$$

From Equation (4.39), Equation (4.40), Equation (4.42) and Equation (4.43), the result of Lemma 4.4 is immediate. ■

Now we state the following theorem to show the performance of DWM algorithm in a SCE.

Theorem 4.3: For any integer $t \geq 1$, DWM algorithm is $(2 + 2\frac{C_c}{C_d})$-competitive in a SCE.

Proof: The proof is directly evident from the results of Lemmas 4.3 and 4.4. From Lemma 4.3 and Lemma 4.4, we know that for an arbitrary σ_o with an IA_o ($IA_o = S(o)$),

$$COST_{DWM}(\sigma_o, IA_o) = \sum_{i=0}^{r} COST_{DWM}(P(i), IA_o(i))$$

$$\leq (2+2\frac{C_c}{C_d})\sum_{i=0}^{r}(COST_{OPT}(P(i), IA_o^*(i))) + K$$

$$= (2+2\frac{C_c}{C_d})COST_{OPT}(\sigma_o, IA_o) + K \qquad (4.44)$$

where $IA_o^*(i)$ is the initial allocation scheme of object o on $P(i)$ after servicing the last request in $P(i-1)$ using the OPT algorithm, $IA_o^*(0) = IA_o$ and $K = \sum_{i=1}^{r} x_i$ $(x_i \in \{K_3, K_4, K_5, K_6\})$ is an additive constant. It may be noted that $K = \alpha_3 K_3 + \alpha_4 K_4 + \alpha_5 K_5 + \alpha_6 K_6$ $(\alpha_3, \alpha_4, \alpha_5, \alpha_6 \geq 0)$ is a linear combination of K_3, K_4, K_5 and K_6 obtained in our analyses of $P(i)(1 \leq i \leq r)$. The values of $\alpha_3, \alpha_4, \alpha_5$ and α_6 depend upon the requests in σ_o. Hence the proof. ■

4. ADRW Algorithm

DWM algorithm is designed for distributed systems with centralized control. Some of the primary issues in OMP of a centralized control system are in realizing efficient concurrency and security control mechanisms. Such concurrency control and security control mechanisms are assumed to be easily taken care by the CCU. In fact, it is intuitively clear that since the control is exercised at one place, it is rather fairly simple to realize the design of DWM algorithm. In DWM algorithm, CCU is fully aware of the allocation and replication scheme of every object in the system. Depending on the arrival of request patterns CCU can dynamically adjust the object allocation schemes so as to minimize the total servicing cost of all the requests. However, as mentioned in Chapter 1, the system reliability of a DDBS with centralized control is lower as there is a single point (CCU) failure. Thus, applicability of DWM is particularly recommended for small-scale systems wherein control and failures can be easily monitored. For large-scale systems where single point failure cannot be tolerable DWM algorithm seems to be inefficient. Thus, in this section, we present a new object allocation and replication algorithm, referred to as *Adaptive Distributed Request Window* (ADRW) algorithm, that is designed for a DDBS with decentralized control mechanism (without CCU) to improve the system reliability. In practice, the design of such a decentralized algorithm must provide the flexibility for the requests to be submitted to any processor[19] for processing (servicing) in a distributed system. Thus, the processing of requests is distributed in the system. The design of ADRW algorithm allows

[19]There is an inherent concurrency control mechanism in each processor.

this feature. This can circumvent the requirements of demanding processing capacity and reliability/fault-tolerance at a single point in the system, as the CCU in the case of centralized control systems. Further, ADRW algorithm involves a distributed request window mechanism in each processor. Based on the local (historical) information, the window mechanism will arrive at a decision on whether a processor should *enter* or *exit* an object allocation scheme to minimize the total servicing cost of future expected requests. Since the decisions are distributed in the system, the communication of "invalidate" messages to the processors can be avoided in ADRW algorithm. We will further describe the distributed request window mechanism following the cost model of ADRW.

Furthermore, in ADRW algorithm, we still assume that for every object o, the initial allocation scheme is given by a fixed server set $S(o)$ ($|S(o)| = t$) which is the t-availability constraint in ADRW algorithm. It should be noted that for different objects, the initial allocation schemes may be different. Without loss of generality, we assume that each processor knows the server set of every object in the system and each processor, which is not a server, knows the "nearest" server of an object in the system[20]. Further, in each processor, we suppose that the status of an object o whether it is in its local memory or not is indicated by either a "1" or a "0" value.

4.1 Cost Model

We now present the cost model of ADRW algorithm to compute the cost of servicing a read request or a write request.

Case A (Read request): Consider servicing a read request $R_o^{p_i}$ and let A_o be the allocation scheme of object o on this request. Then,

$$COST_{ADRW}(R_o^{p_i}) = \begin{cases} 1 & \text{if } p_i \in A_o \\ 1 + C_c + C_d & \text{if } p_i \notin A_o \text{ and } R_o^{p_i} \text{ is not} \\ & \quad \text{a saving-read request} \\ 2 + C_c + C_d & \text{if } p_i \notin A_o \text{ and } R_o^{p_i} \text{ is} \\ & \quad \text{a saving-read request} \end{cases} \tag{4.45}$$

The cost model in Equation (4.45) for servicing a read request is similar to that in Equation (4.23). If $p_i \in A_o$, then the request is satisfied locally. On the other hand, if $p_i \notin A_o$, then p_i will send the read request

[20]The nearest server can be predefined by some system parameters such as processor ID. Additionally, for a processor the nearest server is fixed, as the server set is fixed.

to its nearest server[21] $p_j \in S(o)$. After receiving the read requst, p_j retrieves object o and sends it to p_i. The difference between these two cost models in Equation (4.45) and Equation (4.23) is as follows. In DWM algorithm, whether a read request from a non-data-processor is a saving-read request or not is decided by CCU to minimize the total servicing cost of the request sequence in a phase. However, in ADRW algorithm, this decision is made by p_j based on the distributed request window mechanism to minimize the total servicing cost of future expected read requests.

Once server p_j decides that request $R_o^{p_i}$ is a saving-read request, p_j will add processor p_i into its *data-processor list*, which is a list-based data structure and denoted as *data_list*(o). Similarly, p_i will change its respective status to 1, since p_i is now a data-processor. The key idea behind the operation of adding a data-processor to the *data_list*(o) is that when servicing a following write request for the object o, servers of object o can simply send data-messages to the processors in their respective *data_list*(o) to ensure the object consistency. We will further describe this in Case B as follows.

Case B (Write request): Consider servicing a write request $W_o^{p_i}$ with an allocation scheme A_o on this request. Let A_o' be the allocation scheme after servicing this request. Then, the cost of servicing this request is given by,

$$COST_{ADRW}(W_o^{p_i}) = \begin{cases} (|A_o| - 1)C_d + |A_o'| & \text{if } p_i \in A_o \\ |A_o|C_d + |A_o'| & \text{otherwise} \end{cases} \qquad (4.46)$$

In order to maintain the object consistency, whenever ADRW algorithm services a write request $W_o^{p_i}$, if $p_i \in A_o$, then object o will be transferred to all the data-processors in A_o other than p_i, incurring $(|A_o| - 1)C_d$ units of cost. Whereas, if $p_i \notin A_o$, then object o will be transferred to all the data-processors in A_o, incurring $(|A_o|)C_d$ units of cost. Theoretically, we describe the transferring operation as follows. Firstly, p_i sends the new version to all the servers in $S(o)$. After receiving the new version of object o, all the servers propagate the new version to the processors in their respective *data_list*(o). Finally, according to the distributed request window mechanism, some data-processors in A_o, which are not the servers in S_o, may *exit* the allocation scheme to minimize the total servicing cost of future expected write requests. Only

[21] It should be noted that in ADRW algorithm, only the servers of an object o can receive requests from remote processors to read object o.

those processors in A'_o save the new version into their respective local memories, incurring $|A'_o|$ units of I/O cost. Thus, it may be noted that $A'_o \subseteq A_o$ in this case.

4.2 Distributed Request Window Mechanism

As claimed above, ADRW algorithm can dynamically adjust the allocation scheme of an object o by using a distributed request window mechanism. The objective is to minimize the total servicing cost of future expected requests. We now describe this distributed request window mechanism in detail.

We assume that the initial allocation scheme of an object o is $S(o)$. As explained in the cost model (Equation (4.45)), when a non-data-processor p_i needs to read an object o, it will send a read request $R_o^{p_i}$ to its nearest server p_j in $S(o)$. After receiving the read request, p_j will create a request window $Win(o, p_i)$ for processor p_i unless $Win(o, p_i)$ already exists. It then inserts $R_o^{p_i}$ into $Win(o, p_i)$. $Win(o, p_i)$ is a FIFO type window with size k ($k \geq 1$) bits to track the latest *relevant* k requests (an entry 0 in a bit represents a read request and 1 represents a write request). We assume that the initial values of the k bits are all set[22] to 1. The main objective for using this request window is that based on the number of read/write requests in $Win(o, p_i)$, denoted as N_r and N_w respectively, ADRW algorithm in server p_j will decide whether or not processor p_i should *enter* A_o to minimize the servicing cost of future expected read requests. Furthermore, according to the cost model, we know that the read requests for object o issued from server p_j and the write requests for object o issued from p_i do not influence p_j to make the decision mentioned above. This is due to the fact that the cost of servicing such requests is identical, regardless of whether or not p_i has a replica of an object o in its local memory. Therefore, the *relevant* requests that can be inserted into $Win(o, p_i)$ are the read requests issued from p_i for object o or the write requests for object o issued from processors other than p_i.

As explained before, since p_i is a non-data-processor, each read request $R_o^{p_i}$ will incur $(1+C_c+C_d)$ units of cost and any write requests for object o will not be propagated to p_i, incurring a zero cost. On the other hand, if we assume that p_i is a data-processor, then each read request $R_o^{p_i}$ will be satisfied locally, incurring only 1 unit cost for I/O operation. However, each write request in $Win(o, p_i)$ must be propagated to p_i and hence p_i must update the copy of object o in its local memory, incurring

[22] We can also let the initial values be 0 in this FIFO window.

$(1 + C_d)$ units of cost. Therefore, in server p_j, upon inserting a *relevant* request into $Win(o, p_i)$, if ADRW algorithm finds that $(1+C_c+C_d)N_r \geq N_r + (1 + C_d)N_w$, i.e.,

$$(C_c + C_d)N_r \geq (1 + C_d)N_w \tag{4.47}$$

then p_j would consider p_i as a *read-intensive node.* Thus, p_j will indicate p_i to *enter* A_o and add p_i into its *data_list*(o). Finally, p_j transfers $Win(o, p_i)$ to p_i to continue tracking the *relevant* requests. We refer to this process simply as *Test-and-Enter* (TEN) policy. The pseudocode in Table 4.4 presents the TEN policy of the distributed request window mechanism in server p_j for object o. We assume that the arriving request *Req* is issued from p_i for object o.

Table 4.4. Test-and-Enter (TEN) policy

```
Test-and-Enter();

If (Req is a read request) /* R_o^{p_i} */
    {If(p_i == p_j) /* The read request Req is issued from p_j itself */
            {Exit;} /*satisfy Req locally*/
      Else /*p_i ≠ p_j, p_i must be a non-data-processor */
            {If (Req is the first read request from p_i)
                  {Generate an initial Win(o,p_i);}
             Insert 0 into Win(o,p_i);
             If ((C_c + C_d)N_r ≥ (1 + C_d)N_w) /* implying read-intensive */
                  {Indicate p_i to enter A_o;
                    Add processor p_i into data_list(o);
                    Transfer Win(o,p_i) to p_i;
                    Delete Win(o,p_i) in p_j;
                    p_i saves object o and changes its relative status to 1;
                                                            /*data-processor*/
                  }
            }
    }
Else /*Req is a write request for object o */
    {Insert 1 into all existing request windows for object o in p_j,
     except Win(o,p_i), if it exists
    }
```

It should be noted that although a write request issued from p_i does not affect ADRW algorithm to decide whether or not p_i should enter A_o, it will indeed influence the decisions by p_j for other non-data-processors. Therefore, in Table 4.4, when *Req* is a write request it will be inserted into all the existing request windows in p_j other than $Win(o, p_i)$. Figure 4.5 shows the illustration of how a non-data-processor enters the allocation scheme using the distributed request window mechanism.

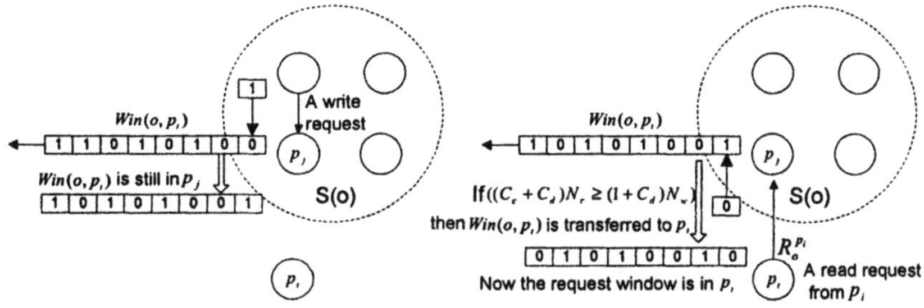

(a) a write request for object o from any processor other than p_i

(b) a read request for object o from p_i, which is considered as a saving-read request

Figure 4.5. Illustration of the *TEN* policy in server p_j for a non-data-processor p_i

From the above description, we know that the *TEN* policy is executed in the servers of an object. Furthermore, there is another operation called *Test-and-Exit* (TEX) policy, which is executed in a data-processor, but not in a server, of an object o. We assume that there is a data-processor of object o, say p_i ($p_i \notin S(o)$), and its nearest server in $S(o)$ is p_j. From the working style of TEN policy, we know that there must be a $Win(o, p_i)$ in p_i. Similarly, in this case, the *relevant* requests (those that can be inserted into $Win(o, p_i)$) are the read requests issued from p_i for object o or the write requests for object o propagated from p_j.

As mentioned above, since p_i is a data-processor each read request $R_o^{p_i}$ will be satisfied locally, incurring only 1 unit cost for I/O operation. Furthermore, all the write requests issued from any other processors for object o must be propagated to p_i by server p_j to maintain the object consistency, which will incur $(1+C_d)$ units of cost for each propagation. On the other hand, if we assume that p_i is a non-data-processor, then each read request $R_o^{p_i}$ will incur $(1 + C_c + C_d)$ units of cost. However, each write request mentioned above will not be propagated to p_i, incurring zero cost. Therefore, whenever p_i inserts a *relevant* request into $Win(o, p_i)$, if ADRW algorithm finds that $N_r + (1 + C_d)N_w > (1 + C_c + C_d)N_r$, i.e.,

$$(C_c + C_d)N_r < (1 + C_d)N_w \tag{4.48}$$

then p_i would consider that the system is a *write-intensive* network. Thus, p_i will decide to *exit* A_o and indicate p_j to delete it from the *data_list*(o) in p_j. Finally, p_i transfers $Win(o, p_i)$ to p_j to continue tracking the *relevant* requests. Theoretically, the pseudocode in Table

4.5 presents the *TEX* policy of the distributed request window mechanism in data-processor p_i when a request *Req* arrives.

Table 4.5. Test-and-Exit (TEX) policy

Test-and-Exit();

If (*Req* is a read request) /* It must be issued by p_i */
    {Insert 0 into $Win(o, p_i)$;}/*satisfy *Req* locally*/
Else /**Req* is a write request*/
    {If (*Req* is issued by p_i)
        {Send the write request to p_j;}
      Else /* *Req* is propagated from p_j */
        {Insert 1 into $Win(o, p_i)$;
         If $((C_c + C_d)N_r < (1 + C_d)N_w)$
            {Indicate p_j to delete it from *data_list*(o);
             Transfer $Win(o, p_i)$ to p_j;
             Delete $Win(o, p_i)$ in p_i;
             Deletes object o from its local memory;
             Changes its relative status to 0; /* non-data-processor */
            }
        }
    }

Figure 4.6 shows the illustration of how a data-processor (not server) exits the allocation scheme under the distributed request window mechanism.

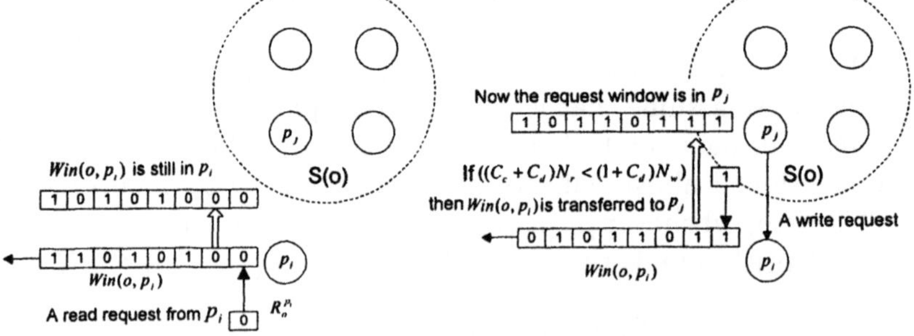

(a) a read request for object o from p_i

(b) a write request for object o propagated from p_j

Figure 4.6. Illustration of the *TEX* policy in a data-processor p_i

We recall that for different objects, the server sets may be different. For example, a processor p_i is a server of an object o. It may also be a data-processor of object o_1 ($p_i \notin S(o_1)$). Therefore, it should be noted that the TEN policy and TEX policy can be carried out concurrently in a processor for different objects.

4.3 Analysis of ADRW Algorithm

In this subsection, using a new Phase Partition technique, Heuristic 4, we state and prove that ADRW algorithm is $\left[k + \frac{1+C_c+2C_d}{C_d} + \frac{C_d}{t}\right]$-competitive in a SCE.

Theorem 4.4: For any integer $t \geq 1$, ADRW algorithm is $\left[k + \frac{1+C_c+2C_d}{C_d} + \frac{C_d}{t}\right]$-competitive in SCE, where k ($k \geq 1$) is the size of a request window.

Proof: Consider an object o with its server set $S(o)$. Suppose that there is a non-data-processor p_i and its nearest server in $S(o)$ is p_j. As explained before, we observe that the request window $Win(o, p_i)$ will track all the *relevant* requests between p_i and p_j, no matter $Win(o, p_i)$ is in p_j or p_i. It should be noted that for each of the read requests issued from servers, the servicing cost using ADRW algorithm is always 1 unit, whereas the servicing cost using an optimal off-line algorithm OPT, which knows the whole read/write request patterns, is at least 1 unit. Thus this does not affect the competitive ratio of our analysis. Therefore, in our analysis, it is sufficient to consider an arbitrary request sequence $\sigma_o = \sigma_o(1), \sigma_o(2), ..., \sigma_o(m)$, which consists of only the *relevant* requests between p_i and p_j for object o. Without loss of generality, we assume that ADRW algorithm and an optimal algorithm OPT, which also satisfies the t-availability constraint, initially start with the same allocation scheme of object o, i.e., $S(o)$.

Heuristic 4

We now introduce the Phase Partition technique Heuristic 4. As shown in Figure 4.7, using Heuristic 4, we partition σ_o into several request phases, $P(0)$, $P(1)$, $P(2)$, ..., $P(r)$, such that each phase consists of either only read requests or only write requests, denoted by *read sub-sequence*(RSS) and *write sub-sequence*(WSS), respectively. A RSS consists of all the consecutive read requests in σ_o, and a WSS consists of all the consecutive write requests in σ_o. For example, if $\sigma_o = R_o^{p_i} R_o^{p_i} R_o^{p_i} W_o^{p_a} W_o^{p_b} W_o^{p_j} R_o^{p_i} R_o^{p_i}$, then $P(0) =< R_o^{p_i} R_o^{p_i} R_o^{p_i} >$, $P(1) =< W_o^{p_a} W_o^{p_b} W_o^{p_j} >$ and $P(2) =< R_o^{p_i} R_o^{p_i} >$. Further, we assume that the number of read requests, each of which immediately follows a write request in σ_o, is N_{raw}.

This implies that the number of RSS and the number of WSS in σ_o are at most $(N_{raw}+1)$, respectively.

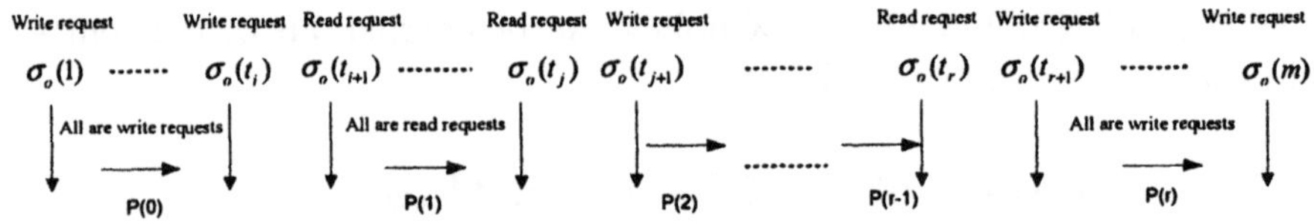

Figure 4.7. Illustration of Phase Partition technique – Heuristic 4

Analysis of RSS

We now analyze the cost to service a RSS $P(i)$ using ADRW algorithm. Based on the cost model in Equation (4.45), we know that if p_i is a data-processor[23] (not a server), then all the read requests in $P(i)$ will be satisfied locally, incurring only I/O cost, i.e.,

$$COST_{ADRW}(P(i)) = |P(i)| \tag{4.49}$$

On the other hand, if p_i is a non-data-processor[24], then each read request in $P(i)$ would incur $(1+C_c+C_d)$ units of cost. However, from Equation (4.47) and the condition that $N_r+N_w=k$, we can obtain that when,

$$N_r \geq \frac{1+C_d}{1+C_c+2C_d}k \tag{4.50}$$

using the distributed request window mechanism, after the first $\lceil\frac{1+C_d}{1+C_c+2C_d}k\rceil$ read requests in $P(i)$, p_i will enter the allocation scheme A_o and become a data-processor. Thus, in this case, the total servicing cost is,

$$COST_{ADRW}(P(i)) = \lceil\frac{1+C_d}{1+C_c+2C_d}k\rceil(C_c+C_d)+1+|P(i)| \tag{4.51}$$

where each of the first $(\lceil\frac{1+C_d}{1+C_c+2C_d}k\rceil-1)$ read requests will incur $(1+C_c+C_d)$ units of cost, the $(\lceil\frac{1+C_d}{1+C_c+2C_d}k\rceil)$-th read request will incur $(2+C_c+C_d)$ units of cost (a saving-read request) and the rest of the requests will incur only I/O cost in p_i.

---

[23]In this case, $Win(o,p_i)$ is in p_i.

[24]In this case, $Win(o,p_i)$ is in server p_j.

Therefore, from Equation (4.49) and Equation (4.51), we can obtain that,

$$COST_{ADRW}(P(i)) \leq \lceil \frac{1 + C_d}{1 + C_c + 2C_d} k \rceil (C_c + C_d) + 1 + |P(i)| \quad (4.52)$$

Analysis of WSS

Similarly, we will now analyze the cost to service a WSS $P(j)$ using ADRW algorithm. According to the cost model in Equation (4.46), if p_i is a non-data-processor, then all the write requests in $p(j)$ will incur zero cost in p_i. On the other hand, if p_i is a data-processor, then each write request in $p(j)$ should be propagated to p_i. However, from Equation (4.48) and the condition that $N_r + N_w = k$, we can obtain that when,

$$N_w > \frac{C_c + C_d}{1 + C_c + 2C_d} k \quad (4.53)$$

using the distributed request window mechanism, after the first $\lceil \frac{C_c+C_d}{1+C_c+2C_d} k \rceil$ write requests in $P(j)$, p_i will exit the allocation scheme A_o and become a non-data-processor. Thus, in this case, the total servicing cost in p_i is,

$$COST_{ADRW}(P(j)) = \lceil \frac{C_c + C_d}{1 + C_c + 2C_d} k \rceil (1 + C_d) - 1 \quad (4.54)$$

where each of the first $(\lceil \frac{C_c+C_d}{1+C_c+2C_d} k \rceil - 1)$ write requests will incur $(1+C_d)$ units of cost in p_i, and the $(\lceil \frac{C_c+C_d}{1+C_c+2C_d} k \rceil)$-th write request will incur C_d units of cost to propagate the new version to p_i (p_i does not save it). The rest of the write requests will not be propagated to p_i and incur zero cost in p_i.

Furthermore, it should be noted that it will incur at most C_d units of cost for a processor to send a write request in $P(j)$ to p_j[25]. In addition, p_j must save the new version into its local memory. Thus, the total servicing cost on $P(j)$ in p_j is,

$$COST_{ADRW}(P(j)) \leq |P(j)|(1 + C_d) \quad (4.55)$$

[25]If the write request is issued by p_j, then it will not cause the data-message transferring cost in p_j.

Therefore, from Equation (4.54) and Equation (4.55), we can obtain that the total servicing cost of all the write requests in $P(j)$ incurred in p_i and p_j is given by,

$$COST_{ADRW}(P(j)) \leq \lceil \frac{C_c + C_d}{1 + C_c + 2C_d} k \rceil (1 + C_d) - 1 + |P(j)|(1 + C_d) \tag{4.56}$$

Finally, from Equation (4.52) and Equation (4.56), the total servicing cost on σ_o by using ADRW algorithm is given by,

$$\begin{aligned} COST_{ADRW}(\sigma_o) &= \sum_i \{COST_{ADRW}(P(i)), P(i) \text{ is a RSS}\} \\ &\quad + \sum_j \{COST_{ADRW}(P(j)), P(j) \text{ is a WSS}\} \\ &\leq (N_{raw} + 1) \left[\lceil \frac{1 + C_d}{1 + C_c + 2C_d} k \rceil (C_c + C_d) + \lceil \frac{C_c + C_d}{1 + C_c + 2C_d} k \rceil (1 + C_d) \right] \\ &\quad + \sum_i \{|P(i)|, P(i) \text{ is a RSS}\} + \sum_j \{|P(j)|(1 + C_d), P(j) \text{ is a WSS}\} \end{aligned} \tag{4.57}$$

Now we consider the servicing of σ_o by the OPT algorithm. It can be observed that at least N_{raw} number of data-messages must be transferred to service σ_o by OPT, incurring $N_{raw}C_d$ units of cost. Furthermore, each read request in σ_o must incur at least 1 unit cost for I/O operation. According to the cost model in Equation (4.46), we know that each write request for object o from the system will incur at most $(1 + C_d)$ units of cost in each server of object o ($|S(o)| = t$). Similarly, for the OPT algorithm, in order to satisfy the t-availability constraint, each write request must also be transferred to at least number of $(t - 1)$ processors. Further, upon receiving the write request, these processors will save the new version into their respective local memories, which implies that using the OPT algorithm, each write request will incur at least $[(t-1)C_d + t]$ units of cost. Thus, although the processor set to which a newly created version (due to a write request) of object o is transferred using the OPT algorithm may be different from the server set $S(o)$ in ADRW algorithm, we can simply consider that the cost incurred in each server (belonging to $S(o)$, including p_j) by using the OPT algorithm to service a write request in σ_o is $[\frac{(t-1)C_d + t}{t}]$ units. Thus, for the OPT algorithm, the total servicing cost of σ_o incurred in p_i and p_j is given by,

$$COST_{OPT}(\sigma_o) \geq N_{raw}C_d + \sum_i \{|P(i)|, P(i) \text{ is a RSS}\}$$

$$+\sum_j \{|P(j)|(1+C_d), P(j) \text{ is a WSS}\}$$
$$-\frac{C_d}{t}\sum_j \{|P(j)|, P(j) \text{ is a WSS}\} \tag{4.58}$$

The difference between Equation (4.57) and Equation (4.58) is,

$$\begin{aligned}
&COST_{ADRW}(\sigma_o) - COST_{OPT}(\sigma_o) \\
&\leq (N_{raw}+1)\left[\lceil \frac{1+C_d}{1+C_c+2C_d}k\rceil (C_c+C_d) + \lceil \frac{C_c+C_d}{1+C_c+2C_d}k\rceil (1+C_d)\right] \\
&\qquad -N_{raw}C_d + \frac{C_d}{t}\sum_j \{|P(j)|, P(j) \text{ is a WSS}\} \\
&\leq (N_{raw}+1)[kC_d+1+C_c+2C_d] - N_{raw}C_d \\
&\qquad +\frac{C_d}{t}\sum_j \{|P(j)|, P(j) \text{ is a WSS}\} \\
&= N_{raw}C_d\left[k-1+\frac{1+C_c+2C_d}{C_d}\right] + \frac{C_d}{t}\sum_j \{|P(j)|, P(j) \text{ is a WSS}\} \\
&\qquad +[kC_d+1+C_c+2C_d] \\
&\leq \left[k-1+\frac{1+C_c+2C_d}{C_d}+\frac{C_d}{t}\right] COST_{OPT}(\sigma_o) \\
&\qquad +[kC_d+1+C_c+2C_d]
\end{aligned}$$

Therefore, we can clearly observe that ADRW algorithm is $\left[k+\frac{1+C_c+2C_d}{C_d}+\frac{C_d}{t}\right]$-competitive, and hence the proof. ■

We rewrite the competitive ratio, denoted as R_{SCE}, in Theorem 4.4 as follows.

$$R_{SCE} = k+2+(1+C_c)/C_d + C_d/t \tag{4.59}$$

Furthermore, in the network system, it is reasonable to assume that the cost of a control message C_c is fixed. Therefore, we can consider that R_{SCE} is a function of C_d, and hence we have,

$$\frac{d^2R_{SCE}}{dC_d{}^2} = \frac{2}{C_d{}^3} > 0 \tag{4.60}$$

Thus, when

$$\begin{aligned}
\frac{dR_{SCE}}{dC_d} &= \frac{1}{t} - \frac{1+C_c}{C_d^2} = 0 \\
&\Rightarrow C_d = \sqrt{t(1+C_c)}
\end{aligned} \tag{4.61}$$

we can obtain the minimal competitive ratio of ADRW algorithm in a SCE as $(k+2+2\sqrt{\frac{(1+C_c)}{t}})$.

5. Concluding Remarks

In this chapter, we considered the OMP in DDBSs which support SCEs. For servicing requests that arrive at a DDBS, we have presented four *deterministic* object allocation and replication algorithms – SA, DA, DWM and ADRW algorithm, respectively. All the four algorithms are designed exclusively for tackling certain special situations in SCEs. The SA algorithm is a static object allocation algorithm, in which the allocation scheme of an object is assumed to be fixed at any time instant. Hence the object consistency constraint is somewhat easy to take care. Fundamental concepts and a collection of other related static object allocation schemes can be found in [OV99]. The DA algorithm, DWM algorithm and ADRW algorithm are dynamic object allocation and replication schemes that can adapt the arriving read/write request patterns. Based on different existing conditions, these three dynamic algorithms are carefully designed to adjust the object allocation schemes to minimize the total servicing cost of current request sequence (DWM) or future expected request sequence (DA and ADRW). Although DWM algorithm is essentially designed for a DDBS with a centralized control unit (CCU), one can extend the basic underlying concept to handle requests in a DDBS with decentralized controls, especially to handle real-time requests in a RTDDBS. We will present this extension later in Chapter 5. Lastly, it may be noted that all the above four algorithms thrive to satisfy the t-availability constraint mentioned in this book to improve the object availability and system reliability.

For each algorithm mentioned above, we first proposed a mathematical cost model that considers the I/O operation, control-message transfer and data-message transfer associated with processing a request, and then we used a competitive analysis to quantify the performance. It should be noted that our main focus in this chapter is on designing schemes to efficiently serve the requests in terms of minimizing their servicing costs. Therefore, in the above four cost models, we ignored the cost of submitting a request, such as the cost for a processor submitting a request to CCU in DWM algorithm. Finally, using Phase Partition techniques Heuristic 3 or Heuristic 4, we state and prove that in a SCE, SA algorithm is $(1+C_c+C_d)$-competitive, DA algorithm is $(2+C_c)$-competitive, DWM algorithm is $(2+2\frac{C_c}{C_d})$-competitive and ADRW algorithm is $[k+\frac{1+C_c+2C_d}{C_d}+\frac{C_d}{t}]$-competitive, respectively.

Chapter 5

OBJECT MANAGEMENT IN MOBILE COMPUTING ENVIRONMENTS

Mobile devices such as laptops, cellular phones, Personal Digital Assistants (PDAs), have recently been of immense use and particularly started getting considerable attention in database systems. Mobile users on the MHs (or mobile devices) may interact with a database system in retrieving objects or they may interact with other mobile devices via wireless network. Hence, a DDBS is expected to support a computer network comprising a number of MHs. As discussed in Chapter 1, due to the mobility and disconnection of MHs, it is important for a DDBS in a MCE to provide a continuous network connectivity to the MHs regardless of their locations [BAI94, IB92]. Additionally, it is very well known that a wireless network bandwidth availability is very limited and hence object management in a MCE poses many challenges to the database designers. Thus, in this chapter, we address the issues of OMPs in MCEs.

To understand the importance of object management in a MCE, we can consider a typical interaction of a user in a MCE. A user with a mobile device, may attempt to modify a file/data (object) and may participate in a co-operative computing processes. In this scenario, the user may first request the file to be downloaded from a site. When this (read) request is made, possibly a most recent version of the file will be transferred to the user. It may be noted that during this interaction, the mobile device may be out of the "scope" of the current *cell*[1] and "hand-off" might have happened. Thus, continuous connectivity becomes an imperative requirement in this service. When the file

[1] A limited geographical area [BAI94].

reaches the user, the user starts to edit (in our context this is an object modification process) and once completed, he/she wants to transfer it back to the DDBS. This submission is what we refer to as a "write request". When this request arrives at the system, object consistency algorithms may be invoked and replicas of this file/data in the system will be replaced with this modified version. Of course, we assume that this process has an inherent locking mechanism (as explained in Chapter 1) by which no subsequent modifications are allowed when the user is currently attempting to modify the file.

Similar to a SCE, in order to maximize the system performance of a wireless network, objects may be replicated on the network to minimize the average request waiting/response time, the request blocking probability, or the cumulative servicing cost of all the requests arriving. Generally, servicing a read/write request in a MCE may incur all the three types of cost[2] introduced in Chapter 4. However, since the bandwidth of wireless communication links in a MCE is very limited, the transfer of data-messages and control-messages over wireless networks incurs very high cost when compared to I/O cost. Therefore, for all practical purposes, the I/O cost can be neglected in a MCE[3]. In other words, in our analysis we consider $C_{io} = 0$ in a MCE.

In this chapter, we again consider the *deterministic* on-line algorithms SA, DA, DWM, and ADRW presented in Chapter 4 and we will discuss on how these algorithms can be adopted in MCEs. As a first step, we modify the cost models of all these four algorithms to consider only the communication cost and then use competitive analysis to quantify their performance. Furthermore, we also modify the DWM algorithm to a new object allocation and replication algorithm that satisfies the requirement of a RTDDBS, referred to as *Real-time Decentralized Dynamic Window Mechanism* (RDDWM) algorithm. RDDWM algorithm also guarantees the t-availability constraint of an object and is capable of servicing requests with hard deadlines[4]. Finally, competitive analysis is used to quantify the performance of RDDWM algorithm under two different extreme conditions, i.e., when the deadline periods of all the requests are sufficiently long and when the deadline periods of all the requests are very short.

---

[2]Control-message transfer cost, data-message transfer cost, and I/O cost.

[3]Refer to [SSZ93, SWH98, WH98].

[4]For the definition of hard deadlines, refer to Chapter 1.

1. Performance of SA Algorithm in a MCE

In this section, we extend our analysis of SA algorithm to the case of a MCE. As mentioned earlier, we consider $C_{io} = 0$ in a MCE. Thus, given a σ_o, we modify the cost model for servicing a request in σ_o as follows.

1.1 Cost Model

As done before, let $S(o)$ be the server set of an object o.

Case A (Read request): Consider servicing a read request $R_o^{p_i}$. Then, the cost of servicing this request is given by,

$$COST_{SA}(R_o^{p_i}) = \begin{cases} 0 & \text{if } p_i \in S(o) \\ C_c + C_d & \text{otherwise} \end{cases} \tag{5.1}$$

Compared to Equation (4.1), in Equation (5.1), we observe that if $p_i \in S(o)$ then object o is directly retrieved from its local memory. This will involve only I/O operation which incurs zero cost as per our assumption in a MCE. On the other hand, if $p_i \notin S(o)$ then p_i will send a read request to a server p_j. After receiving the read request, p_j retrieves object o from its local memory and sends it to processor p_i. The entire process will incur $(C_c + C_d)$ units of cost in a MCE.

Case B (Write request): Consider servicing a write request $W_o^{p_i}$. Then, the cost of servicing this request is given by,

$$COST_{SA}(W_o^{p_i}) = \begin{cases} (|S(o)| - 1)C_d & \text{if } p_i \in S(o) \\ |S(o)|C_d & \text{otherwise} \end{cases} \tag{5.2}$$

Similarly, compared to Equation (4.2), in Equation (5.2), we observe that if $p_i \in S(o)$, then object o will be transferred to all the processors in $S(o)$ other than p_i, incurring $(|S(o)| - 1)C_d$ units of cost. Whereas, if $p_i \notin S(o)$ then object o will be transferred to all the processors in $S(o)$, incurring $(|S(o)|)C_d$ units of cost. Further, the I/O operations carried out by the servers in $S(o)$ for saving the object o into their respective local memories will incur zero cost in a MCE.

1.2 Analysis of SA Algorithm

In this section, we will attempt to derive the competitive ratio of SA algorithm, if it exists, in a MCE. To do so, let us consider an object o and its server set in the system $S(o)$. Without loss of generality, we assume that SA algorithm and an optimal algorithm OPT (which also satisfies the t-availability constraint) initially start with the same allocation scheme of object o $S(o)$.

Let us suppose that there exist two constants α ($\alpha \geq 1$) and β ($\beta \geq 0$), such that for any request sequence σ_o

$$COST_{SA}(\sigma_o, S(o)) \leq \alpha COST_{OPT}(\sigma_o, S(o)) + \beta \qquad (5.3)$$

In other words, we suppose that SA algorithm is α-competitive in a MCE. Now let us consider a request sequence for object o, $\sigma'_o = \sigma'_o(1)$, $\sigma'_o(2), ..., \sigma'_o(m)$, arriving at the system, where $\sigma'_o(i)$ $(1 \leq i \leq m)$ denotes the i-th request in σ'_o. Suppose that all the requests in σ'_o are read requests and are issued from a non-data-processor p_i. According to Equation (5.1), we know that using SA algorithm, each read request in σ'_o is served as a non-saving-read request and incurs $(C_c + C_d)$ units of cost. Thus, the total servicing cost of σ'_o for SA algorithm is given by,

$$COST_{SA}(\sigma'_o, S(o)) = m(C_c + C_d) \qquad (5.4)$$

On the other hand, for the OPT algorithm, the first read request $\sigma'_o(1)$ can be served as a saving-read request, incurring at most (C_c+C_d) units of cost. All the other requests $(\sigma'_o(i), (2 \leq i \leq m))$ will, hence, incur zero cost. Therefore, the total servicing cost of σ'_o for the OPT algorithm is given by,

$$COST_{OPT}(\sigma'_o, S(o)) \leq (C_c + C_d) \qquad (5.5)$$

Thus, when the number of requests in σ'_o is large enough so that $m > \alpha + \frac{\beta}{C_c + C_d}$, we can observe that

$$\begin{aligned} COST_{SA}(\sigma'_o, S(o)) &= m(C_c + C_d) \\ &> \alpha(C_c + C_d) + \beta \\ &= \alpha COST_{OPT}(\sigma'_o, S(o)) + \beta \end{aligned} \qquad (5.6)$$

which contradicts the hypothesis in Equation (5.3). Therefore, we conclude that SA algorithm is not competitive in a MCE. This means that there exists no real constants[5] c and d such that $COST_{SA}(\sigma) \leq c \cdot COST_{OPT}(\sigma) + d$ holds for any request sequence σ. Following theorem formalizes this argument.

Theorem 5.1: For any integer $t \geq 1$, SA algorithm is not competitive in a MCE.

Proof: The above argument clearly establishes the proof. ■

From the definition of competitiveness in Chapter 3, it may be noted that competitive analysis is a strong performance measure capable of

[5] Refer to Chapter 3 for the definition of competitiveness.

quantifying the *worst-case* performance. Although SA algorithm is not competitive in MCEs, it does not mean that SA algorithm always performs worse in MCEs. It should be noted that SA algorithm always maintains a minimum number of copies of an object[6] in the system. Hence, the average servicing cost of a write request is minimized when the t-availability constraint is considered. Therefore, in a write-intensive DDBS, system designers can continue to use SA algorithm as the object management algorithm to obtain better system performance.

2. Performance of DA Algorithm in a MCE

We now consider DA algorithm and quantify its performance in a MCE in this section. Given a σ_o, we modify the cost model for servicing a request in σ_o as follows.

2.1 Cost Model

Let $S(o)$ be the server set of an object o.

Case A (Read request): Consider servicing a read request $R_o^{p_i}$ and let A_o be the allocation scheme of object o on this request. Then,

$$COST_{DA}(R_o^{p_i}) = \begin{cases} 0 & \text{if } p_i \in A_o \\ C_c + C_d & \text{otherwise} \end{cases} \tag{5.7}$$

Compared to Equation (4.8), in Equation (5.7), we observe that if $p_i \in A_o$, then object o is simply retrieved from its local memory incurring zero unit cost. On the other hand, if $p_i \notin A_o$, then as done before, p_i will send a control-message to a server p_j ($p_j \in S(o)$) to inform the read request. As a response, p_j retrieves object o from its local memory and sends it to p_i. After receiving, p_i saves object o into its local memory(saving-read) and thus, the total servicing cost will be $(C_c + C_d)$ units in a MCE. Finally, server p_j will add processor p_i into its invalidate-list $inv\_list(p_j, o)$.

Case B (Write request): Consider servicing a write request $W_o^{p_i}$ and let A_o be the allocation scheme of object o on this request. Then,

[6] $A(o) = S(o)$, and $|S(o)| = t$ which satisfies the t-availability of object o.

$$COST_{DA}(W_o^{p_i}) = \begin{cases} (|S(o)|-1)C_d + \sum_{p \in S(o)} (|inv\_list(p,o)|C_c) & \text{if } p_i \in S(o) \\ |S(o)|C_d + \sum_{p \in S(o)} (|inv\_list(p,o) - \{p_i\}|C_c) & \text{otherwise} \end{cases} \quad (5.8)$$

The cost model for DA algorithm to serve a write request is almost the same as that in Equation (4.9), except that $C_{io} = 0$ as per our assumption in a MCE.

2.2 Analysis of DA Algorithm

With the above described model, in this subsection, we use competitive analysis technique, Phase Partition Heuristic 3, to analyze the performance of DA algorithm in a MCE. We consider an arbitrary request sequence for object o, $\sigma_o = \sigma_o(1), \sigma_o(2), ..., \sigma_o(m)$, arriving at the system, where $\sigma_o(j)$ $(1 \leq j \leq m)$ denotes the j-th request in σ_o. We know that using Phase Partition Heuristic 3, σ_o will be partitioned into *phases* $P(0), P(1), P(2), ..., P(r)$. Further, we assume that the initial allocation scheme of each phase $P(i)$ $(0 \leq i \leq r)$ is $IA_o(i)$ when DA algorithm services σ_o. Without loss of generality, we assume that DA algorithm and an optimal algorithm OPT (which also satisfies the t-availability constraint) initially start with the same initial allocation scheme $IA_o = IA_o(0) = S(o)$. Similar to the competitive analysis of DA algorithm in a SCE, we first state two important lemmas associated with the servicing of each phase and then show that DA algorithm is $(2 + 2\frac{C_c}{C_d})$-competitive in a MCE.

Lemma 5.1: Given a σ_o with an IA_o, $COST_{DA}(P(0), IA_o) \leq (2 + 2\frac{C_c}{C_d})COST_{OPT}(P(0), IA_o)$ in a MCE.

Proof: Using the cost model in Equation (5.7) and referring to Equation (4.11), the total cost for DA algorithm to service the read requests in $P(0)$ is given by,

$$COST_{DA}(P(0), IA_o) \leq |N(0)|(C_c + C_d) + |N(0)|C_c \quad (5.9)$$

For the OPT algorithm, referring to Equation (4.12), when I/O operation incurs zero unit cost, the total cost computed by the OPT algorithm for servicing $P(0)$ is,

$$COST_{OPT}(P(0), IA_o) \geq |N(0)|C_d \tag{5.10}$$

Thus, the difference between Equation (5.9) and Equation (5.10) is,

$$\begin{aligned} COST_{DA}(P(0), IA_o) &- COST_{OPT}(P(0), IA_o) \\ &\leq 2|N(0)|C_c \\ &\leq |N(0)|C_d + 2|N(0)|C_c \\ &\leq (1 + 2\frac{C_c}{C_d})COST_{OPT}(P(0), IA_o) \end{aligned}$$

Alternatively,

$$COST_{DA}(P(0), IA_o) \leq (2 + 2\frac{C_c}{C_d})COST_{OPT}(P(0), IA_o) \tag{5.11}$$

Hence the proof. ■

Lemma 5.2: Given a σ_o with an IA_o, $COST_{DA}(P(i), IA_o(i)) \leq (2 + 2\frac{C_c}{C_d})COST_{OPT}(P(i), IA_o^*(i)) + K$ in a MCE, where $1 \leq i \leq r$, $IA_o^*(i)$ is the initial allocation scheme of object o on $P(i)$ using the OPT algorithm, and K is an additive constant.

Proof: As done in the proof of Lemma 4.2, we suppose that the first request in $P(i)$ $(1 \leq i \leq r)$ is W_o^*, where W_o^* denotes a write request issued from any processor in the system for object o. Referring to Equation (4.16), in a MCE, the total cost to serve the requests in $P(i)$ for DA algorithm is given by,

$$\begin{aligned} COST_{DA}(P(i), A_o(i)) &= COST_{DA}(W_o^*) \\ &\quad + \sum_{j=1}^{|P(i)|-1} COST_{DA}(\text{the } j^{th} \text{ read request in } P(i)) \\ &\leq (|S(o)| + |N(i)|)C_d + (2|N(i)| + 1)C_c \end{aligned} \tag{5.12}$$

For the OPT algorithm, we also consider the following two cases.

Case A: If $|N'(i)| > t$, then referring to Equation (4.17), in a MCE, the total cost of servicing the requests in $P(i)$ for the OPT algorithm is given by,

$$\begin{aligned} COST_{OPT}(P(i), IA_o^*(i)) &\geq (t-1)C_d + (|N'(i)| - t)C_d \\ &= (|N'(i)| - 1)C_d \end{aligned} \tag{5.13}$$

Thus, the difference between Equation (5.12) and Equation (5.13) is,

$$\begin{aligned} & COST_{DA}(P(i), IA_o(i)) - COST_{OPT}(P(i), IA_o^*(i)) \\ \leq\ & (t + |N(i)| - |N'(i)| + 1)C_d + (2|N(i)| + 1)C_c \quad (\text{for } |S(o)| = t) \\ \leq\ & (|N'(i)| - 1)C_d + (2|N(i)| + 1)C_c + 2C_d \\ & \qquad\qquad (\text{for } |N'(i)| > t, |N'(i)| \geq |N(i)|) \\ \leq\ & (|N'(i)| - 1)C_d + 2(|N'(i)| - 1)C_c + 2C_d + 3C_c \\ \leq\ & COST_{OPT}(P(i), IA_o^*(i)) + 2\frac{C_c}{C_d}COST_{OPT}(P(i), IA_o^*(i)) + K_1 \end{aligned}$$

where $K_1 = (2C_d + 3C_c)$ is a constant. Therefore, we obtain,

$$\begin{aligned} & COST_{DA}(P(i), IA_o(i)) \\ & \qquad \leq (2 + 2\frac{C_c}{C_d})COST_{OPT}(P(i), IA_o^*(i)) + K_1 \end{aligned} \tag{5.14}$$

Case B: If $|N'(i)| \leq t$, then referring to Equation (4.19), in a MCE, the total cost of servicing the requests in $P(i)$ for the OPT algorithm is given by,

$$COST_{OPT}(P(i), IA_o^*(i)) \geq (t - 1)C_d \tag{5.15}$$

In this case, the difference between Equation (5.12) and Equation (5.15) is,

$$\begin{aligned} & COST_{DA}(P(i), IA_o(i)) - COST_{OPT}(P(i), IA_o^*(i)) \\ \leq\ & (|N(i)| + 1)C_d + (2|N(i)| + 1)C_c \\ \leq\ & (t - 1)C_d + 2(t - 1)C_c + 2C_d + 3C_c \quad (\text{for } |N(i)| \leq |N'(i)| \leq t) \\ \leq\ & COST_{OPT}(P(i), IA_o^*(i)) + 2\frac{C_c}{C_d}COST_{OPT}(P(i), IA_o^*(i)) + K_2 \end{aligned}$$

where $K_2 = (2C_d + 3C_c)$ is a constant. Therefore, we can obtain that,

$$COST_{DA}(P(i), IA_o(i)) \leq (2 + 2\frac{C_c}{C_d})COST_{OPT}(P(i), IA_o^*(i)) + K_2 \tag{5.16}$$

Thus, from Equation (5.14) and Equation (5.16) the result of Lemma 5.2 is immediate. Hence the proof. ■

The above two lemmas derive competitive ratios for specific phases ($P(0)$ and $P(i)$ ($1 \leq i \leq r$), whenever they exist). The significance of the above two lemmas is as follows. For request patterns in $P(0)$ and phase $P(i)$ $(1 \leq i \leq r)$, Lemmas 5.1 and 5.2 assure that the total cost of the DA algorithm on $P(i)$ $(0 \leq i \leq r)$ is at most $(2 + 2\frac{C_c}{C_d})$ times worse than that of an optimal algorithm, which also satisfies the t-availability constraint. This interesting property will be used in proving our main theorem for a MCE below.

Theorem 5.2: For any integer $t \geq 1$, DA algorithm is $(2 + 2\frac{C_c}{C_d})$-competitive in a MCE.

Proof: From the results of Lemma 5.1 and Lemma 5.2, we know that for an arbitrary σ_o with an IA_o,

$$\begin{aligned} COST_{DA}(\sigma_o, IA_o) &= \sum_{i=0}^{r} COST_{DA}(P(i), IA_o(i)) \\ &\leq (2 + 2\frac{C_c}{C_d}) \sum_{i=0}^{r} (COST_{OPT}(P(i), IA_o^*(i))) + K \\ &= (2 + 2\frac{C_c}{C_d}) COST_{OPT}(\sigma_o, IA_o) + K \qquad (5.17) \end{aligned}$$

where $IA_o^*(i)$ is the initial allocation scheme of object o on $P(i)$ after servicing the last request in $P(i-1)$ using the OPT algorithm, $IA_o^*(0) = IA_o$, and $K = \sum_{i=1}^{r} x_i$ $(x_i \in \{K_1, K_2\})$ is an additive constant. It may be noted that $K = \alpha_1 K_1 + \alpha_2 K_2$ $(\alpha_1, \alpha_2 \geq 0)$ is a linear combination of K_1 and K_2 obtained in our analysis of $P(i)$ $(1 \leq i \leq r)$. The values of α_1 and α_2 depend upon the requests in σ_o. Hence the proof. ■

3. Performance of DWM Algorithm in a MCE

Similarly, in this section, we extend our analysis of DWM algorithm to the case of MCE. Given a σ_o, we modify the cost model for servicing a request in σ_o as follows.

3.1 Cost Model

Let $S(o)$ be the server set of an object o.

Case A (Read request): Consider a read request $R_o^{p_i}$, and let A_o be the allocation scheme of object o on this request. Then,

$$COST_{DWM}(R_o^{p_i}) = \begin{cases} 0 & \text{if } p_i \in A_o \\ C_c + C_d & \text{otherwise} \end{cases} \qquad (5.18)$$

When compared to Equation (4.23), in a MCE we observe that if $p_i \in A_o$, then object o is simply retrieved from its local memory, incurring zero cost. On the other hand, if $p_i \notin A_o$ then no matter whether DWM algorithm decides this read request to be a saving-read request or not, the entire process will only incur $(C_c + C_d)$ units of cost.

Case B (Write request): Consider a write request $W_o^{p_i}$. Let A_o be the allocation scheme of object o on this request and let A_o' be the allocation scheme of object o after servicing this request. Then,

$$COST_{DWM}(W_o^{p_i}) = \begin{cases} (|S(o)| - 1)C_d + |A_o - A_o'|C_c & \text{if } p_i \in S(o) \\ |S(o)|C_d + |A_o - A_o'|C_c & \text{otherwise} \end{cases} \tag{5.19}$$

The cost model for DWM algorithm to serve a write request is almost the same as that in Equation (4.24) except the fact that $C_{io} = 0$ in this case.

3.2 Servicing of Phases

As mentioned in Section 3 of Chapter 4, using the window mechanism of DWM algorithm, a request sequence σ_o will be essentially partitioned into several phases $P(0), P(1), ..., P(r)$. Using the above cost model, the conditions for DWM algorithm to consider a read request as a saving-read request in a MCE are as follows. Referring to the definition of $\Delta(0)$ in Equation (4.25), in a MCE, when servicing phase $P(0)$ of σ_o, if $\Delta(0) > (|N(0)|C_c)$, then DWM considers the first read requests from each of the processors in $N(0)$ as saving-read requests. Otherwise, if $\Delta(0) \leq (|N(0)|C_c)$, DWM algorithm will not consider any of the read requests from processors in $N(0)$ as a saving-read request. It may be noted that $N(0)$ refers to the set of processors that have issued read requests in $P(0)$ but do not belong to the initial allocation scheme. Similarly, when servicing phase $P(i)$ $(1 \leq i \leq r)$ in σ_o, referring to Equation (4.30), if $\Delta(i) > (|N(i)|C_c)$, then DWM considers the first read requests from each of the processors in $N(i)$ as saving-read requests. Otherwise, if $\Delta(i) \leq (|N(i)|C_c)$, DWM algorithm will not consider any of the read requests from processors in $N(i)$ as a saving-read request. Note that $N(i)$ refers to the set of processors that have issued read requests in $P(i)$ and do not belong to A_o after servicing the first write request W_o^* in $P(i)$.

3.3 Analysis of DWM Algorithm

In this section, we state the following theorem to quantify the performance of DWM algorithm in a MCE.

Theorem 5.3: For any integer $t \geq 1$, DWM algorithm is $(2 + 2\frac{C_c}{C_d})$-competitive in a MCE.

Proof: Using the above cost models in Equation (5.18) and Equation (5.19) for servicing read/write requests, as well as the conditions for deciding a saving-read request (Refer to Section 3.2), it can be verified that Lemma 4.3 and Lemma 4.4 stated in Section 3.4 of Chapter 4 hold for a MCE, except that we use $C_{io} = 0$. Further, following the steps of the proof of Theorem 4.3, the result of Theorem 5.3 is evident. ∎

4. RDDWM Algorithm

As mentioned in Chapter 1, a transaction in a RTDDBS, especially a RTDDBS in a MCE, may demand a response on or before a specified deadline period. Thus, one of the primary objectives in a RTDDBS is to design an efficient mechanism to schedule transactions that are associated with time constraints and also guarantee the consistency of the objects in the system. There have been a number of research efforts in recent years that address the problems of scheduling real-time transactions in a RTDDBS. In [PSS93], two real-time active database applications, i.e., the cooperative distributed navigation application and the network services database application, were presented in detail. The former is exclusively for a hard real-time system, whereas the latter is a soft/firm real-time system. The application characteristics in these two real-time systems such as data characteristics and transaction characteristics were introduced in this paper. In [NRP95], a "Two-Phase Approach" was provided to schedule the transactions predictably in a real-time system. The first phase is to gather all the needed information to make the transaction predictable and the second phase is to execute the transactions so as to avoid data and resources contentions.

There are several criteria to evaluate the performance of a RTDDS such as, the percentage of the transactions that can be serviced without missing their time constraints, the total cost of servicing the transactions, the system resources utilization rate, etc. For example, the goal of the Adaptive Earliest Deadline (AED) algorithm introduced in [HCL91] is to schedule the transactions so as to maximize the total value of the *in-time* transactions. It does not consider the execution cost of transactions. In this section, we consider an OMP in a RTDDBS where each request arriving at the system imposes a hard deadline period. We modify the cost model and window mechanism of DWM to satisfy the real-time requirements. Our objective is to service all the requests *on or before* their respective deadline periods and minimize the total servicing cost. To this end, we design a decentralized data allocation and replication algorithm, referred to as *Real-time decentralized dynamic Window Mechanism* (RDDWM) algorithm. RDDWM algorithm also satisfies the t-availability constraint mentioned earlier. Using competitive analysis, we study the performance of RDDWM algorithm under two different extreme conditions, i.e., when the deadline period of each request is sufficiently long and when the deadline period of each request is very short.

As each request consists of a respective deadline period in a RTDDBS, we need to slightly redefine a read request from processor p_i for object o with deadline period[7] k as $R_o^{p_i}(k)$. Similarly, we redefine a write request from processor p_i for object o with deadline period k as $W_o^{p_i}(k)$. As done in DWM algorithm, we assume that the initial allocation scheme of an object o in RDDWM algorithm is given by a fixed server set $S(o)$ ($|S(o)| = t$). It should be reminded that for different objects, the server sets may be different. Further, we assume that all the processors in the system know the initial allocation scheme (server set) of every object.

In RDDWM algorithm, there is no a CCU in the system. All requests for objects are assumed to arrive at the processors in the system. Requests arrive at a processor concurrently and there is a concurrency control mechanism at the processor to serialize[8] them for processing. When a processor p_r prefers to read an object o, if the latest version of object o is in its local memory, then object o is directly retrieved from its local memory; Otherwise, since p_r knows $S(o)$, p_r will send a read request to the nearest server[9] in $S(o)$. Further, without loss of generality, each processor can issue a write request for any object in a RTDDS. Thus, the request arriving at a processor q can be a read request from processor q for an object o in its local memory, a write request from processor q for any object in the system, or a read request from a remote processor for an object o' if processor q is a server of object o'.

4.1 Cost Model

We now present the cost model used in RDDWM algorithm to compute the cost of servicing a read request or a write request arriving at a processor q. Let $S(o)$ be the server set of an object o.

[7] Measured in number of time units.

[8] Refer to Section 3 of Chapter 4.

[9] This is different from DWM algorithm in which CCU can randomly choose a server to service the read request. As done in ADRW algorithm in Chapter 4, the nearest server can be predefined by some system parameters such as processor ID. Further, for a given processor, the nearest server is fixed.

Case A (Read request): Consider servicing a read request $R_o^{p_i}(k)$ and let A_o be the allocation scheme of object o known by processor q. Then,

$$COST_{RDDWM}(R_o^{p_i}(k)) = \begin{cases} 0 & \text{if } p_i \in A_o \\ C_c + C_d & \text{otherwise} \end{cases} \tag{5.20}$$

Lemma 5.3. Consider servicing a read request $R_o^{p_i}(k)$ that arrives at processor q. Let A_o be the allocation scheme of object o in processor q by RDDWM. If $p_i \in A_o$, then p_i must be the processor q itself.

Proof: The proof of Lemma 5.3 is straightforward to realize, since otherwise, p_i will not send a read request to processor q, as object o is in its local memory. Hence the proof. ■

The cost model in Equation (5.20) is similar to that in Equation (5.18). If $p_i \in A_o$, then according to Lemma 5.3, object o is directly retrieved from the local memory of q, incurring zero cost. On the other hand, if $p_i \notin A_o$, then q retrieves object o from its local memory and sends it to p_i. After p_i receives object o, no matter whether RDDWM algorithm in q decides this read request to be a saving-read request or not, the entire process will incur $(C_c + C_d)$ units of communication cost, including the control-message transferring cost for processor p_i sending $R_o^{p_i}(k)$ to q. Further, once q decides that request $R_o^{p_i}(k)$ is a saving-read request, q and p_i will change their respective allocation schemes of object o from A_o to $A_o \cup \{p_i\}$. Further, server q will add p_i into an invalidate-list[10] for object o, denoted as $inv\_list(q, o)$. The key idea behind this operation is that when servicing a following write request from processor p_j for object o in the system, the servers in $S(o)$ can simply send "invalidate" control-messages to the processors in their respective invalidate-lists for object o, except p_j (if p_j is in an invalidate-list), to invalidate the redundant copies of object o.

Case B (Write request): Consider servicing a write request $W_o^q(k)$ and let A_o be the allocation scheme of object o known by processor q.

[10]The *invalidate-list* can be referred to DA algorithm in Section 2 of Chapter 4.

Then, the cost of servicing this request is given by,

$$COST_{RDDWM}(W_o^q(k)) = \begin{cases} (t-1)C_d + \sum_{p \in S(o)} |inv\_list(p,o)|C_c & \text{if } q \in S(o) \\ tC_d + \sum_{p \in S(o)} |inv\_list(p,o) - \{q\}|C_c & \text{otherwise} \end{cases} \tag{5.21}$$

where $inv\_list(p, o) - \{q\}$ denotes the set of processors in $inv\_list(p, o)$, except processor q. Similar to Equation (4.9), in RDDWM algorithm, when processor q services a write request from itself for an object o, if $q \in S(o)$, then object o will be transferred to all processors in $S(o)$ other than q, incurring $(|S(o)| - 1)C_d$ units of data-transferring cost. Whereas, if $q \notin S(o)$, then object o will be transferred to all processors in $S(o)$, incurring $(|S(o)|)C_d$ units of cost. In both cases, the processors in $S(o) \cup \{q\}$ will save object o into their respective local memories.

After receiving the new version of object o from processor q, all the servers in $S(o)$ will send control-messages to the processors in their corresponding invalidate-lists except processor q (if q is in an invalidate-list) to "invalidate" the redundant replicas of object o, remove these processors from their A_o and corresponding invalidate-lists. Similarly, after receiving the "invalidate" control-messages, the processors in the invalidate-lists invalidate the copy of object o in their respective local memories and remove themselves from their respective A_o. Finally, if processor $q \notin S(o)$ and q is not in any invalidate-list for object o then q will add itself into its A_o and its nearest server in $S(o)$ will add processor q into its A_o and corresponding invalidate-list. The purpose of this process is to invalidate the copy of object o in processor q when another processor services a following write request for object o. Thus, in Equation (5.21), $\sum_{p \in S(o)} |inv\_list(p,o) - \{q\}|C_c$ and $\sum_{p \in S(o)} |inv\_list(p,o)|C_c$ denote the cost for sending "invalidate" control-messages by the processors in $S(o)$ when processor q is in an invalidate-list and processor q is not in any invalidate-list, respectively.

4.2 Window Mechanism of RDDWM Algorithm

In RDDWM algorithm, as CCU is removed from the system, each processor has a request window mechanism. The decentralized request window mechanism of RDDWM algorithm is a modified version of the window mechanism designed for DWM algorithm. There are multiple dynamic request windows[11] with size τ in each processor, one for each requested object. As done in DWM algorithm, we denote a request window for an object o in a processor as $win(o)$. Further, we associate two counters, TC_o^1 and TC_o^2, for each $win(o)$. TC_o^1 has the same function of TC_o in DWM algorithm and TC_o^2 will track the deadline periods of requests in $win(o)$. We now describe the window mechanism of RDDWM algorithm in a processor q in Table 5.1.

From Table 5.1, it may be observed that the processing of requests in a request window can be driven by the deadline requirement of a particular request and not completely constrained by the formation of the request window. In fact, there are three conditions that can trigger immediate servicing of the requests in a $win(o)$.

- A write request arrives
- $TC_o^1 == 0$
- A request in the window will miss its deadline ($TC_o^2 == 0$)

Further, whenever TC_o^1 of a $win(o)$ in processor q reaches 0 the $win(o)$ will be deleted from q and RDDWM algorithm will reset A_o in q to $S(o)$. At the same time, if q is a server of object o, then q will send "invalidate" control-messages to the processors[12] in $inv\_list(q, o)$ to invalidate the replicas of object o and empty $inv\_list(q, o)$. The next request for object o arriving at processor q will be considered as the first request for object o and $win(o)$ will be regenerated by our window mechanism. Thus, we consider the request sequence inserted into $win(o)$ during its individual lifetime as σ_o. Similar to DWM algorithm, using the window mechanism of RDDWM algorithm in Table 5.1, a σ_o will be essentially partitioned into several request sub-sequences $ReqSS(1), ReqSS(2), ..., ReqSS(r)$. Each request sub-sequence belongs to either Type I (σ^{ss1}) or Type II (σ^{ss2}). A σ^{ss1} sub-sequence consists of several read requests and a σ^{ss2} sub-sequence consists of a write request followed by several read requests. However, it should be noted that the partition heuristic used in RDDWM algorithm is not the same as that in DWM algorithm due to the deadline requirement of each request. This is shown in the following example.

Example 5.1: Let us consider a request sequence

$$\sigma_o = R_o^{p_7}(k_1)R_o^{p_5}(k_2)W_o^{q}(k_3)R_o^{q}(k_4)R_o^{p_3}(k_5)R_o^{q}(k_6)R_o^{p_3}(k_7)$$

Using DWM algorithm, σ_o will be divided into two phases, $P(0) =< R_o^{p_7}(k_1)R_o^{p_5}(k_2) >$ and $P(1) =< W_o^{q}(k_3)R_o^{q}(k_4)R_o^{p_3}(k_5)R_o^{q}(k_6)R_o^{p_3}(k_7) >$.

---

[11]The complete description of a request window can be obtained in Section 3.2 of Chapter 4.
[12]These processors are not servers of object o and the processor q must be their nearest server of object o in the system.

Table 5.1. Window mechanism of RDDWM algorithm

For (Each time unit)
{ If (There is a request *Req* for an object o with deadline period τ_{Req})
  { If ($win(o)$ does not exist)
        /**Req* is the first request for object o arriving at q*/
    { Generate $win(o)$ and insert *Req* into $win(o)$;
      $TC_o^1 = \tau$; $TC_o^2 = \tau_{Req}$;
    }
   Else /**Req* is not the first request for object o arriving at q*/
    { If (*Req* is a read request)
        { Insert *Req* into $win(o)$; TC_o^2 = Min(TC_o^2,τ_{Req});}
      Else /**Req* is a write request*/
        { Service the requests in $win(o)$;
              /* $win(o)$ is empty after servicing */
          Insert *Req* into $win(o)$; $TC_o^1 = \tau$; $TC_o^2 = \tau_{Req}$;
        }
    }
  }
 For (Each currently existed request window $win(o')$ in processor q)
    /* No matter whether there is a request in this time unit or not */
  { $TC_{o'}^1$=$TC_{o'}^1 - 1$; $TC_{o'}^2$=$TC_{o'}^2 - 1$;
   If ($TC_{o'}^1$ == 0)
    { Service the requests in $win(o')$; Delete $win(o')$;
      If (q is a server of object o')
        {Invalidate the copies of o' in processors that
          belong to $inv\_list(q, o')$;
         Empty $inv\_list(q, o')$;
        }
      $A_{o'} = S(o')$;
    }
   Else /*Check whether there is a request that will miss its deadline or not*/
    {If ($TC_{o'}^2$ == 0)
        {Service the requests in $win(o')$; $TC_{o'}^1 = \tau$; $TC_{o'}^2 = \infty$;}
    }
  }
}

However, using RDDWM algorithm, σ_o may be divided into three request sub-sequences, $ReqSS(1) =< R_o^{p_7}(k_1)R_o^{p_5}(k_2) >$, $ReqSS(2) =< W_o^q(k_3)R_o^q(k_4)R_o^{p_3}(k_5) >$, and $ReqSS(3) =< R_o^q(k_6)R_o^{p_3}(k_7) >$, since the deadline period of the fifth request $R_o^{p_3}(k_5)$ is not sufficiently long and will be missed before the sixth request arrives.

Finally, it may be noted that if the deadlines imposed by the requests are too short for the system to process, certain requests may be dropped by the system. Without loss of generality, we assume that the deadline imposed by a request that can be successfully processed by the system is at least equal to 1. The dropped requests, otherwise referred to as *blocked* requests will either leave the system or can be resubmitted, depending on the underlying application. Thus the fraction of the requests that are dropped (also referred to as *blocking probability*) can be monitored periodically to sense the performance of the system and hence the number of future requests that can be admitted for servicing can be controlled. This, in a way, refers to an *admission control* mechanism that is inherent to the design of OMP in our RDDWM algorithm.

Below, we describe on how RDDWM algorithm at processor q serves the request sub-sequences in σ_o to minimize the cumulative servicing costs.

4.3 Servicing of Request Sub-sequences

The servicing of request sub-sequences in RDDWM algorithm is similar to that in DWM algorithm. Let $n_r(p, i)$ be the total number of read requests issued by processor p in a sub-sequence $ReqSS(i)$. Further, when servicing a $ReqSS(i)$ belonging to σ^{ss1}, let $N(i)$ be the set of processors which are not in the initial allocation scheme $IA_o(i)$ on $ReqSS(i)$ and have issued read requests in $ReqSS(i)$; when servicing a $ReqSS(i)$ belonging to σ^{ss2}, let $N(i)$ be the set of processors which are not in the allocation scheme A_o after the servicing of the first write request and have issued read requests in $ReqSS(i)$. Thus, we define

$$\triangle(i) = \Big(\sum_{p \in N(i)} (n_r(p, i)) - |N(i)| \Big)(C_c + C_d) \tag{5.22}$$

As done in DWM algorithm, when servicing $ReqSS(i)$, if $\triangle(i) > |N(i)|C_c$, then RDDWM considers all the first read requests from processors in $N(i)$ as saving-read requests. Otherwise, RDDWM will not consider any of the read requests from processors in $N(i)$ as a saving-read request.

4.4 Analysis of RDDWM Algorithm

Based on the above described model, we now use competitive analysis to quantify the performance of RDDWM algorithm in a MCE. As RDDWM algorithm is a decentralized algorithm and the window mechanisms are distributed in each processor and work independently, it is sufficient for us to analyze the performance of RDDWM algorithm in a single processor.

Theorem 5.4: For any integer $t \geq 1$, if the deadline period of each request is at least τ, then RDDWM algorithm is $(2+2\frac{C_c}{C_d})$-competitive. However, if the deadline period of each request is 1, then RDDWM algorithm is not competitive.

Proof: Using the window mechanism of RDDWM algorithm in Table 5.1, it can be observed that when the deadline period of each request is sufficiently long ($\geq \tau$), the working style of RDDWM algorithm is identical to that of DWM algorithm in a MCE. Hence, referring to Theorem 4.3 and Theorem 5.3, it is obvious that RDDWM algorithm is $(2+2\frac{C_c}{C_d})$-competitive in this case.

On the other hand, if the deadline period of each request is very short ($= 1$)[13], RDDWM algorithm must service each request immediately when the request arrives. In this case, according to the window mechanism, each request would be considered as a request sub-sequence, either Type I or Type II. Since there is only one request in a sub-sequence, $\Delta(i) < |N(i)|C_c$ is always true. Thus, RDDWM algorithm will not consider any read request in $ReqSS(i)$ as a saving-read request. Therefore, the working style of RDDWM algorithm is almost the same as that of SA algorithm in a MCE. Following the proof of Theorem 5.1 (by way of contradiction), we can realize[14] that RDDWM algorithm is not competitive in this case.

Hence the proof. ■

5. Performance of ADRW algorithm in a MCE

In this section, we shall show how ADRW algorithm can be used in a MCE. We first modify the cost model of ADRW algorithm to suit a MCE as follows.

5.1 Cost Model

Case A (Read request): Consider servicing a read request $R_o^{p_i}$ and let A_o be the allocation scheme of object o on this request. Then,

$$COST_{ADRW}(R_o^{p_i}) = \begin{cases} 0 & \text{if } p_i \in A_o \\ C_c + C_d & \text{otherwise} \end{cases} \tag{5.23}$$

[13]This is the minimum deadline period imposed by a request that can be successfully processed by the system.

[14]We leave the complete proof to interested readers.

Case B (Write request): Consider servicing a write request $W_o^{p_i}$ with an allocation scheme A_o on this request. Then, the cost of servicing this request is given by,

$$COST_{ADRW}(W_o^{p_i}) = \begin{cases} (|A_o| - 1)C_d & \text{if } p_i \in A_o \\ |A_o|C_d & \text{otherwise} \end{cases} \tag{5.24}$$

It may be observed that, in a MCE, except for the fact that $C_{io} = 0$, the cost models of ADRW algorithm in Equation (5.23) and Equation (5.24) are the same as those in Equation (4.45) and Equation (4.46), respectively.

5.2 Distributed Request Window Mechanism

Referring to Section 4.2 of Chapter 4, let us consider a request window $Win(o, p_i)$, a non-server processor p_i ($p_i \notin S(o)$) and its nearest server p_j ($p_j \in S(o)$). As shown for a SCE, when servicing the *relevant* requests in $Win(o, p_i)$ we have two policies, TEN and TEX. In TEN policy, the nearest server p_j uses the condition in Equation (4.47) to determine whether or not the non-data-processor p_i should enter the allocation scheme A_o. In the case of a MCE, because $C_{io} = 0$ we must modify the condition discussed in Equation (4.47) as follows.

$$(C_c + C_d)N_r \geq C_d N_w \tag{5.25}$$

Similarly, for TEX policy, we also need to modify the condition discussed in Equation (4.48) as follows,

$$(C_c + C_d)N_r < C_d N_w \tag{5.26}$$

for the data-processor p_i ($p_i \notin S(o)$) to decide whether or not it should exit from the allocation scheme A_o.

5.3 Analysis of ADRW Algorithm

In this section, according to the modified cost model and TEN/TEX policy, we use competitive analysis to study the performance of ADRW algorithm in a MCE.

Theorem 5.5: Using the request window mechanism, if $t = 1$, then ADRW algorithm is not competitive in a MCE.

Proof: Consider an object o and its server in the system is p_j (i.e., $t = 1$). Suppose that there is a non-data processor p_i and the requests arrive at the system are all write requests from p_i. Using an OPT algorithm, the total servicing cost of these requests would be zero, since the OPT algorithm will just consider p_i as the unique data processor in the system and will not send the new version of object o to p_j. However, using ADRW algorithm, each write request from p_i will incur C_d units of cost and the total servicing cost of these requests will be unboundedly higher than that of the OPT algorithm when the number of such requests increases. Therefore, ADRW algorithm is not competitive when $t = 1$, and hence the proof. ■

Now we shall attempt to derive the competitive ratio of when $t > 1$.

Theorem 5.6: Using the request window mechanism, if $t > 1$, then ADRW algorithm is $\left\lceil (1 + \frac{C_c}{C_c+2C_d})k + \frac{C_c+2C_d}{C_d} \right\rceil$-competitive in a MCE, where k ($k \geq 1$) is the size of a request window.

Proof[15]*:* Consider an arbitrary request sequence $\sigma_o = \sigma_o(1), \sigma_o(2), ...,$ $\sigma_o(m)$, which consists of only the *relevant* requests between a non-server processor p_i and its nearest server p_j for object o. Without loss of generality, we assume that ADRW algorithm and an OPT algorithm, which also satisfies the t-availability constraint, initially start with the same allocation scheme of object o, $S(o)$. Using Phase Partition Heuristic 4, σ_o will be partitioned into several phases, $P(0)$, $P(1)$, $P(2)$, ..., $P(r)$, belonging to either RSS or WSS. Referring to (4.52) and (4.56), we can obtain that the total servicing cost of a RSS $P(i)$ in σ_o is,

$$COST_{ADRW}(P(i)) \leq \lceil \frac{C_d}{C_c + 2C_d} k \rceil (C_c + C_d) \tag{5.27}$$

and the total servicing cost of a WSS $P(j)$ in σ_o is,

$$COST_{ADRW}(P(j)) \leq \lceil \frac{C_c + C_d}{C_c + 2C_d} k \rceil C_d + |P(j)| C_d \tag{5.28}$$

Therefore, we can obtain that the total servicing cost of σ_o using ADRW algorithm is given by,

$$\begin{aligned} COST_{ADRW}(\sigma_o) &= \sum_i \{COST_{ADRW}(P(i)), P(i) \text{ is a RSS}\} \\ &\quad + \sum_j \{COST_{ADRW}(P(j)), P(j) \text{ is a WSS}\} \\ &\leq (N_{raw} + 1) \left[\lceil \frac{C_d}{C_c + 2C_d} k \rceil (C_c + C_d) + \lceil \frac{C_c + C_d}{C_c + 2C_d} k \rceil C_d \right] \\ &\quad + \sum_j \{|P(j)| C_d, P(j) \text{ is a WSS}\} \end{aligned} \tag{5.29}$$

---

[15]The proof follows similar steps used in the prooof of Theorem 4.4.

Similarly, for the OPT algorithm, the total servicing cost of σ_o is given by,

$$COST_{OPT}(\sigma_o) \geq N_{raw}C_d + \sum_j \{|P(j)|\frac{(t-1)C_d}{t}, P(j) \text{ is a WSS}\} \tag{5.30}$$

The difference between (5.29) and (5.30) is,

$$\begin{aligned}
&COST_{ADRW}(\sigma_o) - COST_{OPT}(\sigma_o) \\
&\leq (N_{raw}+1)\left[\lceil\frac{C_d}{C_c+2C_d}k\rceil(C_c+C_d) + \lceil\frac{C_c+C_d}{C_c+2C_d}k\rceil C_d\right] - N_{raw}C_d \\
&\qquad + \frac{C_d}{t}\sum_j \{|P(j)|, P(j) \text{ is a WSS}\} \\
&\leq (N_{raw}+1)\left[\frac{2(C_c+C_d)C_d}{C_c+2C_d}k + C_c + 2C_d\right] - N_{raw}C_d \\
&\qquad + \frac{C_d}{t}\sum_j \{|P(j)|, P(j) \text{ is a WSS}\} \\
&= N_{raw}C_d\left[\frac{2(C_c+C_d)}{C_c+2C_d}k - 1 + \frac{C_c+2C_d}{C_d}\right] \\
&\quad + \left[\frac{2(C_c+C_d)C_d}{C_c+2C_d}k + C_c + 2C_d\right] + \frac{C_d}{t}\sum_j \{|P(j)|, P(j) \text{ is a WSS}\} \\
&\leq \left[\frac{2(C_c+C_d)}{C_c+2C_d}k - 1 + \frac{C_c+2C_d}{C_d}\right] COST_{OPT}(\sigma_o) \\
&\qquad + \left[\frac{2(C_c+C_d)C_d}{C_c+2C_d}k + C_c + 2C_d\right]
\end{aligned} \tag{5.31}$$

Therefore, we can clearly observe that our ADRW algorithm is $\left[(1+\frac{C_c}{C_c+2C_d})k + \frac{C_c+2C_d}{C_d}\right]$-competitive in a MCE and hence the proof. ■

The competitive ratio of ADRW algorithm in Theorem 5.6, denoted as R_{MCE}, can be rewritten as follows.

$$R_{MCE} = k + 2 + \frac{C_c}{C_c+2C_d}k + \frac{C_c}{C_d} \tag{5.32}$$

Let $\alpha = C_d/C_c$, we have

$$R_{MCE} = k + 2 + \frac{k}{1+2\alpha} + \frac{1}{\alpha} \tag{5.33}$$

It can be observed that R_{MCE} decreases when α increases, which implies that the larger the ratio between a data-message transferring cost and a control-message transferring cost, the better ADRW algorithm performs in a MCE. Thus, we can obtain that the minimal competitive ratio of ADRW algorithm is $(k+2)$ in a MCE when α tends to infinity and $t > 1$.

6. Concluding Remarks

In this chapter, we considered the OMP in DDBSs exclusively for MCEs. There have been a number of research efforts in recent years that address the problems of data management in DDBSs in MCEs. A thorough and cohesive overview of recent advances in wireless and mobile data management was provided in [PS98]. The focus of this book is on the impact of mobile computing on data management beyond the networking level. In [DH94], an operational system model in a MCE was introduced and issues of designing efficient distributed algorithms in a MCE were discussed. The work in [WHH98] evaluated various communication styles operated in conventional distributed systems concerning about MCEs.

For servicing requests that arrive at a DDBS in a MCE, we have modified the cost models of SA, DA, DWM, and ADRW algorithms which are presented in Chapter 4, and extended their competitive analysis to a MCE. The analysis shows that algorithms that are in place for a SCE can be tuned to suit the conditions of a MCE. Table 5.2 summarizes the results of Chapters 4 and 5, which in a way compares the competitive ratios derived for the respective environments.

The results summarized in Table 5.2 provides a considerable flexibility in the choice of an algorithm for a particular environment. We observe that the SA algorithm, which is competitive in a SCE is no longer competitive in a MCE. For DA algorithm, the competitive ratios in a SCE and a MCE are different. However, the competitive ratio of the DWM algorithm remains unchanged for both the SCE and MCE. Further we note that the competitive ratio of the DA and DWM algorithms are identical in a MCE. Finally, we observe that in a MCE, SA algorithm is not competitive for all values of t whereas ADRW algorithm is not competitive only for the case when $t = 1$. Hence, we realize that the competitive feature of an on-line algorithm may vary when the system environments are subject to changes. Furthermore, we also modified DWM algorithm to RDDWM algorithm to satisfy the real-time requirements. Using competitive analysis, we quantified the performance of RDDWM algorithm under two different extreme conditions, i.e., when

Table 5.2. Competitive ratios of SA, DA, DWM, and ADRW algorithm in a SCE and a MCE

Algorithms	SCE	MCE
SA	$1 + C_c + C_d$	Not competitive
DA	$2 + C_c$	$2 + 2\frac{C_c}{C_d}$
DWM	$2 + 2\frac{C_c}{C_d}$	$2 + 2\frac{C_c}{C_d}$
ADRW	$\left[k + \frac{1 + C_c + 2C_d}{C_d} + \frac{C_d}{t}\right]$	Not competitive when $t = 1$ $\left[(1 + \frac{C_c}{C_c + 2C_d})k + \frac{C_c + 2C_d}{C_d}\right]$ when $t > 1$

the deadline periods of all the requests are sufficiently long ($\geq \tau$) and when the deadline periods of all the requests are very short ($= 1$).

Thus depending on the respective values of C_d, C_c, and C_{io}, one may prefer to choose the algorithms for minimizing the total cost in the respective environments. However, the wider choice on algorithms is the demand from the underlying application domain that truly restricts the choice. For instance, most of the time-critical transactions in a DDBS prefer the use of the RDDWM algorithm when compared to the DWM algorithm or ADRW algorithm. In fact, most of the transactions involved with applications such as banking, air-line reservation systems, etc, may directly use RDDWM algorithm in SCEs and MCEs. The design and analysis presented in Chapters 4 and 5 show conclusively the power of competitive analysis in deriving the bounds of performance of the on-line algorithms.

Chapter 6

OBJECT MANAGEMENT IN REGULAR NETWORK TOPOLOGIES

So far we have been describing the OMP in arbitrary networks under a specific objective, namely the (monetary) cost optimization. Chapters 4 and 5 have clearly exposed certain models that are suited for stationary and mobile computing environments and shown how the performance is influenced by several parameters. There have been numerous studies in this area of DDBS on a variety of issues and it is beyond the scope of this book to deal with all of them. However, what has not been so far mentioned is on the performance quantification for regular or known topologies. Conducting performance studies on known topologies is always a natural interest to implementation specialists and researchers. In this chapter, we will present two specific examples on known topologies, i.e., (a). star networks and (b). multi-level generic tree networks. We use the parameters defined in Chapters 4 and 5 to analyze the performance and our objective remains the same namely, the minimization of the monetary cost involved in servicing the requests. However, it may be noted that the parameters influencing the performance may differ on different topologies as each case is a special case. Also, it depends on the underlying assumptions made.

In this Chapter, we consider the object replication issues in star networks in a SCE domain and the object migration issues[1] in generic multi-level tree networks in a MCE domain. We present a randomized on-line algorithm for each of the above mentioned domains, referred to as *Randomized Object Replication* (ROR) algorithm and *Randomized Object*

[1]Refer to Chapters 1 and 2 for the details of object replication and object migration issues in DDBSs.

Migration (ROM) algorithm, respectively. We use competitive analysis[2] to demonstrate the differences in performance of these two algorithms. Further, it may be noted that the competitive analysis conducted in Chapters 4 and 5 have specifically used phase partition technique to quantify the competitive ratios. As mentioned in these chapters, it is possible to use other competitive techniques to derive these bounds. Thus, in this chapter we take this opportunity to use potential function method (Refer to Chapter 3) to quantify the performance, as readers who are looking for the applicability of potential function method may find this exercise useful.

1. ROR Algorithm in Star Networks

Star topology is one of the widely used structures in data communication systems, especially in LANs and WANs. An illustration of a star network is shown in Figure 1.3(d). In a star network, all *peripheral nodes* (workstations or other devices) are directly connected to a common *central computer*[3]. The central computer is usually a computer with large computation/memory capacity such as a minicomputer or a mainframe. Workstations can only communicate each other by accessing the central computer. As such, a star network configuration is appropriate for systems that demand centralized control. The star network was predominant in the 1960s and early 1970s because it was easy to control. The main advantages of a star network are as follows.

- Easy to add/remove workstations to/from the network.
- Easy to diagnose link problems. In a star network, each workstation has its own individual cable connecting to the central computer. A cable failure will only isolate the workstation that it links to the central computer. All the other workstations will continue to function normally, except that they will not be able to communicate with the isolated workstation.
- Easy to handle the security control and concurrency control due to the centralizing nature.

However, it should be noted that if the central computer goes down, the entire network will exhibit a degraded performance or may fail completely.

In this section, we consider the object replication problem in a star topology network in a SCE. The replication problem was first defined in

[2]Refer to Chapter 3 for the competitiveness of a randomized on-line algorithm.
[3]In some star networks, the central computer can also operate as a workstation.

[BS89] in which an object (page) is read-only. In other words, a write request is disallowed in the replication problem. The VOR and VOD applications mentioned in Chapter 2 are such examples. The object replication problem can be considered as a *finite game* where replicas of an object can be made in the system and never be discarded. We have to determine (in an on-line fashion) which nodes should have the replicas in their respective local memories and the objective is to minimize the over all servicing cost incurred. When all the nodes in the system have the copy of the object, the game comes to a completion. This object replication problem is also addressed in the literature [ABF93, K93, AK94, FS00].

Formally we describe the object replication problem in a star network (undirected) as follows. Without loss of generality, we assume that there are n nodes, $p_0, p_1, ..., p_{n-1}$, in the system, where p_0 is the central computer and p_i $(1 \leq i \leq n-1)$ is a workstation, and the distance between any workstation and the central computer is 1. We generally concentrate on one particular object o and initially, only the central computer has the object, i.e., $IA_o = \{p_0\}$. We now describe the ROR algorithm as follows.

ROR Algorithm (for star networks): When servicing a read request from node p_i $(0 \leq i \leq n-1)$, if p_i holds a copy of object o, then the request will be satisfied locally. On the other hand, if p_i does not have object o, then p_i[4] will obtain object o from the central computer and with probability $\frac{1}{2}$, the central computer will consider this read request as a saving-read request[5].

The cost model for ROR algorithm to serve a read request in a SCE is almost the same as defined in Equation (4.23). The main difference is that, in DWM algorithm, CCU determines a saving-read request based on the request sequence in a request window, whereas in ROR algorithm, the central computer will consider a read request from a non-data-processor as a saving-read request with probability $\frac{1}{2}$.

1.1 Analysis of ROR Algorithm

We now quantify the performance of ROR algorithm in a SCE by using the potential function method introduced in Chapter 3. The competitive ratio is given by the following theorem.

[4]In this case, p_i must be a workstation.

[5]Considering each request equivalent to a Bernoulli trial with probabilities of non-saving-read and saving-read requests as $\frac{1}{2}$ each.

Theorem 6.1: The ROR algorithm is $(C_c + \frac{3}{2})$-competitive in a SCE against any oblivious adversary[6].

Proof: Let us consider an arbitrary request sequence generated by an oblivious adversary ADV, $\sigma_o = \sigma_o(1), \sigma_o(2), ..., \sigma_o(m)$, where $\sigma_o(i)$ $(1 \leq i \leq m)$ denotes the i-th request in σ_o. As mentioned in Chapter 3, by using the potential function method to prove Theorem 6.1, we shall construct a non-negative potential function[7] Φ, such that the following inequality holds for any request $\sigma_o(i)$ in σ_o.

$$\mathbf{E}[COST_{ROR}(\sigma_o(i))] + \mathbf{E}[\Phi(i) - \Phi(i-1)] \leq (C_c + \frac{3}{2})COST_{ADV}(\sigma_o(i)) \qquad (6.1)$$

where $\Phi(i)$ denotes the value of the potential function after ROR and ADV serve the request $\sigma_o(i)$. Summing up Equation (6.1) for all i $(1 \leq i \leq m)$, we will obtain,

$$\mathbf{E}[COST_{ROR}(\sigma_o)] + \mathbf{E}[\Phi(m) - \Phi(0)] \leq (C_c + \frac{3}{2})COST_{ADV}(\sigma_o) \quad (6.2)$$

which implies that the ROR algorithm is $(C_c + \frac{3}{2})$-competitive. Thus, it remains to construct the potential function Φ and verify that the inequality in Equation (6.1) holds for every request in σ_o.

We now construct the potential function as follows.

$$\Phi = 2C_d|A'_o - A_o| \qquad (6.3)$$

where A'_o and A_o denote the allocation scheme of object o by using ADV and ROR to serve σ_o, repectively, and $A'_o - A_o$ denotes the set of processors in A'_o but not in A_o. Without loss of generality, we assume that the ADV and ROR start with the same object allocation scheme, i.e., $A'_o = A_o = \{p_0\}$, where p_0 is the central computer.

Upon servicing an arbitrary request $\sigma_o(i)$ $(1 \leq i \leq m)$ from processor p_j $(0 \leq j \leq n-1)$, we have to consider following distinct cases.

Case 1: $p_j \in A_o$

In this case, $\sigma_o(i)$ will be satisfied locally by ROR algorithm, and thus

$$COST_{ROR}(\sigma_o(i)) = 1 \qquad (6.4)$$

[6] Refer to the working style of an oblivious adversary in Chapter 3.
[7] Typically, we will choose a potential function such that $\Phi(0) = 0$.

Now consider the oblivious adversary ADV. If $p_j \in A'_o$, then $COST_{ADV}(\sigma_o(i)) = 1$ and the value of the potential function remains unchanged. On the other hand, if $p_j \notin A'_o$, then at least one I/O cost and one data-message transferring cost will be incurred for ADV to serve $\sigma_o(i)$. Thus, $COST_{ADV}(\sigma_o(i)) \geq 1 + C_d$. Further, it can be observed that the value of the potential function remains unchanged, no matter whether or not ADV considers $\sigma_o(i)$ as a saving-read request.

From the above description, we obtain that

$$\begin{aligned} & COST_{ROR}(\sigma_o(i)) + (\Phi(i) - \Phi(i-1)) \\ = \;& 1 < (C_c + \frac{3}{2})COST_{ADV}(\sigma_o(i)) \end{aligned} \tag{6.5}$$

Case 2: $p_j \notin A_o$

In this case, if ROR algorithm does not consider $\sigma_o(i)$ as a saving-read request, then the servicing cost is $(1+C_c+C_d)$ units. Otherwise, the servicing cost would be $(2 + C_c + C_d)$ units. Thus,

$$\begin{aligned} \mathbf{E}[COST_{ROR}(\sigma_o(i))] &= \frac{1}{2}(1 + C_c + C_d) + \frac{1}{2}(2 + C_c + C_d) \\ &= \frac{3}{2} + C_c + C_d \end{aligned} \tag{6.6}$$

For the ADV, as usual, we need to consider following two cases.

Case 2(a): $p_j \in A'_o$

If $p_j \in A'_o$, then $COST_{ADV}(\sigma_o(i)) = 1$. Further, with probability $\frac{1}{2}$, p_j will be added into A_o by ROR algorithm, thus

$$\mathbf{E}[\Phi(i) - \Phi(i-1)] = \frac{1}{2}[0 + (-2C_d)] = -C_d$$

Thus, we can obtain that

$$\begin{aligned} & \mathbf{E}[COST_{ROR}(\sigma_o(i))] + \mathbf{E}[(\Phi(i) - \Phi(i-1))] \\ \leq \;& (C_c + \frac{3}{2}) \leq (C_c + \frac{3}{2})COST_{ADV}(\sigma_o(i)) \end{aligned} \tag{6.7}$$

Case 2(b): $p_j \notin A'_o$

In this case, if $p_j \notin A'_o$ after ADV serves $\sigma_o(i)$, then $COST_{ADV} \geq 1+C_d$, and the value of the potential function remains unchanged. It is clear that

$$\begin{aligned} & \mathbf{E}[COST_{ROR}(\sigma_o(i))] + \mathbf{E}[(\Phi(i) - \Phi(i-1))] \\ = \;& (\frac{3}{2} + C_c + C_d) \leq (C_c + \frac{3}{2})COST_{ADV}(\sigma_o(i)) \end{aligned} \tag{6.8}$$

On the other hand, if $p_j \in A'_o$ after ADV serves $\sigma_o(i)$, then $COST_{ADV} \geq 2 + C_d$ and $\mathbf{E}[\Phi(i) - \Phi(i-1)] = \frac{1}{2}[0 + 2C_d] = C_d$. Thus, we obtain that

$$\begin{aligned} &\mathbf{E}[COST_{ROR}(\sigma_o(i))] + \mathbf{E}[(\Phi(i) - \Phi(i-1))] \\ &= (\frac{3}{2} + C_c + 2C_d) \leq (C_c + \frac{3}{2})COST_{ADV}(\sigma_o(i)) \quad (6.9) \end{aligned}$$

Thus we can verify that the inequality in Equation (6.1) holds for every request in σ_o, and hence the proof. ∎

Remarks: It may be noted that the choice of the above potential function defined in Equation (6.3) is purely based on the working style of ROR algorithm. It may be possible to choose other functions, however, they must adhere to the working style of ROR and must account all the possibilities as done above. Also, it may be observed that any change in potential function with our choice is in steps of $2C_d$ at most while servicing each request. Further, to ease the comparison, the parameter C_d is figuring in our potential function since $C_d > C_c$. Finally, in this section, although our ROR algorithm considers a uniform star network[8], it can be easily extended to a non-uniform star network, and the competitive ratio remains unchanged.

2. ROM Algorithm in Multi-level Generic Tree Networks

A multi-level tree topology is basically a hierarchical configuration. Figure 1.3(c) illustrates a multi-level generic tree topology. Essentially, a tree network consists of a *root node* (the uppermost node), which is an *ancestor* of all the other nodes in the system. Each node is either a *leaf* or an *internal node.* An internal node has one or more *child* nodes and is called the *parent* of its child nodes. A star network introduced in Section 1 can be considered as a single-level tree network, where the central computer represents the root and all the workstations represent the children of the root. Further, in a tree network, a node can only directly communicate with its parent or children and thus it should be noted that there is only one path between any two nodes in the system.

As mentioned in our previous chapters, if objects are writable and there are multi-copies of an object existing in the system, then object consistency control becomes a crucial issue to deal with. One way to handle this is to assume that there exists only one copy of each object in the entire distributed system at any time instant. Thus, read and write

[8]The distance between any workstation and the central computer is 1.

requests arriving at the system must all access the node that holds the copy of the requested object. Black and Sleator defined this problem as the migration problem in [BS89]. In this section, we consider an object migration problem in a multi-level generic (undirected) tree network in a MCE. Our objective is to devise sophisticated strategies to determine a *vantage node* that should hold a copy (only copy) of an object so as to minimize the communication cost in servicing the arriving read/write request sequence.

Formally, we are given a multi-level generic (undirected) tree network with n nodes, $p_0, p_1, ..., p_{n-1}$, where p_0 is the root of the tree network. We denote the distance between any two nodes, p_i and p_j $(0 \leq i, j \leq n-1)$, as $d(p_i, p_j)$. As usual, we concentrate on one particular object o in the system and describe ROM algorithm proposed below to solve our problem.

ROM Algorithm (for multi-level generic tree networks): When servicing a read request from node p_i, if p_i holds the copy of object o, then the request will be satisfied locally without incurring any cost[9]. On the other hand, if p_i does not have object o, then p_i will send a control-message to the node p_j that holds the object to inform about the read request and obtain object o from p_j, incurring $d(p_i, p_j)(C_c + C_d)$ units of cost. Finally, with probability $\frac{1}{2}$, p_j will send a control-message to p_i to inform about the object migration, incurring $d(p_i, p_j)C_c$ units of cost. As a result, p_i will save object o into its local memory and p_j will delete object o from its local memory without incurring any cost.

Similarly, when servicing a write request from node p_i, if p_i holds the copy of object o, then the request will be satisfied locally without incurring any cost. Otherwise, p_i will send the new version of object o to the node p_j that holds the object, incurring $d(p_i, p_j)C_d$ units of cost. Finally, with probability $\frac{1}{2}$, p_j will send a control-message to p_i to inform about the object migration, incurring $d(p_i, p_j)C_c$ units of cost. As a result, p_i will save object o into its local memory and p_j will delete object o from its local memory without incurring any cost.

2.1 Analysis of ROM Algorithm

We now quantify the performance of ROM algorithm in a MCE by deriving its competitive ratio using the potential function method.

[9] $C_{io} = 0$ as per our assumption in a MCE.

Theorem 6.2: The ROM algorithm is 5-competitive in a MCE against any adaptive on-line adversary[10].

Proof: Let us consider an arbitrary request sequence generated by an adaptive on-line adversary ADV, $\sigma_o = \sigma_o(1), \sigma_o(2), ..., \sigma_o(m)$, where $\sigma_o(i)$ $(1 \leq i \leq m)$ denotes the i-th request in σ_o. We now construct the potential function as follows.

$$\Phi = 5d(p_{ROM}, p_{ADV})C_d \tag{6.10}$$

where p_{ROM} and p_{ADV} denote the node that holds object o by using ROM and ADV to serve σ_o, respectively. Without loss of generality, we assume that initially $p_{ROM} = p_{ADV} = p_0$, where p_0 is the root of the tree network.

As mentioned before, in order to prove Theorem 6.2, we shall show that the following inequality holds for any request $\sigma_o(i)$ in σ_o.

$$\begin{aligned} \mathbf{E}[COST_{ROM}(\sigma_o(i))] + \mathbf{E}[\Phi(i) - \Phi(i-1)] \\ \leq 5\mathbf{E}[COST_{ADV}(\sigma_o(i))] \end{aligned} \tag{6.11}$$

Without loss of generality, we assume that ROM algorithm and ADV serve each request in σ_o simultaneously. Our proof proceeds by analyzing separately the changes in Φ after servicing each request due to the object migration being carried out (if need arises) by the ADV and due to the service of a request by both ROM and ADV, assuming that the ADV does not implement the object migration. Thus, we have accounted all the operations in servicing a request for both ROM algorithm and ADV.

For servicing a request $\sigma_o(i)$ $(1 \leq i \leq m)$ from node p_j $(0 \leq j \leq n-1)$, we first analyze the case that ADV migrates the object.

ADV migrates the object: The ADV migrates object o from node p_{ADV} to node p'_{ADV}. In this case, we know that,

$$COST_{ADV}(\sigma_o(i)) \geq d(p_{ADV}, p'_{ADV})C_d$$
$$COST_{ROM}(\sigma_o(i)) = 0$$

and since the distance function in a tree network satisfies the triangle inequality[11], we obtain that,

$$\begin{aligned} \Phi(i) - \Phi(i-1) &= 5[d(p_{ROM}, p'_{ADV}) - d(p_{ROM}, p_{ADV})]C_d \\ &\leq 5d(p_{ADV}, p'_{ADV})C_d \\ &= 5COST_{ADV}(\sigma_o(i)) - COST_{ROM}(\sigma_o(i)) \end{aligned}$$

[10]Refer to the working style of an adaptive on-line adversary in Chapter 3.
[11]Refer to the Equation (3.1) in Section 1 of Chapter 3.

Alternatively,

$$COST_{ROM}(\sigma_o(i)) + [\Phi(i) - \Phi(i-1)] \leq 5COST_{ADV}(\sigma_o(i)) \quad (6.12)$$

Thus, we can observe that the inequality in Equation (6.11) holds in this case.

ROM and ADV serve the request[12]: In this case, we have to consider the following distinct cases.

Case 1: $\sigma_o(i)$ is a read request

In this case, if node p_j holds object o by using ROM algorithm, i.e., $p_j = p_{ROM}$, then $COST_{ROM}(\sigma_o(i)) = 0$ and the value of the potential function remains unchanged. On the other hand, if $p_j \neq p_{ROM}$, then

$$\begin{aligned}\mathbf{E}[COST_{ROM}(\sigma_o(i))] &= d(p_{ROM}, p_j)(C_c + C_d) + \frac{1}{2}d(p_{ROM}, p_j)C_c \\ &= d(p_{ROM}, p_j)C_d + \frac{3}{2}d(p_{ROM}, p_j)C_c \\ &\leq \frac{5}{2}d(p_{ROM}, p_j)C_d\end{aligned}$$

$$COST_{ADV}(\sigma_o(i)) \geq d(p'_{ADV}, p_j)C_d$$

$$\mathbf{E}[\Phi(i) - \Phi(i-1)] = \frac{5}{2}[d(p'_{ADV}, p_j) - d(p'_{ADV}, p_{ROM})]C_d$$

Thus, again using the triangle inequality, we obtain that

$$\begin{aligned}&\mathbf{E}[COST_{ROM}(\sigma_o(i))] + \mathbf{E}[\Phi(i) - \Phi(i-1)] \\ \leq\ & \frac{5}{2}[d(p_{ROM}, p_j) - d(p'_{ADV}, p_{ROM}) + d(p'_{ADV}, p_j)]C_d \\ \leq\ & 5d(p'_{ADV}, p_j)C_d \\ =\ & 5COST_{ADV}(\sigma_o(i)) \qquad (6.13)\end{aligned}$$

Case 2: $\sigma_o(i)$ is a write request

In this case, if $p_j = p_{ROM}$, then $COST_{ROM}(\sigma_o(i)) = 0$ and the value of the potential function remains unchanged. On the other hand, if $p_j \neq p_{ROM}$, then

$$\mathbf{E}[COST_{ROM}(\sigma_o(i))] = d(p_{ROM}, p_j)C_d + \frac{1}{2}d(p_{ROM}, p_j)C_c$$

[12] Assuming that ADV does not carry out the object migration.

$$
\begin{aligned}
& < & \frac{5}{2}d(p_{ROM}, p_j)C_d \\
COST_{ADV}(\sigma_o(i)) & \geq & d(p'_{ADV}, p_j)C_d \\
\mathbf{E}[\Phi(i) - \Phi(i-1)] & = & \frac{5}{2}[d(p'_{ADV}, p_j) - d(p'_{ADV}, p_{ROM})]C_d
\end{aligned}
$$

Thus, referring to Equation (6.13), we obtain that

$$
\begin{aligned}
\mathbf{E}[COST_{ROM}(\sigma_o(i))] + \mathbf{E}[\Phi(i) - \Phi(i-1)) \\
\leq 5COST_{ADV}(\sigma_o(i))
\end{aligned}
\quad (6.14)
$$

Based on the above analysis, we observe that the inequality in Equation (6.11) holds for any request in σ_o. Hence the proof. ■

3. Concluding Remarks

In this chapter, we considered issues (object replication and object migration) of OMP in DDBSs with regular topologies. We have proposed a randomized on-line algorithm for both object replication issues in star networks in SCEs and object migration issues in multi-level generic tree networks in MCEs, i.e., ROR algorithm and ROM algorithm, respectively. Using potential function method, we quantified and proved that ROR algorithm is $(C_c + \frac{3}{2})$-competitive against any oblivious adversary and ROM algorithm is 5-competitive against any adaptive on-line adversary.

Object replication and migration issues are extensively studied problems in the literature. In terms of competitiveness, the object replication issues are more complex than the object migration issues [BRICS96]. On-line replication algorithms achieving a constant competitive ratio are only known for specific network topologies, such as tree networks, fully connected uniform networks[13] and ring networks. For tree networks and fully-connected uniform networks, the best deterministic on-line replication algorithm is 2-competitive given in [BS89]. Research contributions in [LRWY99] and [AK94] considered the object replication problem for the same network topologies and derived optimal randomized algorithms which are approximately 1.58-competitive against oblivious adversaries. In [AK94] the authors also present a randomized replication algorithm for the above network topologies that is 2-competitive against adaptive on-line adversaries and subsequently, it was shown in [LRWY99] that no randomized algorithm for replication problem can be better

[13]Networks in which any two nodes are connected by an edge of identical length, as shown in Figure 1.3(e).

than 2-competitive against any adaptive on-line adversary. Furthermore, [AK94] considered the replication problem in ring networks and presented general techniques that transform c-competitive algorithms for tree networks into $2c$-competitive algorithms for ring networks. As a result, [AK94] gave two randomized on-line replication algorithm for ring networks that are 3.16-competitive against oblivious adversaries and 4-competitive against adaptive on-line adversaries, respectively. Recently, [FS00] presented a new randomized replication algorithm for ring networks which is 2.37297-competitive against oblivious adversaries, improving the best previous result of 3.16 in [AK94]. They also showed that no randomized replication algorithm is better than 1.75037-competitive on ring networks. Lastly, for general (arbitrary) networks, it was shown in [BFR92] that no deterministic or randomized on-line replication algorithm can achieve a competitive ratio smaller than $O(logn)$, where n is the number of nodes in the network.

For object migration, [BS89] gave optimal 3-competitive deterministic algorithms for tree networks and full connected uniform networks. Optimal $(2 + \frac{1}{2D})$-competitive randomized object migration algorithms against oblivious adversaries for fully-connected uniform networks are dealt in [LRWY99] and for tree networks these can be found in [CLRW93]. For general networks, [ABF93] gave the first deterministic on-line migration algorithm with a competitive ratio of 7 and later [BCI97] gave an approximately 4.086-competitive deterministic algorithm for the object migration problem. Work in [CLRW93] obtained a general lower bound, approximate 3.148, for deterministic migration algorithm for some network topologies. Further, for general networks, [W94] obtained a 3-competitive randomized object migration algorithm against an adaptive on-line adversary and a $(1+\phi)$-competitive randomized object migration algorithm against an oblivious adversary, where $\phi \approx 1.62$ is the golden ratio. Using the results[14] in [BBKTW94], this leads to a $3(1 + \phi)$-competitive deterministic algorithm for the object migration problem on arbitrary networks.

Thus, as shown above, there has been an immense interest in the object replication and migration problems in distributed systems. Designing efficient object replication and migration algorithms depends on the assumptions of underlying applications such as network topologies and cost models. There are several interesting open problems such as designing competitive (either deterministic or randomized) replication algorithm for arbitrary networks, obtaining a randomized migration al-

[14]Theorems 3.1 and 3.2 in our Chapter 3.

gorithm with optimal competitive ratio for arbitrary networks. The content in this chapter serves as a basis in providing the underlying concept and two practically important examples for interested readers to attempt some of the above-mentioned open problems.

Chapter 7

FUTURE DIRECTIONS

Due to the need for DDBSs that has grown in many facets of our lives, as mentioned in Chapter 1, DDBSs are finding their way into a wider range and previously inconceivable application domains such as medical diagnostics, computer-aided manufacturing, etc. Designing an intelligent and efficient OMP in such a DDBS always poses considerable challenges to the system designers and implementation specialists. For different application domains[1], the requirements of OMPs such as system security/reliability and object consistency may be different and thus the performance measurements of OMPs may significantly vary (Refer to Section 5 of Chapter 1). Recently, the rapid proliferation of mobile devices and their utility in several application domains also pose several other challenges for DDBS applications. As mobile bandwidth availability is an inherent constraint to several applications, service providers are expected to provide with a guaranteed and reliable service infrastructure to the users interacting over mobile networks. DDBS applications over mobile networks will be promising and a viable technology only when service providers put their best effort to maximize the resource utilization and at the same time proposing a very cost-effective solution. The strategies we have put in place to demonstrate the cost analysis in MCEs clearly reflect the fact that mobile technology is indeed promising, as we can directly compare the competitive ratios between identical applications operating in SCEs and MCEs. From service providers perspective, monetary cost is a parameter of direct and relevant interest and the analysis covered in this book indeed captures this metric. Of course, the

[1]Refer to Chapter 2 for more details.

cost is a function of several components which are not merely influenced by strategies that one may design but also depending on the availability and use of resources in the network.

All the analysis in the Chapters 4, 5, and 6 are directly suitable for the existing technological trends. As number of request transactions handled in a DDBS is enormous, one of the unavoidable issues to address is the amount of storage space expected to be available at each site in the network. While in a distributed system the storage can be spread over several sites, to some extent replication and allocation algorithms take care in managing the space available with the system. On the other hand, in the case of centralized control systems (such as star networks/single-level tree networks), it is expected that the database storing the objects must be sufficiently large. In either case, one would expect that constraints imposed by storage space availability cannot be circumvented as it indeed becomes one of the deciding factors for superior performance. However, with current technological trends and promises, cheaper and cheaper solutions make this issue virtually non-existent. For instance, one to two decades back, storage was indeed an imperative issue to be considered in the design as it will ultimately reflect in the number of customers/requests that can be entertained at a time. With the current day storage technology, storing several Terabytes of data is a trivial or easy-to-take-care issue. Although there were several studies attempted to show the effect of limited memory storage capacity on the performance, these are much akin to systems with respect to paging and file management applications (exclusively for small-scale systems). Some useful references closer in this context include the studies presented in [AK95, BFR92, TTBSJ00], to quote a few.

As a side note, we want to stress that the issue of storage becomes more meaningful to consider depending on the underlying applications. In Chapter 2, we have identified certain application domains that share several common features in designing OMPs. Among these, applications, such as VOD and/or VOR on network, demand a very large storage infrastructure, especially when handling movie-on-demand requests. The size of an object in this case may be rather large (100s of Mega-Bytes or several Giga-bytes magnitude), and hence the limited storage space availability becomes a bottleneck. To handle such applications, designing efficient and high-fidelity replacement algorithms, which in a way is a part of OMP, becomes a challenging task. For instance, a multimedia object stored in a node may be evicted to reserve sufficient space for another object that will be replicated in the node. Thus, when the memory capacity is taken into account, efficient memory replacement algorithms play a key role. The algorithms such as LRU, LFU, and

FIFO designed for paging problems (Refer to Chapter 3) can be easily applied to this area. However, for a large class of DDBS applications, the storage of data remains a secondary issue as system storage technology is so advanced at present, especially in handling database applications. Moreover the size of the data or the object that is considered in such environments is several order magnitudes less when compared to objects in multimedia or web applications. Thus the analysis presented in our Chapters 4 through 6 neither warrant an explicit mention of the storage space availability nor the object size.

In this book, we exposed the reader to highlight the usefulness of the competitive analysis technique(s) that are in place in the DDBS domain. Although in Chapter 2 we have considered several application domains that share a common set of issues in the design of OMP, our emphasis was focused on design and analysis of strategies to minimize the overall (monetary) cost of servicing user requests in a DDBS domain. Competitive analysis serves as a powerful analytical tool in quantifying the performance of on-line algorithms. We introduced the fundamental concepts of competitive analysis by using a well-known on-line paging algorithm (LRU) in Chapter 3. As our focus was to devise strategies that can minimize the associated (monetary) cost of serving requests that arrive at a DDBS, we considered two domains that are in place - *Stationary Computing Environment* (SCE) domain and *Mobile Computing Environment* (MCE) domain. We emphasized the issues (object allocation and replication) of OMP in the application domains in SCEs in Chapter 4. We proposed four deterministic on-line object allocation and replication algorithms (one static algorithm (SA) and three dynamic algorithms (DA, DWM, ADRW), or in other words, one centralized algorithm (DWM) and three decentralized algorithms (SA, DA, ADRW)) and we have analyzed their performance. Further, we extended the competitive analysis of these four algorithm to the application domains in MCEs in Chapter 5. In the application domains of *Real-time Distributed Database systems* (RTDDBSs) in a MCE, we have modified the cost model and window mechanism of DWM algorithm to RDDWM algorithm to satisfy the real-time requirements of on-line requests. Competitive analysis was chosen to quantify the performance of RDDWM algorithm under two extreme conditions. It may be noted that the DDBSs considered in Chapters 4 and 5 are symmetric networks, as the cost of transferring an object between any two nodes and the cost of passing control-messages are always constants (C_d and C_c, respectively). However, it appears possible to extend our designs and competitive analysis for non-symmetric networks.

Further, in order to satisfy the t-availability constraint of an object o in the system, there is a server set $S(o)$ ($|S(o)| = t$) in each of the algorithms presented in Chapters 4 and 5. Though obtaining an optimal server set $S(o)$ for an object o in a general network may be a *NP*-complete[2] problem, system designers are expected to choose those processors, which have larger processing capacities and/or higher reliabilities in the system, as the servers of an object. This is of course, an implementation level issue to be considered.

As emphasized in Chapters 1 and 2 that OMP involves object migration and replication, it would be curious to sense how these issues affect the system performance. In order to clearly understand the impact of these issues, we have considered some standard regular topologies in Chapter 6. Typically, we present a randomized on-line algorithm for object replication in star networks/single-level tree networks in SCEs and a randomized on-line algorithm for object migration in multi-level generic tree networks in MCEs. Here too, we used competitive analysis to quantify the performance of these two randomized on-line algorithms. Finally, closely related previous works available in the literature on OMPs in regular topologies are enumerated.

The contributions made in this book and their applicability are multifold. Firstly, the importance of identifying issues that must be in place for a design of OMP for a particular application is stressed. This can be seen from Chapter 2. Secondly, we have highlighted how each of the chosen issues critically influences the system performance. It is clearly demonstrated how identical set of issues may take different roles in two different environments. For instance, with more-or-less same operational style in a SCE and a MCE, the performance of algorithms seem to be radically different. Thus, how one manages the request handling part (such as request submission phase, concurrency control, etc), object replication, etc, depends on the design process and carefully identifying the influencing issues. The contributions made in this book are directly useful to algorithm designers, system designers, operation research and modeling specialists, and finally to implementation specialists. Finally, although the major focus in this book was on designing OMPs in DDBSs, the concepts and issues seem to be applicable to a wide variety of application domains as exemplified in Chapter 2. For example, the DWM algorithm can be easily presented in a VOR system, where the VWHs can be considered as the server set of objects (objects in this case are

[2] It was shown in [KPE74] that the data allocation algorithm is *NP*-complete in general. In [WM91], it was also proved that the problem to determine an optimal *residence set* (equivalent to our server set in this book) is *NP*-complete, in general.

multimedia documents) and PSAs form a centralized control unit (CCU) that collects requests for a certain time period and then serve these requests to deliver a near-optimal performance. As a second example, the ADRW algorithm can be adopted to solve Web Caching problems on WWW, where each web proxy represents a node in the network and a web server can be considered as an object (web-page) server. The web server can then decide whether or not a web-page should be replicated in a web proxy based on the TEN policy of ADRW algorithm. Similarly, a web proxy can also decide whether or not a web-page should be discarded based on the TEX policy of ADRW algorithm.

A complete object model *Common Object Request Broker Architecture* (CORBA) is built in [OMG95], including object types, parameters, interfaces, attributes, etc. Under the CORBA standards, an object is defined as follows. *"An object is an identifiable, encapsulated entity that provides one or more services that can be requested by a client."* In this book, we have exclusively considered an object as an indivisible entity[3] such as a multimedia document, a web-page, or a small text file, as per the underlying application domain. This means that an entity cannot be partitioned and supplied to the requested site. However, in case when an object can be partitioned or allowed to be partitioned into several *fragments*[SWZ96, ZWC91], a single request may be serviced by several processors concurrently, each responding for one or more fragments of the object. As an example, in VOD and VOR applications, when large movie files are partitioned and delivered to the clients, each server and hence a request for that server are assigned deadlines. These deadlines are *hard* in the sense that, any violation will result in movie presentation incontinuity at the client site. In such a scenario, in addition to the issues identified for the design of OMP, load balancing is an additional issue to be considered. It is certainly beyond the purview of this book to expose issues and algorithms on load balancing. Readers can refer to [HJ86, HJ88, HL95, SWZ96] for details on load balancing. Further, the study of the case when objects are divisible illuminates us to consider a DDBS where each request arriving can demand several objects. The contents of this book certainly serve as a basis for designing competitive on-line algorithms to handle such requests.

Furthermore, as mentioned in Chapters 1 and 2, using an on-line object management algorithm, an object in the system may be dynamically replicated in several new locations (nodes) or migrated from one location to another, as per the arriving request patterns, to improve certain

[3]Also refer to [PJF97, pp.151].

system performance. Practically, the object allocation scheme (Refer to Chapter 4) serves as a *directory* that indicates the locations of an object. It may be noted that the process such as object replication and object migration are essentially modifying this directory. Thus, essentially we are confronted with a problem on deciding whether this directory be made centralized, distributed, partitioned, or replicated in the system. In addition, we must also address on how the concurrency control can be taken care to maintain the consistency when the directory is updated. Furthermore, we must also account on the frequency of this updates, as very frequent updates incur several large overheads. As a result, from the viewpoint of OMP, this object directory can also be considered as an object in a DDBS. Designing judicious directory management mechanisms therefore presents a potential research area for the database designers, especially in a MCE where a mobile host (MH) is often disconnected[4] and the directory has to be updated frequently.

Thus, in this book a number of competitive object management algorithms that are suitable for managing, transporting, and processing the requests are presented and analyzed. The content of this book, although focused on DDBSs, we strongly believe that it can serve as a good starting point to understand the concept of designing competitive object management algorithms in several other related application domains.

[4]Due to the mobility and disconnection properties of a MH, refer to Chapter 1.

References

[ABCD96] V.Almeida, A.Bestavros, M.Crovella, and A.De Oliveira, "Characterizing Reference Locality in the WWW", *Proceedings of 1996 International Conference on Parallel and Distributed Information Systems*, pp.92-103, 1996.

[ABF93] B.Awerbuch, Y.Bartal, and A.Fiat, "Competitive Distributed File Allocation", *Proc. of the 25th Ann. ACM Symp on Theory of Computing*, May 1993.

[ACDFJ99] M.F.Arlitt, L.Cherkasova, J.Dilley, R.Friedrich, and T. Jin, "Evaluating Content Management Techniques for Web Proxy Caches", *Proceedings of the 2nd Workshop on Internet Server Performance*, May 1999.

[ACN00] D.Achlioptas, M.Chrobak, and J.Noga, "Competitive Analysis of Randomized Paging Algorithms", *Theoretical Computer Science*, Vol. 234, pp. 203-218, 2000.

[AFJ00] M.F.Arlitt, R.Friedrich, and T.Jin, "Performance Evaluation of Web Proxy Cache Replacement Policies", *Performance Evaluation*, 39, pp.149-164, 2000.

[AK94] S.Albers and H.Koga, "New On-Line Algorithms for the Page Replication Problem", *Proceedings of the 4th Scandinavian Workshop on Algorithm Theory* (SWAT'94), 1994.

[AK95] S.Albers, H.Koga, "Page Migration with Limited Local Memory Capacity", *Workshop on Algorithms and Data Structures*, 1995.

[AMT99] T.Asaka, H.Miwa and Y.Tanaka, "Distributed Web Caching Using Hash-based Query Caching Method", *Proceedings of the 1999 IEEE International Conference on Control Applications*, vol. 2, pp. 1620-1625, 1999.

[ASF98] M.Afonso, A.Santos and V.Freitas, "QoS in Web Caching", *Computer Networks and ISDN Systems*, Vol.30, Issues 22-23, 25, pp. 2093-2103, November 1998.

[AW96] M.F.Arlitt and C.L.Williamson, "Web Server Workload Characterization: The Search for Invariants", *Proceedings of the ACM SIGMETRICS '96 Conference*, Philadelphia, PA, Apr. 1996.

[AW97] M.F.Arlitt and C.L.Williamson, "Internet Web Servers: Workload Characterization and Performance Implications", *IEEE/ACM Trans.on Networking*, 5, pp.631-645, 1997.

[AW98] H. Attiya and J. Welch, "Distributed Computing: Fundamentals, Simulations, and Advanced Topics", *McGrawHill Companies*, UK, 1998.

[AWY99] C.Aggarwal, J.L.Wolf and P.S. Yu, "Caching on the World Wide Web", *IEEE Transactions on Knowledge and Data Engineering*, Vol.11, No.1, pp.94 -107, Jan.-Feb., 1999.

[B97] A.Bestavros, "WWW Traffic Reduction and Load Balancing through Server-Based Caching", *IEEE Concurrency*, pp. 56-67, Jan./Mar., 1997.

[BAI94] B.R.Badrinath, Arup Acharya, and Tomasz Imilelinski, "Designing Distributed Algorithms for Mobile Computing Networks", *Computers and Communications*, 1994.

[BBKTW94] S.Ben-David, A.Borodin, R.M.Karp, G.Tardos, and A.Wigderson, "On the Power of Randomization in On-line Algorithms", *Algorithmica*, 11:2-14, 1994.

[BC89] D.P. Bertsekas and D.A. Castanon, "Auction Algorithm for Transportation Problem", *Annals of Operations Research*, pp.67-96, 1989.

[BCFPS99] L.Breslau, P.Cao, L.Fan, G.Phillips and S.Shenker, "Web Caching and Zipf-like Distributions: Evidence and Implications", *Proceedings of INFOCOM '99*, Vol.1, pp.126 -134, 1999.

[BCI97] Y.Bartal, M.Charikar, and P.Indyk, "On Page Migration and Other Relaxed Task Systems", In *Proc. 8th Ann. ACM-SIAM Symp. on Discrete Algorithms*, 1997.

[BE98] Allan Borodin and Ran El-Yaniv, "Online Computation and Competitive Analysis", *Cambridge University Press*, 1998.

[BFR92] Y.Bartal, A.Fiat, and Y.Rabani, "Competitive Algorithms for Distributed Data Management", In *Proc. of the 24th Ann. ACM Symp. on Theory of Computing*, May 1992.

[BH98] A.Belloum and L.O.Hertzberger, "Replacement Strategies in Web Caching" *Conference ISIC/CIRA/ISAS'98*, Gaithersburg, Maryland USA, September 1998.

[BHG87] P. Bernstein, V. Hadzilacos, and N. Goodman, "Concurrency Control and Recovery in Database Systems", *Addison Wesley*, Massachusetts, 1987.

[BK91] Naser S.Barghouti and Gail E.Kaiser, "Concurrency Control in Advanced Database Applications", *ACM Computing Surveys*, 23(3), pp.269-317, September 1991.

[BO00] G.Barish and K.Obraczke, "World Wide Web Caching: Trends and Techniques",*IEEE Communications Magazine*, Vol.38 5, pp. 178-184, May 2000.

[BP96] C. C. Bisdikian, and B. V. Patel, "Cost-based Document Allocation for Distributed Multimedia Systems", *IEEE Multimedia*, pp. 62-72, Fall 1996.

[BRICS96] S. Albers, "Competitive Online Algorithms", *BRICS* LS-96-2,LSSN 1395-2048, September 1996.

[BS89] D.L. Black and D.D.Sleator, "Competitive Algorithms for Replication and Migration Problems", *Technical Report CMU-CS-89-201*, Department of Computer Science, Carnegie Mellon University, 1989.

[BY02] V. Bharadwaj, and E.M.Yew, "Network Caching Strategies for Reservation-based Multimedia Services on High-speed Networks", *Data&Knowledge Engineering* 41, pp.85-103, 2002.

[C69] W.W.Chu, "Optimal File Allocation in a Multiple Computer system", *IEEE Trans. on computers C-18(10)*, October 1969.

[C72] R.G.Casey, "Allocation of Copies of a File in an Information Network", *Proc. AFIPS 1972 Spring Joint Comput. Conf.*, AFIPS Press, pp.617-625, 1972.

[CDNSW96] A.Chankhunthod, P.B.Danzig, C.Neerdaels, M.F.Schwartz, and K.J.Worrell, "A Hierarchical Internet Object Cache", *Proceedings of the 1996 USENIX Technical Conference*, Jan. 1996.

[CG90] D.Corner and J.Griffioen, "A New Design for Distributed Systems: the Remote Memory Model", *Summer USENIX*, 1990.

[CI97] P.Cao and S.Irani, "Cost-aware WWW Proxy Caching Algorithms", *Proc. 1st USENIX Symp. on Internet Technologies and Systems*, Monterey, California, pp.193-206, 1997.

[CKV90] M.Chrobak, H.Karloff, T.Payne, and S.Vishwanathan, "New Results on Server Problems", In *First Annual ACM-SIAM Symposium on Discrete Algorithms*, pp.291-300, San Francisco, January 1990.

[CL96] M.Chrobak and Lawrence L.Larmore, "An Optimal On-line Algorithm for k Servers on Trees", *SIAM Journal on Computing*, 1996.

[CLR94] T.H. Cormen, C.E. Leiserson, and R.L. Rivest, "Introduction to Algorithms", *The MIT Press*, Cambridge USA, 1994.

[CLRW93] M.Chrobak, L.Larmore, N.Reingold, and J.Westbrook, "Optimal Multiprocessor Migration Algorithms Using Work Functions", in *Proc. of the 4th Syrup. on Algorithms and Computation*, 1993.

[DA99] J.Dilley and M.Arlitt, "Improving Proxy Cache Performance: Analysis of Three Replacement Policies", *IEEE Internet Computing*, Vol.3 6, pp.44 -50, November-December 1999.

[DF82] L.Dowdey and D.Foster, "Comparative Models of the File Assignment Problem", *Computing Surveys*,Vol.14,No.2, pp.287-313, June 1982.

[DH94] Daniel Barbara, Hector Garcia-Molina, "Replicated Data Management in Mobile Environments: Anything New Under the Sun?", on *Application in Parallel and Distributed Computing*, 1994.

[DJ92] B.David and G.Jane, "Distributed Database Systems", *Addison-Wesley Publishing Company, Inc.*, 1992.

[DJD99] S.G.Dykes, C.L.Jeffery, and S.Das, "Taxonomy and Design Analysis for Distributed Web Caching", *Proceedings of the 32th Hawaii International Conference on System Sciences - 1999, Distributed Caching and Replication Minitrack*, Jan. 1999.

[DS96] A. Dan and D.Sitaram, "A generalized Interval Caching Policy for Mixed Interactive and Long Video Environments", *Multimedia Computing and Networking Conference*, January 1996.

[DS97] A.Dan and D. Sitaram, "Multimedia Caching Strategies for Heterogeneous Applications and Server Environments", *Multimedia Tools and Applications*, Vol. 4, pp. 279-312, May 1997.

[DV03] L.Dong and B.Veeravalli, "GEMA: An Object Replacement Algorithm for Cooperative Web Proxy Systems", To appear in *Multimedia Tools and Applications*, Kluwer Academic, 2003.

[E74] K.Eswaran, "Placement of Records in a File Allocation in a Computer Network", *Proc IFIP Conf.* Stockholm Sweden, August 1974.

[FCJ99] L.Fan, P.Cao, and Q.Jacobson, "Web Prefetching Between Low-Bandwidth Clients and Proxies: Potential and Performance", *Proceedings of the Joint International Conference on Measurement and Modeling of Computer Systems (SIGMETRICS '99)*, Atlanta, GA, May 1999.

[FHH99] A.P.Foong, Yu-Hen Hu, D.M.Heisey, "Logistic Regression in An Adaptive Web Cache", *IEEE Internet Computing*, Vol.3 5, pp. 27 -36, Sept.-Oct. 1999.

[FKLMSY91] Amos Fiat, Richard M. Karp, Michael Luby, Lyle A. McGeoch, Daniel D. Sleator, and Neal E. Young, "Competitive Paging Algorithms", *Journal of Algorithms*, Vol.12, No.4, pp.685-699, December 1991.

[FS00] R.Fleischer and S.Seiden, "New Results for Online Page Replication", In Proceedings of the *International Workshop on Approximation Algorithms for Combinatorial Optimization*, 2000.

[FZ91] E.W.Felten and J.Zahorjan, "Issues in Implementation of a Remote Memory Paging System", *Technical Report 91-03-09*, Dept. of Computer Science, University of Washington, 1991.

[GK00] D. Ghose and H-J. Kim, "Scheduling Video Streams in Video-on-Demand Systems: A Survey", *Multimedia Tools and Applications*, 11, pp.167-195, 2000.

[GN72] R.S.Garfinkel and G.L.Nemhauser, "Integer Programming", *John wiley and Sons*, 1972.

[GR93] J.Gray and A.Reuter, "Transaction Processing: Concepts and Techniques", *Morgan Kaufmann Publishers, Inc.*, San Mateo, CA, 1993.

[GVW96] G.A.Gibson, J.S.Vitter, and J.Wilkes, "Strategic Directions in Storage I/O Issues in Large-Scale Computing", *ACM Computing Surveys*, Vol.28, No.4, pp.779 - 793, 1996.

[HCL91] J.R.Haritsa, M.J.Carey, and M.Livny, "Earliest Deadline Scheduling for Real-Time Database Systems", *Proceedings of the Real-Time Systems Symposium*, Dec. 1991.

[HJ86] A.Hac and T.Johnson, "A Study of Dynamic Load Balancing in a Distributed System", *Proceedings of the ACM SIGCOMM conference on Communications architecture & protocols*, September 1986.

[HJ88] A.Hac and X.Jin, "Dynamic Load Balancing in a Distributed System Using a Sender-Initiated Algorithm", *Proceedings of the 13th Conference on Local Computer Networks*, pp.172-180, 1988.

[HL95] Mounir Hamdi and Chi-Kin Lee, "Dynamic Load Balancing of Data Parallel Applications on a Distributed Network", *Proceedings of the 9th International Conference on Supercomputing*, pp.170-179, 1995.

[HVZ02] C. Hammacher, Z. Vranesic, and S. Zaky, "Computer Organization", *McGrawHill* 5th edition, 2002.

[HX00] K. Hwang and Z. Xu,"Scalable Parallel Computing-Technology, Architecture, Programming", *McGraw-Hill Publishers*, 2000.

[IB92] T. Imielinski and B. R. Badrinath. "Querying in Highly Mobile and Distributed Environment", *Proceeding of the 18th International Conference on Vary Large Data Bases*, pp.41-52, August 1992.

[IMMN98] S.Inohara, Y.Masuoka, J.Min and F.Noda, "Self-organizing Cooperative WWW Caching", *Proceedings of 18th International Conference on Distributed Computing Systems*, pp.74 -83, 1998.

[J94] H. A. Jessel, "Cable Ready: the High Appeal for Interactive Services", *Broadcasting and Cable*, May 23, 1994.

[JB00] S. Jin and A.Bestavros, "Popularity-aware Greedy Dual-size Web Proxy Caching Algorithms", *Proceedings of 20th International Conference on Distributed Computing Systems*, pp. 254 -261, 2000.

[JBa00] S. Jin and A.Bestavros, "Greedy dual* Web Caching Algorithm: Exploiting the Two Sources of Temporal Locality in Web Request Streams", *Proc. 5th Int. Workshop on Web Caching and Content Delivery*, Lisboa, Portugal, 2000.

[JLC00] J.Jung, D.Lee and K.Chon, "Proactive Web Caching with Cumulative Prefetching for Large Multimedia Data", *Computer Networks*, Vol.33, Issues 1-6, pp. 645-655, June 2000.

[K93] H.Koga, "Randomized On-line Algorithms for the Page Replication Problem", In *Proc. 4th International Symposium on Algorithms and Computation*, 1993.

[KH93] K.Hwang, "Advanced Computer Architecture: Parallelism, Scalability, Programmability", *McGraw-Hill Companies, Inc.*, 1993.

[KH98] A. Karmouch,, E. Horlait, "Agent-based Multimedia Communication on Internet", *IEEE Canadian Conference on Electrical and Computer Engineering*, Vol. 2, pp.734-737, 1998.

[KPE74] K.P.Eswaran, "Placement of records in a file and file allocation in a computer network", *IFIP Conference Information Proceedings*, pp.304-307, August 1974.

[KSBBDIKMY99] D.Karger, A.Sherman, A.Berkheimer, B.Bogstad, R.Dhanidina, K.Iwamoto, B.Kim, L.Matkins and Y.Yerushalmi, "Web Caching with Consistent Hashing", *Computer Networks*, Vol.31, Issues 11-16, 17, pp. 1203-1213, May 1999.

[KW99] B.Krishnamurthy and C.E.Wills, "Proxy Cache Coherency and Replacement-towards a More Complete Picture", *Proceedings of 19th IEEE International Conference on Distributed Computing Systems*, pp.332 -339, 1999.

[L97] A.Luotonen, "Web Proxy Servers", *Prentice Hall PTR*, Upper Saddle River, NJ 07458, 1997.

[LCCNMC97] D. Lee, J. Choi, H. Choe, S.H.Noh, S.L.Min, and Y. Cho, "Implementation and Performance Evaluation of the LRFU Replacement Policy", *EUROMICRO 97*, pp.106 -111, 1997.

[LG90] T.D.C. Little and A. Ghafoor, "Synchronization and Storage Models for Multimedia Objects", *IEEE Journal of Selected Areas of Communication*, Vol. 8, No. 3, pp. 413-427, April 1990.

[LGIDS99] B. Li, M.J.Golin, G.F.Italiano, X. Deng and K.Sohraby, "On the Optimal Placement of Web Proxies in the Internet", *Proceedings of INFOCOM '99*, Vol.3, pp.1282 -1290, 1999.

[LRWY99] C.Lund, N.Reingold, J.Westbrook, and D.Yan, "Competitive On-line Algorithms for Distributed Data Management", *SIAM Journal on Computing*, vol.38, no.3, pp.1086-1111, Mar 1999.

[LW00] Ch. Lindemann and O. Waldhorst, "Evaluating Hardware and Software Web Proxy Caching Solutions", *Report for Milestone 1 of the Project "Analysis of the Effectiveness of Web Caching in the Gigabit Research Network G-WiN"*, supported by the DFN-Verein with Funds of the BMBF, November 2000.

[LWY91] A.Leff, J.Wolf, and P.S.Yu, "Policies for Efficient Memory Utilization in a Remote Caching Architecture", *First Intl. Conf. On Parallel and Distributed Information Systems*, pp.198-207, December 1991.

[LWY92] A.Leff, J.Wolf, and P.S.Yu, "LRU-based Replication Strategies in a LAN Remote Caching Architecture", in *Proc. 17th Annu. Conf. Local Comput. Networks*, Minneapolis, MN, September 1992.

[LWY93] A.Leff, J.Wolf, and P.S.Yu, "Replication Algorithms in a Remote Caching Architecture", *IEEE Trans. Parallel and Distributed Systems*, Vol.4, No.11, pp.1185-1204, November 1993.

[LWY96] A.Leff, J.Wolf, and P.S.Yu, "Efficient LRU-based Buffering in a LAN Remote Caching Architecture", *IEEE Trans. Parallel and Distributed Systems*, Vol.7, No.2, pp.191-206, Feb.1996.

[M00] J.C.Mogul, "Squeezing More Bits out of HTTP Caches", *IEEE Network*, Vol.14 3, pp.6 -14, May-June 2000.

[M95] J.C.Mogul, "Network Behaviour of a Busy Web Server and its Clients", *WRL Research Report 95/5. Western Research Laboratory DIGITAL*, 1995.

[MC98] E.P.Markatos and C.E.Chronaki, "A TOP-10 Approach to Prefetch on Web", *Proceedings of INET'98*, 1998.

[MJA98] Mikhail J. Atallah, "Algorithms and Theory of Computation Handbook", *Boca Raton, FL:CRC Press*, 1998.

[MMS88] M.S.Manasse, L.A.McGeoch, and D.D.Sleator, "Competitive Algorithms for On-line Problems", *Proceedings 20th Annual ACM Symposium on Theory of Computing*, ACM, New York, pp.322-333, 1988.

[MNRZFJ98] S.Michel, K.Nguyen, A.Rosenstein, Lixia Zhang, S.Floyd and V.Jacobson, "Adaptive Web Caching: Towards a New Global Caching Architecture", *Computer Networks and ISDN Systems*, Vol.30, Issues 22-23, pp. 2169-2177, November 1998.

[MPKD99] M.Makpangou, G.Pierre, C.Khoury and N.Dorta, "Replicated Directory Service for Weakly Consistent Distributed Caches", *ICDCS'99*, Austin, Texas, May 1999.

[MR95] R.Motwahl and P.Raghavan, "Randomized Algorithms", *Cambridge University Press*, 1995.

[N95] J.-P, Nussbaumer, "Networking Requirements for Interactive Video On Demand", *IEEE Journal on Selected Areas in Communications*, Vol.13, No.5, pp.779-787, June 1995.

[NL91] B.Nitzberg, V.Lo, "Distributed Shared Memory: A Survey of Issues and Algorithms", *IEEE computer*, Vol.24, pp.52-60, August 1991.

[NNW93] E.J.O'Neil, P.E.O'Neil, G.Weikum, "The LRU-K Page Replacement Algorithm for Database Disk Buffering", *Proceedings of ACM SIGMOD*, 1993.

[NRP95] P.E.O'Neil, K.Ramamritham and C.Pu, "A Two-Phase Approach to Predictably Scheduling Real-Time Transactions", *Performance of Concurrency Control Algorithms in Centralized Database Systems*, V.Kumar(ed.), Prentice-Hall, Englewood Cliffs, NJ, 1995.

[ODV94] M.Tamer Ozsu, U.Dayal, and P.Valduriez, "Distributed Object Management", *Morgan Kaufmann Publishers*, San Mateo, California, 1994.

[OMG95] Object Management Group, "The Common Object Request Broker: Architecture and Specification", Revision 2.0, July 1995.

[ORBS94] B. Ozden, R. Rastogi, A. Biliris, and A. Silberschatz, "A Low Cost Storage Server for Movie-On-Demand Databases", In the *Proceedings of Twentieth International Conference on Very Large Databases*, Santiago, September 1994.

[ORP95] P.E.O'Neil, K.Ramamritham and C.Pu "A Two-Phase Approach to Predictably Scheduling Real-Time Transactions', *Performance of Concurrency Control Algorithms in Centralized Database Systems, V.Kumar(ed.), Prentice-Hall*, Englewood Cliffs, NJ, 1995.

[OV99] T.M.Ozsu and P.Valduriez, "Principles of Distributed Database Systems", *Patrick Valduriez Prentice Hall*, ISBN 0-13-659707-6, 1999.

[PFSYW91] C.Pu, D.Florissi, P.Soares, P.S.Yu and K.L.Wu, "Performance Comparison of Sender-Active and Receiver-Active Mutual Data Serving", *Tech. Rept. CUCS-025-091*, Columbia University, 1991.

[PH97] D.Povey and J.Harrison, "A Distributed Internet Cache", *Proceedings of the 20th Australasian Computer Science Conference*, February 1997.

[PJF97] Paul J.Fortier, "Database Systems Handbook", *McGraw-Hill Companies, Inc.*, 1997.

[PLKC90] C.Pu, A.Leff, F.Korz, and S.W.Chen, "Redundancy Management in a Symmetric Distributed Main-Memory Database", *Tech. Rep. CUCS-014-090*, Columbia Univ., 1990.

[PRVS95] C. H, Papadimitriou, S. Ramanathan, P. Venkat Rangan, and S.Sampathkumar, "Multimedia Information Caching for Personalized Video-On-Demand", *Computer Communications*, Vol. 18, No.3, pp. 204-216, March 1995.

[PS98] E.Pitoura and G.Samaras, "Data Management for Mobile Computing", *Kluwer Academic Publishers*, 1998.

[PSS93] B.Purimetla, R.M.Sivasankaran, and J.Stankovic,"A Study of Distributed Real-Time Active Database Applications", *IEEE Workshop on Parallel and Distributed Real-time Systems*, April 1993.

[RCG98] M.Rabinovich, J.Chase, and S. Gadde, "Not All Hits Are Created Equal: Cooperative Proxy Caching over a Wide-area Network", *Computer Networks and ISDN System*, 30, 1998.

[RS89] P.Raghavan and M.Snir, "Memory Versus Randomization in On-line Algorithms", In *16th International Colloquium on Automata, Languages and Programming*, Vol. 372 of Lecture Notes in Computer Science, Springer-Verlag, pp. 687-703, July 1989.

[RSB99] P.Rodriguez, C.Spanner, and E.W.Biersack, "Web Caching Architectures: Hierarchical and Distributed Caching", *Proceedings of WCW'99*, 1999.

[RV00] L.Rizzo, L.Vicisano, "Replacement Policies for a Proxy Cache", *IEEE/ACM Transaction on Networking*, Vol.8, No.2, April 2000.

[RV93] P. V. Rangan and H. M. Vin, "Efficient Storage Techniques for Digital Continuous Multimedia", *IEEE Transactions on Knowledge and Data Engineering*, 5(4), pp. 564-573, August 1993.

[Reed83] D.P.Reed, "Implementing Atomic Actions on Decentralized Data", *ACM Trans. on Computer Systems*, Vol.1, No.1, pp.3-23, 1983.

[S88] A. Sikeler, "Var-Page-LRU: a Buffer Replacement Algorithm Supporting Different Page Sizes", In G. Goos and J. Hartmanis, editors, *Lecture Notes in Computer Science 303*, Springer Verlag, pp.336–351, 1988.

[SB89] M.Schroeder and M.Burrows, "Performance of Firefly", *Proc. of the 12th Symposium on Operating Systems Principles ACM/SIGO*, December 1989.

[SD91] B.N.Schilit and D.Duchamp, "Adaptive Remote Paging for Mobile Computers", *Tech. Rep. CUCS-004-91*, Columbia Univ., 1991.

[SGG00] A. Silberschatz, P. Galvin, and G. Gagne, "Applied Operating System Concepts", *John Wiley & Sons, Inc.*, 1st edition, 2000.

[SKW99] Y.Smaragdakis, S.Kaplan, and P.Wilson, "EELRU: Simple and Effective Adaptive Page Replacement", *Measurement and Modeling of Computer Systems*, 1999.

[SRT99] S.Sen, J.Rexford, D.Towsley, "Proxy Prefix Caching for Multimedia Streams", *INFOCOM '99* Volume:3, pp. 1310 -1319, 1999.

[SSV97] P.Scheuermann, J.Shim, and R.Vingralek, "A Case for Delay-Conscious Caching of Web Documents", *Computer Networks and ISDN Systems*, Volume 29, Issues 8-13, pp.997-1005, September 1997.

[SSZ93] Swarup Acharya and Stanley B.Zdonik, "An Efficient Scheme for Dynamic Data Replication", *Technical Report* CS-93-43, Department of Computer Science, Brown University, September 1993.

[ST85] D.D.Sleator and R.E.Tarjan, "Amortized Efficiency of List Update and Paging Rules", *Communications of the ACM*, 28(2), pp.202-208, 1985.

[SWH98] A.Prasad Sistla,O.Wolfson and Y.Huang, "Minimization of Communication Cost Through Caching in Mobile Environments", *IEEE Transactions on Parallel and Distributed Systems*, Vol. 9, No. 4, pp.378-390, April 1998.

[SWZ96] P.Scheuermann, G.Weikum, P.Zabback, "Data Partitioning and Load Balancing in Parallel Disk Systems", *The Very Large Data Bases (VLDB) Journal*, 7(1), pp.48-66, February 1998.

[TDVK98] R.Tewari, M.Dahlin, H.M.Vin, and J.Kay, "Beyond Hierarchies: Design Considerations for Distributed Caching on the Internet", *Technical Report CS98-04*, Department of Computer Sciences, UT Austin, Texas, USA, May 1998.

[TS02] Andrew S. Tanenbaum and Maarten Van Steen, "Distributed Systems: Principles and Paradigms", *Prentice Hall*, 2002.

[TTBSJ00] Mitchell D. Theys, Min Tan, Noah B. Beck, Howard Jay Siegel, and Michael Jurczyk, "A Mathematical Model and Scheduling Heuristics for Satisfying Prioritized Data Requests in an Oversubscribed Communication Network", *IEEE Transactions on Parallel and Distributed Systems*, Vol. 11, No. 9, pp.969-988, September 2000.

[V00] B. Veeravalli, "Document Caching Policies on High-Speed Distributed Networks for Personalized Multimedia Services", *Proceedings of the 8th IEEE International Conference on Networks*, Singapore, pp. 215-219, September, 2000.

[VR01] P.Verissimo and L.Rodrigues, "Distributed Systems for System Architects", *Kluwer Academic Publishers*, USA, 2001.

[VY02] B. Veeravalli, E.M.Yew, "Network Caching Strategies for Reservation-based Multimedia Services on High-speed Networks", *Data&Knowledge Engineering*, pp.85-103, 2002.

[W84] B.W.Wah, "File Placement in Distributed Computer Systems", *IEEE Computer*, Vol.17, No.1, pp.23-32, Jan. 1984.

[W94] J.Westbrook, "Randomized Algorithms for Multiprocessor Page Migration", *SIAM Journal on Computing*, 1994.

[W99] J.Wang, "A Survey of Web Caching Schemes for the Internet", *ACM Computer Communication Review*, Vol. 29, pp.36-46, October 1999.

[WA97] R.P.Wooster and M.Abrams, "Proxy Caching that Estimates Page Load Delays", *Computer Networks and ISDN Systems*, Volume 29, Issues 8-13, pp. 977-986, September 1997.

[WASAF96] S.Williams, M.Abrams, C.R.Standridge, G.Abdulla, and E.A.Fox, "Removal Policies in Network Caches for World-Wide Web Documents", *Conference Proceedings on Applications, Technologies, Architectures, and Protocols for Computer Communications*, Palo Alto, CA USA, August 1996.

[WH98] O. Wolfson and Y. Huang, "Competitive Anynasis of Caching in Distributed Databases", *IEEE Transactions on Parallel and Distributed Systems*, Vol.9, No.4, pp.391-409, April 1998.

[WHH98] Jun Wei, Tao He, and Tao Huang, "Challenges of Communication in Mobile Computing", *Technology of Object-Oriented Languages, TOOLS 27. Proceedings*, pp.196-203, 1998.

[WJH97] O. Wolfson, Shushil Jajodia, and Yixiu Huang, "An Adaptive Data Replication Algorithm", *ACM Transactions on Database Systems*, 22(2), pp.255-314, 1997.

[WM91] O.Wolfson and A.Milo, "The Multicast Policy and Its Relationship to Replicated Data Placement", *ACM Transactions on Database Systems*, vol.16, no.1, pp.181-205, 1991.

[WS99] Y. Won and J. Srivastava, "Strategic Replication of Video Files in a Distributed Environment", *International Journal of Multimedia Tools and Applications*, Vol. 8, No.1, pp. 249-283, March 1999.

[WVSCKL99] A.Wolman, G.M.Voelker, N.Sharma, N.Cardwell, A.Karlin, and H.M.Levy, "On the Scale and Performance of Cooperative Web Proxy Caching", *17th ACM Symposium on Operating Systems Principles (SOSP '99)*, Kiawah Island, SC, Dec.1999.

[Y91] N.Young, "On-line Caching as cache Size Varies", Proceedings of the Second Annual ACM-SIAM Symposium on Discrete Algorithms, San Francisco, California, 28-30, pp. 241-250, January 1991.

[ZWC91] Weining Zhang, Ke Wang, and Siu-Cheung Chau, "Data partition: A Practical Parallel Evaluation of Datalog Programs", *Proceedings of the First International Conference on Parallel and Distributed Information Systems*, pp.98-105, 1991.

Index

MIX
Papier aus verantwortungsvollen Quellen
Paper from responsible sources
FSC® C105338

If you have any concerns about our products,
you can contact us on
ProductSafety@springernature.com

In case Publisher is established outside the EU,
the EU authorized representative is:
Springer Nature Customer Service Center GmbH
Europaplatz 3, 69115 Heidelberg, Germany

Printed by Libri Plureos GmbH
in Hamburg, Germany